REBELS ON THE NIAGARA

Tom Sweeny

Andrew Johnson

George Meade

O'Neill

Grant

Lincoln

Nameless US + CS
veterans of Irish
descent

REBELS ON THE NIAGARA

The Fenian Invasion of Canada, 1866

LAWRENCE E. CLINE

excelsior editions

AN IMPRINT OF STATE UNIVERSITY OF NEW YORK PRESS

Cover image: *The Green Above the Red [an imaginary incident during the Fenian Raids of 1866].* Credit: Library and Archives Canada, Acc. No. R9266-3319 Peter Winkworth Collection of Canadiana. Copyright: expired.

Published by State University of New York Press, Albany

© 2018 State University of New York

All rights reserved

Printed in the United States of America

No part of this book may be used or reproduced in any manner whatsoever without written permission. No part of this book may be stored in a retrieval system or transmitted in any form or by any means including electronic, electrostatic, magnetic tape, mechanical, photocopying, recording, or otherwise without the prior permission in writing of the publisher.

Excelsior Editions is an imprint of State University of New York Press

For information, contact State University of New York Press, Albany, NY
www.sunypress.edu

Production, Jenn Bennett
Marketing, Kate Seburyamo

Library of Congress Cataloging-in-Publication Data

Names: Cline, Lawrence E., author.
Title: Rebels on the Niagara : the Fenian Invasion of Canada, 1866 / Lawrence E. Cline.
Description: Albany : State University of New York Press, 2018. | Series: Excelsior editions | Includes bibliographical references and index. | Description based on print version record and CIP data provided by publisher; resource not viewed.
Identifiers: LCCN 2016059902 (print) | LCCN 2016059172 (ebook) | ISBN 9781438467535 (ebook) | ISBN 9781438467528 (pbk. : alk. paper) | ISBN 9781438467511 (hardcover : alk. paper)
Subjects: LCSH: Canada—History—Fenian Invasions, 1866–1870. | Fenians.
Classification: LCC F1032 (print) | LCC F1032 .C63 2017 (ebook) | DDC 971.04/8—dc23
LC record available at https://lccn.loc.gov/2016059902

10 9 8 7 6 5 4 3 2 1

To Priscilla for the patience,
and to Liz and Lucy for the love

Contents

Acknowledgments

The author would like to thank the Buffalo History Museum, Missisquoi Historical Society, and Library and Archives Canada for their great assistance in gathering material. He also would like to thank Professor Thomas Mockaitis and Doctor Peter Vronsky for their valuable comments on the initial manuscript.

Maps

Maps are by the author. Location details for the Battle of Ridgeway map are from Alexander Somerville, *Narrative of the Fenian Invasion of Canada*. Hamilton: J. Lyght, 1866. Location details of the Eccles Hill map are from Hereward Senior, *The Last Invasion of Canada: The Fenian Raids, 1866–1870*. Toronto: Dundurn Press, 1991.

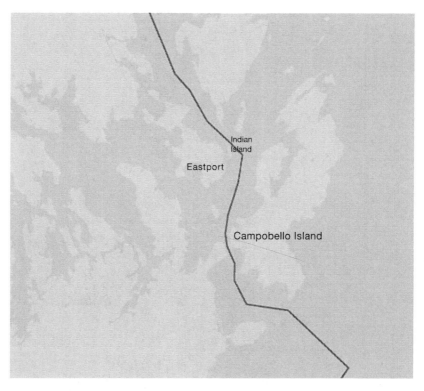

Map 1. Campobello Island raid

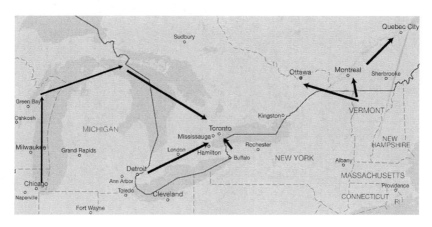

Map 2. Fenian Strategy for the 1866 Invasion

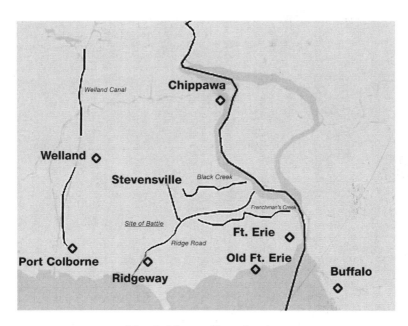

Map 3. Niagara Campaign Area

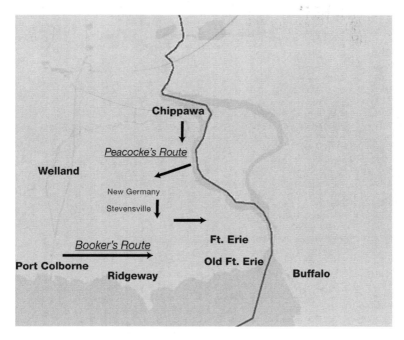

Map 4. Canadian Movements Leading to the Battle of Ridgeway

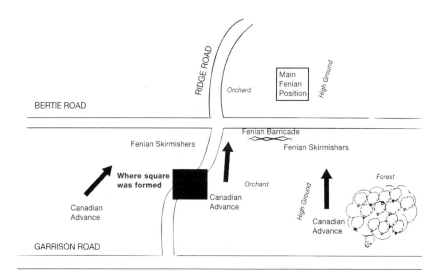

Map 5. Battle of Ridgeway

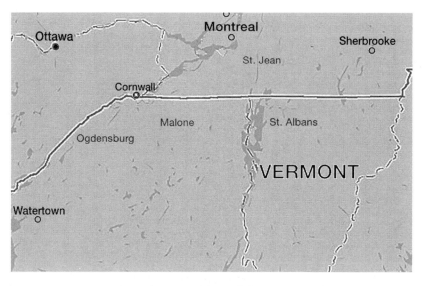

Map 6. Eastern Wing of the Invasion

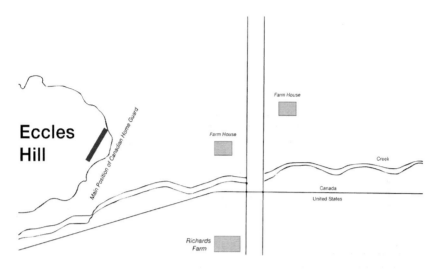

Map 7. Eccles Hill

Map 8. Trout River

Foreword

In June 1866, Americans invaded Canada along the Niagara Frontier. Although now somewhat a footnote in US and New York history, the military operations at the time were viewed with major alarm. The British and Canadians mobilized forces, battles were fought, and the United States sent troops to the Niagara Frontier. The situation could have exploded into a major crisis. As such, the 1866 invasion and its aftermath deserve more attention than commonly given.

The interesting twist on the 1866 fighting was that it was not government-to-government inspired, but rather operations by Canadian forces facing what now would be termed insurgents, namely the Fenian Brotherhood. The Fenian movement in the nineteenth century tried using militant tactics to fight for the independence of Ireland. In many ways, this group was stronger in the United States than it was in Ireland, and may have had more significance in America. At the end of the US Civil War, Fenian leaders decided to try to use Irish Americans, many of them combat veterans of the Civil War, to seize Canada and to make it the "New Ireland" as a means to force the British from "old" Ireland. For some Fenians, it was viewed as a "mega-hostage" operation to extract concessions from the British government. Others perceived it for the Fenians to ignite a larger US-British war. In either event, the ultimate goal was Irish independence.

The Fenian invasion of Canada in 1866 had many roots in the United States and particularly New York State, which was both the epicenter of Fenian leadership and a key support base and staging area for the military operations. Both the larger 1866 efforts and the smaller 1870 operation involved a relative flood of Fenians into New York. After two battles in 1866 and a small skirmish in 1870, the "invasions" turned into fiascoes, in many ways the result of US government responses in Upstate New York. The events leading up to the invasions and the political movement surrounding the Fenian Brotherhood continued to have significant impacts on the region.

The Larger Background

The Irish, of course, had struggled for many years for independence from Britain. The 1798 uprising was particularly widespread and violent, mainly because it involved French intervention, however weak and ill-timed. This was followed by a smaller uprising led by Robert Emmet in 1803. Both led to increased immigration to the United States by Irish with significant grievances, which almost certainly were passed along to their descendants. Much of the later Fenian leadership and many of its members, in fact, were the sons or grandsons of those who had fought in 1798.

In Ireland, after the failure of the 1798 movement, a group called the Young Irelanders emerged as a nationalist movement not based on religion. Their significance increased sharply as the Irish Potato Famine began ravaging the Irish population. The famine also created a fresh wave of embittered Irish immigrants to the US, most of whom settled in New York at least initially. Although the Young Irelanders, in part inspired by the revolutionary environment in Europe in 1848, tried to initiate an uprising in Ireland in 1848, it failed miserably. After the collapse of the movement, many of its leaders fled, several of whom were instrumental in creating the Fenian movement.

Although the focus of this book is on the US Fenians, some notes should be added about allied movements elsewhere. The first was the Irish Republican Brotherhood (IRB), which in early days also was called by some the Irish Revolutionary Brotherhood. In contemporary accounts, the IRB commonly was known as the Irish Fenians, both by its members and by outsiders. To avoid confusion in this book, however, it will be referred to simply as the IRB. This group, led by James Stephens, remained in close contact with the US Fenian Brotherhood, particularly because Stephens and John O'Mahony, the first leader of the US Fenians, had been allied in the 1848 uprising and had fled in exile (for Stephens, only a brief while before returning to Ireland) together. Stephens, in fact, was viewed as a mediator among the US Fenian leadership as the group faced its early splits. Likewise, the IRB received funding and some support from the Fenian Brotherhood in the United States. Interestingly, the impetus for forming the IRB actually came from the United States and founders of the Fenian Brotherhood in New York City. They sent a representative to Ireland to visit Stephens urging him to form a movement and offering to finance its start.[1] As it turned out, the Americans rarely provided the extent of funds the IRB thought it required—and there were significant tensions as a result—but the IRB and American Fenians continued to cooperate in the main.

The Canadian provinces also had their Fenians, but the movement in Canada was much weaker than that in the United States. Perhaps a key issue for the Canadian Fenians, which will receive more discussion later, was that in many ways they were less an Irish Nationalist movement than a religious movement representing Irish Catholics against Irish Protestant Orangemen. As such, they were somewhat a minority within a minority, and they never reached critical mass. By one author's estimate, the total number of Fenians in Canada never exceeded 3,000 among all the provinces; this can be compared to about 50,000 members of the Orange Order in Canada West alone.[2] Nevertheless, as the American Fenians grew ever stronger in the 1860s, the various Canadian governments became increasingly alarmed about the prospects of a Canadian Fenian Fifth Column.

One note should be made on the discussion in this book; this is that the term "Canada" is normally used for descriptions of the operations by the Fenians. This is somewhat of a misnomer. At the time of the 1866 invasion, Canada was still split into the Province of Canada, commonly still identified as Canada West and Canada East, each comprising a relatively small portion of the land, together with the separately controlled colonies of Newfoundland, New Brunswick, Prince Edward Island, Nova Scotia, British Columbia, and Vancouver Island. These smaller areas and the Province of Canada were not confederated until 1867, after the Fenian invasion. Some historians, in fact, have persuasively argued that the Fenian threat was one of several critical reasons for British attempts to unify Canada. For simplicity's sake, however, the term Canada is used except when further specificity is required.

The Fenians in the three countries certainly had multiple contacts and mutual political support. In many ways, this movement was one of the very early examples of a transnational violent (and during at least part of its existence, some would argue terrorist) organization. The problem it faced, however, was in actual coordination and cooperation among the wings of the overall movement. It is most accurate to view these various wings of the Fenians as having the same ultimate objectives, but typically they had differing views on how to get there. In the case of the Americans, this same situation prevailed, leading to major splits within the group.

One other issue should be noted. It is impossible to discuss the American Fenian Brotherhood and its immediate successors without describing the IRB. As such, the focus on the Irish side of the nationalist movement is on the IRB. For about a decade, the IRB was the predominant actor in Irish nationalism, but never represented the only approach to resolving Irish aspirations. Both prior to and following the IRB, there were multiple strands (and groups) in Ireland. In general, these could be divided into two approaches: independence through violence or a more gradual campaign through political means. These two strands never were "clean" distinctions; the relations between politics-first leaders and the militants were very convoluted. This became particularly true during the latter life of the IRB, with the emergence of the Land League, an Irish political movement. At the time (and since), there was considerable debate as to whether the "political" leaders were, in fact, independent actors or if they simply were the open political face of the larger violent movement. Even though the Irish independence movement never was monolithic, during the period under discussion, the IRB clearly was the strongest and most deserving of attention.

The Irish in New York

As one author noted, "In 1860, 40 per cent of all foreign-born immigrants were Irish, and they primarily resided in poor conditions in Northern cities. The combined Irish-born settlers in New York City, Brooklyn, Boston and Philadelphia alone was 400,000 people, or more than a quarter of Canada West's *entire* population."[3] Focusing specifically on New York State, in 1860, the Irish-born population in New York City was 203,740; Brooklyn, 56,710; Albany, 14,780, Buffalo, 9,279; and Rochester, 6,786.[4] It should be stressed that these figures include only those actually born in Ireland and not second-generation Irish. Based on recent patterns with ethnic émigré groups, second-generation Irish, having grown up on tales of Irish resistance to the English, may have been even more militant.

This formed an excellent population base for recruiting a militant movement. Some Irish groups, most notably the Hibernians, which over time became a fraternal rather than militant organization, predated the Fenians or were founded at much the same time. Likewise, other ethnic groups certainly formed associations of varying degrees of willingness to use violence to protect their perceived interests. The Fenians, however, in many ways were in a category all their own. The size of the group, its interconnectivity with both the US government and the military, its willingness to use organized violence to achieve its aims, and its transnational goals all made the Brotherhood a particularly significant group. Although short-lived and with some of its military operations being somewhere between farce and tragedy, the Fenian Brotherhood had an important impact on nineteenth-century New York and the United States.

There are several ways to approach an examination of the Fenians and more specifically the American wing, the Fenian Brotherhood. In recent years, probably the most common have been largely military studies of their operations in 1866 and 1870, of which there have been several excellent studies. These have tended to be very heavily Canadian-focused (and usually written by Canadians) in terms of details of the skirmishes and the units involved. This certainly was the case in near-contemporary accounts, which dealt almost exclusively with the Canadian side, and many of which were very jingoistic. The other strand of writing, much of which now is rather dated, on the American Fenians was on their organizational and political developments. Finally, a body of work is available on the IRB, with the Americans somewhat as supporting cast.

This book unapologetically is focused on the American side of Fenianism, because this has received relatively less attention. It attempts to meld the political and military sides of Fenianism in the United States. Without understanding both the internal political dynamics and their impact on the Brotherhood's armed forays and how these operations in turn impacted the group's political course, considerable nuance is lost. The largest segment of the book surrounds the 1866 efforts to invade Canada because this represented the high watermark of the Fenian Brotherhood's military efforts. The invasion of the Niagara Frontier was both dramatic in its own right and had the most direct impact on New York State and the US in their need to respond. The Fenians, however, continued to be important, and it is equally important to trace their history until their fading.

Ch 1 + Ch 2

Background on
Fenian movement
in U.S. + IRB
Ireland.
(And to lesser
extent Canada)

Chapter 1

The Fenian Brotherhood in New York and the US

Irishmen still, thank God, leave their country with the hatred of England lying deep in their souls. For them there is no pretence [sic] of union of hearts, nor of anything but war with England, for which they are at all times willing to supply the sinews.[1]

—John O'Leary, recollections of Fenians and Fenianism

The genesis of the Fenian Brotherhood was the Emmet Monument Association that was established in the United States for the ostensible purpose of erecting a monument to Robert Emmet, who was executed by the British after leading an Irish rebellion in 1803. Although the group publicly had relatively narrow goals, there was a somewhat coded message in its very name. While Emmet was at trial, his closing speech included the words:

> Let no man write my epitaph; for as no man who knows my motives dare now vindicate them, let not prejudice or ignorance, asperse them. Let them and me rest in obscurity and peace, and my tomb remain uninscribed, and my memory in oblivion, until other times and other men can do justice to my character. When my country takes her place among the nations of the earth, *then and not till then*, let my epitaph be written.

At least among the Irish community, this implied that any group devoted to establish such a monument must also be involved in the nationalist struggle. This certainly was the case with the Emmet Monument Association, which had a secret wing devoted to armed action against Britain. In support of this goal, it reportedly entered into secret talks with the Russian government for an alliance during the period of the Crimean War, but these talks came to nothing.[2] Also note that during every period in which relations were strained between the Russians and the British, the Fenians made similar approaches to Russian officials, but there never were any practical advantages for the Fenians. The major organizers of the Emmet Monument Association were Colonel Michael Doheny, Chairman of the Committee; John O'Mahony (also spelled O'Mahoney in several contemporaneous sources), Pat O'Rourke, Captain Michael Corcoran, Thomas J. Kelly, Oliver Byrne, James Roache, and John Reynolds. Both Doheny and O'Mahony were veterans of the 1848 uprising in Ireland. Most of these figures became key members of the emerging Fenian Brotherhood.

The American members began trying to link with the nationalist movement in Ireland itself. Joseph Denieffe, a member, had to return to Ireland in June 1855 to visit his ill father. At that time, he was instructed to meet with Irish nationalist leaders. The Association had considerable confidence in itself. When Joseph Denieffe departed, he was told: "You may assure them . . . the time [for armed uprising] will be September. We have thirty thousand men ready now, and all we need is money, and arrangements are under way to provide it. We propose to issue bonds and some of the wealthiest men of our race are willing to take them."[3] At the same time, to give some indication of how shaky the Irish nationalist network actually was at this time, Denieffe did not know who to meet with in Ireland.

Denieffe finally met with James Stephens, a veteran of the 1848 uprising. Stephens had fled to Paris after the failure of that movement, where he had associated with John O'Mahony, who also had been in the 1848 movement before emigrating to the US and working with the Emmet Association. This led to links being established between Stephens and the erstwhile leaders of the Emmet Monument Association, which essentially had died by this time. They sent Owen Considine to Ireland with a letter offering help in fall 1857. The principal immediate request by Stephens was for funding for the nationalist movement in Ireland. By Denieffe's account, there were considerable problems in fundraising, with many Irish Americans disillusioned with the Irish nationalist movements, if not necessarily with the concept of Irish independence. It took him two months to raise 400 dollars. When he returned to Dublin in 1858 with the money, Stephens formally founded the Irish Republican Brotherhood (IRB) on March 17, 1858.[4] At about the same time, O'Mahony and others formally established the Fenian Brotherhood, which replaced the Emmet Monument Association. The American Brotherhood reportedly started with forty members, all in New York City.[5] Very quickly, both branches of the movement became known as the Fenians, taking its name from an ancient Irish militia. The group was headquartered in New York City. Along with O'Mahony, Michael Doheny, James Roche, and Oliver Byrne formed the nucleus of the new group. Although the American Fenian Brotherhood was a very distinct organization, its leaders pledged allegiance to Stephens as the overall leader of the Irish nationalist movement.

O'Mahony was the undisputed leader of the American branch of the Brotherhood for the first few years of its existence. He was born in County Limerick and had family members who had been involved in the Irish uprising of 1798. He was well educated and noted as a scholar before emigrating to the US in 1854. One senior Fenian claimed—while extolling O'Mahony's virtues—that he had suffered a temporary "fit of insanity" early in life, but that "I am confident O'Mahony was quite sane during the rest of his life."[6] In reality, although briefly institutionalized well before his involvement in the Brotherhood, this appeared to be more as a result of exhaustion rather than psychological problems. During the Civil War, O'Mahony organized and served as the colonel commanding the 99th New York State Militia, which did not serve in combat, but was assigned to guard Confederate prisoners.

The description by the *New York Times* (which consistently over the years denigrated the Fenians) of the early days of the Fenian movement in New York may represent the prevailing opinion of outsiders of the group at the time: "It was first a weak organization of ambitious Irishmen, who sought by combination to extort office from the Democratic party."[7] Likewise, when James Stephens, leader of the Irish Republican Brotherhood, visited the US, the *New York Times* argued, "There need be no apprehensions, however, that the Fenian leader will disturb the peace of this country, or embroil us in a foreign war, after he gets here. He may agitate for a while, as Kosuth and other exiles have done in other times; but he will be quite certain to subside very soon into a quiet and respectable citizen, obtaining his livelihood by honest labor of one kind or another, in Wall-street or the Bowery. . . ."[8] Very quickly, however, the Fenians proved themselves to be very serious politically, and with very broad aspirations.

The Fenian Brotherhood Organization

The Fenian Brotherhood was organized in the form of "circles." The actual number of Fenian circles was fluid, with contemporary sources claiming somewhere between 500 and 900 circles at its peak.[9] Each circle reportedly had between 100 and 500 members, but in many cases these figures were prone to exaggeration. A good snapshot of the state of the Fenian Brotherhood circles was provided during the 1865 Cincinnati convention. The movement had not been particularly open about its strength previously, but as part of the convention report a full listing of the circles was published. As of that date, the existing circles included:

> Massachusetts: 38 (including 2 "in bad standing"); Rhode Island: 5; Maine: 1; Connecticut: 6 (1 in bad standing); New Hampshire: 7; Vermont: 4; NYC: Manhattan: 20; New York State: 27 (with Rome being in bad standing); New Jersey: 3; Pennsylvania: 16 (with 4 in bad standing); Ohio: 17 (one in bad standing); Illinois: 24 (one in bad standing); District of Columbia: 1; Iowa: 14 (two in bad standing); Wisconsin: 10 (one in bad standing); Michigan: 7; Minnesota: 2; Indiana: 23 (3 in bad standing); Missouri: 5; Tennessee: 3 (one in bad standing); Kentucky: 4 (one in bad standing); Kansas: 3; Oregon, Utah, Nevada, and Idaho: 4; California: 13; British Provinces: 2.[10]

For obvious reasons, the Fenian circles were focused in Northern-controlled and border states during the Civil War. Interestingly, though, at the 1863 convention O'Mahony stated that the New Orleans circle had continued some communications with New York.[11] Union forces had occupied New Orleans prior to this convention, so it is unclear if O'Mahony was referring to a "Union" or a "Confederate" circle. If the latter, it is possible that there were some quiet Fenian circles in Confederate-held areas. In either event, shortly after the war ended, Fenian circles were established (or reestablished) in Southern states, with many former Confederate soldiers and officers as members of the Brotherhood.

It should be noted that the plurality of circles was in New York State, with sufficient strength in New York City itself that it was viewed as a separate Centre. Likewise, at least anecdotally, the New York circles had some of the highest number of members in each circle. The total number of members of the Fenians has been subject to considerable argument, but a realistic estimate would likely be in the range of 50,000 members by the end of the Civil War, with followers and supporters of varying commitment numbering more than 200,000.

It might also be noted that along with the Brotherhood, there also was a Fenian Sisterhood, which provided various fund-raising and support services. According to *The Belfast News* of February 28, 1865, the first public meeting of the Sisterhood took place on February 1, 1865, in New York City. According to this report, ". . . members must be attentive and obedient; that each candidate must 'solemnly pledge her sacred word of honour' that she will 'labour to foster and extend feelings of harmony, and intense and intelligent love of country, among Irish men and women.'" The Sisterhood was to be organized with a head directress and each branch with a directress, secretary, and treasurer. The first Head Directress was a "Miss O'Shea." During a later period, women also were reputed to being used as low-level smugglers of messages and weapons into Ireland because they were much less likely to be searched by the authorities than were men.

Membership in the Fenian Brotherhood was open to anyone, although certainly most welcoming to Irish Americans and Irish immigrants. A person had to pay one-dollar initiation fees and in 1863, at least five cents a week dues, increasing to a dime a week by 1865. These fees were established in the national constitution, which authorized local circles to charge higher fees.[12] Although seemingly not a major sum, this should be compared to the daily wage for a nonfarm laborer or for a skilled carpenter in 1870 (which had seen considerable inflation from the earlier period): $1.04 and $1.70, respectively.[13] As such, the dues alone represented a relatively high degree of financial commitment by individual members. Each member also had to agree to attend weekly meetings to remain in good standing.

Fenians and Society

Early Fenian public events seemed to be a cross between political rallies, state fairs, and circuses. In many ways, they were a microcosm of nineteenth-century society. A somewhat lengthy excerpt from an early description of the Fenian national fair held in Chicago in 1864 will give a flavor of these events:

> Among the articles contributed by Ireland to the fair are three photographic portraits by the venerable Archbishop McHale; "a Whole Irishman" sends a moire antique gent's vest; others send

a piece of Lord Edward Fitzgerald's coffin; a pocket-handker-chief . . . a jar of whisky which had not paid the excise duty; a bog-oak neglige; a copy of a letter from France on Irish bravery; a sword picked up on Bunker's Hill by an Irish-English soldier; a pistol used in '98; a lump of stone, on which the broken treaty was signed by the illustrious Sarsfield; a bird's-eye view of the Protestant Reformation; a pair of lady's boots worked with a '98 pike; a Scotch claymore taken in Wexford in '98; a large doll, dressed as the Tipperary man's dark-haired Mary; a sod of Wolfe Tone's grave; a watch-pocket, worked by lady who hopes that it will be worn next a manly heart . . . a gross of pies "specially manufactured for the fair."[14]

A description of a second event, held in Bergen, New Jersey on August 3, 1865, further describes some of the social side of the Brotherhood at a local level. It relates the "First Grand Annual Pic-Nic [sic] of the Fenian Brotherhood of the New Jersey Department," involving about 700 members:

From Jersey City ferry the body marched to the grove in the following order:

Manahan's Band, 20 instruments; Fenian Brotherhood, 350 strong; the 90th New York State National Guard, 100 men; Fenian Brotherhood, 350 men. . . . On the route windows were thrown up, handkerchiefs waved, and loud cheers greeted them as they passed. . . . The Fenian sisters received their patriotic brethren at the grove, and with true sisterly affection dispensed some of the daisies which they had provided for the occasion. The perspiring and patriotic brothers were cooled off by draughts of fresh lager, or the more sparkling soda water. . . . The blind Irish fiddler . . . was there, and the ring was formed around him, and the Irish jig, hornpipe, and reel went on. . . .[15]

All this was followed by speeches from Brotherhood leaders. These examples of some of the social side of the Fenians are not presented to belittle the seriousness of the group. Rather, they should be reminders of how intertwined the Fenians became with the larger Irish American community, particularly in the cities in New York and surrounding states. Again using modern terminology, whether intentional or socially instinctive, the Fenian Brotherhood in the US clearly won the hearts and minds of the surrounding Irish people. In a real sense, the Brotherhood became synonymous with the local communities. Particularly for local and state governments, dealing with the Fenians meant dealing with the overall Irish American community.

More broadly, the Fenians were somewhat a variant of two major trends in nineteenth-century society. The first was the virtual explosion in private associations, such as lodges, workers' associations, gentlemen's clubs, and local service groups. Members joined on the basis of occupation, religious affiliation, social status, or ethnicity. None of these were mutually exclusive: it was common to have groups combining aspects of several or all these reasons for participation. Most males in society were "joiners" with memberships in several social, ethnic, and occupational groups. Although most represented a "man's world," virtually all of them had associated women's auxiliaries.

The second pattern was that of active membership in local militias. Virtually all towns and particularly cities in New York had local militia forces. In an earlier period, these militias were critical in local self-defense. By the mid-nineteenth century, however, much of their earlier necessity had been lost along the Eastern Seaboard. Although occasionally called out for riots and the like, in many ways a significant portion of these armed groups were more akin to social organizations than effective fighting forces. Some basic military training, such as drill and weapons practice, certainly was conducted, but for most of the militia groups, their main purpose seemed to be the opportunity to wear fancy uniforms and to conduct parades. The Fenians had loftier aspirations, but these were not always immediately apparent to outside observers in the early days of the movement. Nevertheless, the Fenian militias grew rapidly, with William D'Arcy noting forty Fenian militia units by November 1859.[16] Some Irish observers in the pre–Civil War period were less than enthralled with the internal dynamics and efficiency of militia units in general. As one example:

> The officers were very generally so unlettered, untutored and even rude that association with them was disagreeable. You can have no conception of them from anything you experienced in the committee of the R[epeal] A[ssociation] because there after all education or rank commanded respect and deference whereas here the inevitable tendency of equality between an educated and uneducated and a superior and inferior man is to beget rudeness by way of an assertion of the equality.[17]

In fairness, the quality of a particular militia varied particularly on whether a unit was a full member of the state forces, whether just associated with more formalized units, or completely independent. In either event, after some initial problems in the Civil War, many of these forces acquitted themselves very well in combat once they became better trained and more experienced. The other aspect of the local militias was that they tended to be ethnically based, particularly in the larger cities:

> By 1852, 4,000 out of 6,000 members [of militias in New York City] were foreign-born, including: 2,600 Irish in the Emmet Guard, the Irish Rifles, the Irish-American Guards, and the Ninth and Sixty-ninth Regiments; 1,700 Germans in their own regiments; the Italian Garibaldi Guard, and the French Garde Lafayette attached to the Twelfth Regiment. On the other extreme, 2,000 "American" residents of the Lower East Side joined such stoutly nativist militia companies as the American Rifles and the American Guard.[18]

Both the prevalence of civil associations and local militias meant that at first sight the Fenians did not seem to be particularly out of the mainstream, especially when compared to the strong ethnic basis for many of the surrounding groups. There was one significant difference, however. Even though members of German- and Italian-based militias almost certainly had strong connections with what was going on in their native countries and likely supported such issues as the reunification of Italy or the unification of Germany, these primarily were political aspirations rather than active armed support. The Fenians, on the other hand, made no secret of their desire to achieve their goals through armed action.

Although the Fenian Brotherhood had many aspects of a secret—or at least secretive—society, before 1866 in particular it tried to downplay this aspect in public. Members had to swear an oath to join the movement, but this was a matter of public knowledge and rather anodyne:

> I solemnly pledge my sacred word and honour as a truthful and honest man, that I will labour with earnest zeal for the liberation of Ireland from the yoke of England, and for the establishment of a free and independent government on Irish soil; that I will implicitly obey the commands of my superior officers in the Fenian Brotherhood; that I will faithfully discharge the duties of

my membership, as laid down in the Constitution and By-Laws thereof; that I will do my utmost to promote feelings of love, harmony, and kindly forbearance among all Irishmen ; and that I will foster, defend and propagate the aforesaid Fenian Brotherhood to the utmost of my power.

Despite this show of openness, there were continued questions as to what went on within the movement's meetings and planning. In particular, rumors of "inner circles" unknown to the US public continued to circulate. As one early account noted, the Fenians made "a subsequent admission that there is an inner circle, an unnamed council of ten, who direct the proceedings of the Brotherhood, and who are not called upon 'to make any report as to the methods and means by which they are endeavouring to carry forward the avowed ends of the Brotherhood.'"[19] In many ways, this was a perfectly understandable organizational strategy for the Fenians as a militant group. Using modern terminology, such operational security was essential for any group even contemplating armed actions. At the same time, however, this certainly raised concerns—especially among the non-Irish population in the US—as to what the Fenians actually were up to. Although the Brotherhood made moves toward maintaining security about its operations and plans, one envoy from the Irish Republican Brotherhood who was dispatched to New York to meet with the group observed that he was greeted with a brass band, had a reception with militia officers, and was expected to give a public address to a large crowd of supporters. As he noted in retrospect, "It struck me, of course, at the time, as no doubt it will strike many of my readers now, that it was a queer sort of proceeding to give a public, or semipublic, reception to a secret envoy."[20]

The Fenians and the Civil War

The outbreak of the Civil War was a somewhat mixed blessing for the Fenians. It provided both training in military tactics for existing members and a recruitment pool of young Irishmen in the various federal and state military units, many of which were heavily or almost exclusively Irish. In some cases, in fact, Irish nationalist leaders who were well known reportedly were used to recruit for Irish regiments.[21] This served both the interests of the US and state governments in recruiting units and the Fenian Brotherhood itself in getting the "right" people in positions of authority.

The presence of Fenians in the Union forces certainly was not a secret; in fact, Fenian circles were formally established in a number of units. As of January 1865, army and navy circles included those in the 10th Ohio Regiment, 15th Michigan Regiment; Corcoran Legion (comprising a major portion of the New York Regiments in the Irish Brigade); and in the naval vessels *New Ironsides, Huntsville, Port Royal,* and *Brooklyn.* Units at Morris Island and around Washington D.C. formed separate circles.[22] The Army of the Potomac, the Army of the Cumberland, and the Army of Tennessee had larger circles comprising individual soldiers from multiple regiments. Also, many of the senior Irish officers in the Union army were simultaneously either members or leaders of the Fenian Brotherhood. As one example, "[Major] Downing's deep connection to the Fenian Brotherhood was not a secret. It is likely that most commanders knew that while Downing was frequently serving as a recruiting officer in New York he scheduled and held meetings of the Fenian Brotherhood at the Whitney House on the corner of Broadway and Twelfth Street. Notices for these meetings were published in the Irish American newspaper."[23] On the other hand, the large membership of fighting troops and officers came with significant risks for the Fenians. As O'Mahony noted in 1865:

> Many whole circles had entered the American army in a body. . . . In fine, no less than fifty of our branches had become extinct or dormant, and the remainder had lost considerably in ardor and efficiency, through the absence of their choicest spirits in the field. . . . At the Chicago Congress 68 circles were represented, with a constituency of about 15,000 men, half of whom, at least, were in the armies of the Union, and of the others many were apathetic.[24]

Many of the regiments with a preponderance of Irish, particularly the volunteer regiments, took heavy casualties during the Civil War. A particularly significant individual casualty for the Fenians was General Michael Corcoran, one of the founders of the movement and member of the Fenian Brotherhood Supreme Central Council. Corcoran was born in County Sligo in Ireland, son of an Irish officer in the British army. Corcoran joined an Irish opposition movement called the Ribbonmen before he emigrated to the US in 1849. He became active both in the New York City Democratic Party political machine and in the local militia. Corcoran had gained considerable notoriety prior to the war when as commander of the 69th New

York Militia, he refused to parade the unit as part of the visit of the Prince of Wales to New York City. Although he was facing court martial charges at the start of the war due to this refusal of orders, the charges were dropped due to military necessity, and he rejoined the unit. He was captured at the battle of Bull Run early during the Civil War, but his conduct as a prisoner before his release in 1862 by the Confederates was viewed as very heroic. Corcoran as a brigadier general of volunteers then formed the Corcoran Legion with four regiments plus some understrength units. He died on December 22, 1863, after being thrown from a runaway horse. The Fenian Brotherhood clearly had viewed Corcoran as being a prime candidate for the leader of its military wing, and his loss hit them hard.

During the Civil War, the redesignated 69th New York Infantry—which due to its war record became known as "The Fighting 69th"—was combined with the 63rd New York Infantry and the 88th New York Infantry to form the Irish Brigade. The 28th Massachusetts Infantry and the 116th Pennsylvania Infantry later merged into the Brigade. All these units had strong a Fenian presence. Thomas Francis Meagher, well known as a very vocal proponent of Irish independence, was selected as the brigade commander. The Irish Brigade became renowned for its courage, but this came at a price: a total of 7,715 men served in the brigade throughout the course of the war, and 961 were killed or mortally wounded, and about 3,000 were wounded. These figures represented in total more than the actual authorized strength of the brigade. The casualties included a large number of Irish officers. Obviously, many of the troops and officers would have been prime material for the Fenians if they had not been lost. Likewise, the 42nd New York Volunteer Infantry, known as the Tammany Regiment and with strong Fenian influence, had a casualty rate of about fifty percent.[25] In many ways, in fact, this unit and many others gradually lost their "Irishness" as the war ground on and their ranks began filling with draftees and draft substitutes. Wexler noted that by the middle of the war, the "Tammany regiment now had as many men of German descent as there were Irishmen."[26]

There may, however, have been one important intangible additional benefit for the Fenians and the Irish more generally as a result of their Civil War service and the casualties they suffered in it. Irish Americans in the nineteenth century generally were considered as being near the bottom of the social structure, and almost always were viewed as being "different" from the mainstream American culture, in large measure due to their predominant Catholicism. The Irish record in the Civil War certainly did not resolve this completely—particularly given such incidents as the New

Point made also in book on Irish in C.W.

York City draft riots, in which Irish Americans were deeply involved, and increasing reluctance by the Irish to serve in uniform as the war dragged on—but it is likely that the blooding of the Irish regiments in the Civil War at least raised the public perception of the Irish overall and somewhat reduced their image as the "other."

The Catholic Church and the Fenians

The secrecy of the Brotherhood did present particular complications in their relationship with the Catholic Church. Although it might be assumed that there would be an affinity between the Irish Fenians and the Church, many Catholic leaders came out very strongly against the Brotherhood. For example, the Archbishop of Cincinnati argued that the Fenian Brotherhood was "an oath-bound, secret society, and as such to be shunned and avoided by every sincere and loyal Catholic"[27] The *Brooklyn Daily Eagle* on December 17, 1864, also noted that the Fenians in Jersey City "have secured in some way the enmity of the Catholic clergy." It reported that priests actually talked some 200 Fenians from attending a meeting there. Likewise, an aide to Bishop Duggan of Chicago wrote to the *Chicago Republican*:

> There is an irreconcilable difference between Catholics and Fenians, or any other body of men who belong to societies condemned by the Church. The Bishop has, on the contrary, instructed his clergy not to administer the sacraments to Fenians, and to refuse Christian burial to such of them as die in membership with that society.[28]

What this meant in practice was demonstrated in Buffalo when the Fenians tried to have a Catholic burial for a casualty of the 1866 invasion; when the uniformed honor guard tried to enter the church, the priest refused to admit them, and they had to hold the burial without formal church services.[29]

Dating somewhat later, Pope Pius IX himself formally denounced the group in 1870 as part of an overall condemnation of secret societies by the Vatican. The Fenians clearly saw the impact of these denunciations on their recruiting and mobilization efforts and were obviously rankled by them. The Brotherhood passed resolutions at both the 1863 Chicago and the 1865 Cincinnati conventions claiming that it was being unjustly accused of being a secret society.[30] Fenian leaders frequently tried, albeit with limited success, to differentiate between maintaining a required level of secrecy to conduct their operations from being a secret society. O'Mahony, for example, in 1859 wrote:

> Our association is neither anti-Catholic nor irreligious. We are an Irish army, not a secret society. We make no secret of our objects and designs. We simply bind ourselves to conceal such matters as are needful to be kept from the enemy's knowledge, both for the success of our strategy and for the safety of our friends. It is better to avoid their denunciatory attacks by modifying the form of our pledge so as not to be obnoxious to spiritual censure, even by the most exacting ecclesiastic in America.[31]

Despite condemnations by senior Catholic clergy, however, there clearly were mixed messages being sent by the Church hierarchy. Overall, there were various levels and forms of support by individual members of the clergy.[32] Catholic priests continued to support (and join) the Fenians. Likewise, prominent local Fenians continued to be fully accepted in the Church, with many of them being stalwarts of their parishes.[33]

One interesting aspect of the American Fenians and religion was that they seemed to attempt to be nonsectarian. Both Irish Catholics and Irish Protestants were members. The Fenian constitution, in fact, stated that "all subjects relating to differences in religion, be absolutely and forever excluded from the councils and deliberations of the Fenian Brotherhood. . . ."[34] The majority of Fenians were Catholic, but there certainly were Protestant members. Peter Vronsky notes that of fifty-eight Fenians held in Toronto jail after the Ridgeway battle, nineteen were Protestant.[35] Likewise, John Rafferty of the Lavelle Circle in a speech to a group of about 200 members and supporters in the Tara Circle in Brooklyn said "I believe that seven-eighths of the Fenian Brotherhood are children of that [the Catholic] church. . . ."[36] Although obviously far from a scientific appraisal of the sectarian breakdown of the Fenians, this might be a reasonably fair assessment of the Catholic–Protestant composition of the group. Also, a considerable proportion of the senior military leadership of the Brotherhood were Protestant. This was in sharp contrast to the Fenian organization in Canada, where its members represented Catholic Irish Canadians versus Protestant "Orange" Canadians; arguably, in Canada the conflict was more between the Catholic and Protestant Irish than between the Irish and the government.[37]

Fenian Leadership

The Manhattan Circle initially coordinated the other circles, but as the movement grew, a more formal leadership structure was established. In many ways, this eventually was modeled after the US government structure, with a president, cabinet, and senate. In the early days, however, the governing system was somewhat ad hoc. By the time of the 1863 Chicago national convention, the leadership structure had become more regularized. O'Mahony was the Head Centre, supported by a Central Council of five, which at that point included two army officers. Although the naming is initially somewhat confusing, the Fenians used "centre" as the title for the leader rather than its conventional use. Despite this nod toward a broader leadership structure, the Head Centre—at that point synonymous with O'Mahony—clearly was predominant. In the Fenian constitution presented at the convention, it was specified that the council was subject to the call of the Head Centre "when he may deem it expedient."[38] Likewise emphasizing the power of the central leadership, the rule was established at the Cincinnati convention that "No correspondence whatever can be held with Ireland or Europe on the business of the organization, except through the Head Centre. . . . Any member or office derogating from this law shall be considered a traitor."[39]

One parenthetical note should be made about this convention. Both at Chicago and the later Cincinnati convention, the delegates made a particular point about passing a resolution supporting the independence struggles of the Poles.[40] While focused on Irish independence, the Fenian Brotherhood at least institutionally displayed a broader interest in democratic movements in general.[41] In part, this may have been tactical, but many of the Fenian leaders sincerely believed in what might be called international democratization and self-rule, with some of them having been involved with various stripes of international socialism.

The Cincinnati convention of January 1865 further expanded the central leadership so that Head Centre would be "assisted" by a ten-person (in reality, of course, ten-man) Central Council, treasurer, assistant treasurer, and corresponding secretary. Each of these leaders was to be elected annually. Although the system in theory provided considerable internal democracy, O'Mahony continued to be elected unanimously, suggesting either an unusual level of popularity or (more likely) carefully staged elections. This centralized rule was further emphasized by the system whereby members of central council were nominated by Head Centre, and only then put up for elections by the members. The remainder of the leadership structure was formally established as State Centres to direct states and centers for each circle.

Another Fenian national congress was held in Buffalo in July 1865, but few details emerged as to deliberations. There were no public announcements as to changes in the leadership structure. This congress included General O'Neill, James Gibbons of Philadelphia, the Vice President, and senate representatives from Cincinnati, New Jersey, Michigan, Utica, New York City, Troy, Rochester, Buffalo, Albany, Cleveland, Peoria, and Louisville, Kentucky. Although the proceedings were held in secret, some large hints were provided to sympathetic journalists: "The communicativeness which formerly prevailed among those nigh in authority in the organization, no longer enables us to spread before our readers a record of the proceedings, but we are empowered to say that something or other of great moment has been determined upon, and Canada, and the British Empire generally, will see what they will see before long."[42]

Chapter 2

The American and Irish Fenians

He would gladly go; can pay his passage and furnish a rifle. He says he has an old mother in Ireland who would be glad to see him on one condition—fighting for his country.

—Summary of a letter from an Irish American in Wisconsin, 1859[1]

The Fenian Brotherhood represented one of the earlier transnational organized violent groups. Without stretching the historical analogy too far, many of the issues it faced have, in fact, been reflected in more recent movements. Although the emphasis in this book is on the American Fenian movement, its actions and dynamics cannot be particularly well understood without some examination of the Irish Fenians; aka, the Irish Republican Brotherhood (IRB). A short summary would be that the Irish movement probably had fewer active members and lower potential capabilities than did the Americans. Also, it might be noted that in contrast to the ultimate fate of the American Fenians, many of the Irish Fenians eventually were hanged or imprisoned.

A brief description of James Stephens, the leader of the IRB, is necessary to understand the dynamics of the relationship between the Irish Fenians and the Irish American Fenian Brotherhood. As previously noted, Stephens was a veteran of the 1848 uprising. He was wounded in the course of operations; the British mistakenly thought he had been killed (and, in fact, there was a mock funeral for him to reinforce this belief). Stephens was able to flee to France, where he worked a series of odd jobs, including as a teacher and translator. While there, Stephens reportedly met with several revolutionary leaders from other countries, especially Italian nationalists in exile in France.[2]

Stephens returned to Ireland in 1856 and began what he termed his "3,000 mile walk." During this, he walked throughout much of Ireland, in the process regaining contacts with some of the veterans of the 1848 movement. By 1857, he was ready to begin the movement that became the Irish Republican Brotherhood. One allied movement arose at about the same time as the IRB. This was the Phoenix National and Literary Society, a society formed by members of the Young Ireland movement in Dublin in 1856. It was established by Jeremiah (or Diamuid in Gaelic, which he tended to prefer) O'Donovan Rossa "for the liberation of Ireland by force of arms." It quickly became an arm of the IRB. Some contemporary sources, in fact, used "Phoenix men" as a synonym for the Fenians, at least in its early days.

A key difference with the IRB from earlier Irish nationalist groups was its demographics. Earlier movements had been comprised predominantly of intellectuals, well-educated members, and generally upper-middle to upper class. Although the IRB certainly had its share of these types of members, particularly in the leadership, the bulk of its members came from the working classes. John Devoy, one of the earlier members and subsequently a senior leader, noted that the early recruiting grounds were among several drapery companies, building trades, shoemakers, and tailors.[3]

The IRB was intended to be a very cellular structure, with individual members of one cell not knowing the members of other cells; this, of course, continues to be the preferred concept for terrorist or insurgent cells. The Irish structure was generally similar to that of the American Fenians: a "centre" (usually considered to be the equivalent of a colonel) was intended to recruit nine captains, who, in turn, would recruit nine sergeants, who then would recruit nine privates for a theoretical strength in each circle of 820 members. For security purposes, rather than using ranks, the members were supposed to be designated as "A" for colonel, "B" for captain, "C" for sergeant, and "D" for private. The Bs, Cs, and Ds in theory were supposed to know only the identities of their fellow members in the cell and their immediate superiors. Again, at least in theory, a system was established under which a seniority system enabled a quick replacement of any senior leaders who were killed or arrested, without breaching the security of individual cells. Unfortunately for the IRB, the security structure broke down rather rapidly, with individual cells becoming very closely tied together and knowledge of leaders' identities at all levels. This made it much easier for British police forces to take down multiple cells simultaneously rather than having to attack one cell at a time. Likewise, the actual strength level of the individual circles varied widely; Devoy noted two circles that had more than 2,000 members. He also cited several centres who would not work within the normal circle structure. As one of those centres stated, he "didn't want to play second fiddle to no man."[4]

During the early days of the organization of the Fenian Brotherhood in the United States and its sister organization, even while both groups began creating their network in the two countries, a relatively high level of skepticism as to the capabilities of each group was shown. In an era of strong nationalism, this likely was almost inevitable, but Irish Americans (even those who were very recent immigrants) clearly had some misgivings as to the abilities of the Irish nationalists who were to form the IRB in that country. As one Irish Fenian noted, "It is hard to get the mass of the Irish in New York to believe that any one can be serious who speaks of freeing Ireland. They have had their hopes disappointed, when raised to the highest pitch, twice or three times within the five years I have been here."[5] In many ways, the American Fenians seemed to view the Irish as potentially capable foot soldiers, but in dire need of leadership to be furnished by Americans.

These types of jaded views were reciprocated by the Irish toward the Irish Americans. Comments by John O'Leary, who was a member of the Irish branch, probably exemplify a typical attitude: "These working men [Fenian members and potential supporters] were, so far as I could at all gather then or since, very good fellows, indeed, in nearly every way; certainly very enthusiastic Irishmen, but mostly men of very ordinary intelligence—to my mind, rather inferior to the men of the same class whom I knew to belong to the organization in Dublin."[6]

Likewise, James Stephens had what appeared to be a prejudice against Americans and Irish Americans in general. Even before he first visited the US, in a private letter he wrote, "I am sick of Irish Catholics in America. I am sick of Yankee-doodle twaddle, Yankee-doodle selfishness and all Yankee-doodledum!"[7] During his first visit to the US, he also privately expressed his disdain for both the country overall and more specifically virtually all the Irish American nationalists he met.[8]

From the Irish perspective, the two greatest contributions the American Fenians could make were fund raising and practical support by providing weapons and key personnel. Stephens was very clear as to his demands in a letter dated January 1, 1858:

I undertake to organize in three months . . . at least 10,000, of whom about 1500 shall have firearms and the remainder pikes. . . . You [American Fenians] must then be able to furnish from 80[pounds] to 100 [pounds] a month. . . . I believe it essential to success that the centre of this or any similar organization should be perfectly unshackled; in other words, a provisional dictator. On this point I can conscientiously concede nothing.[9]

In general, the Irish Fenians were disappointed in both areas.

A recurring theme in the American and Irish Fenian branches was an almost constant fight over the funds sent to the IRB by the American Fenians. At the beginning of the movement, fund raising was rather informal: "The men were called together again, and the necessity of immediate financial aid to the men in Ireland was explained to them. Captain Corcoran, who always was an essentially practical man, proposed that everyone present empty his pockets on the table, and the amount thus realized was, I think, £80, which was given to Denieffe, who promptly forwarded it to Ireland."[10] Speaking of the early days, Denieffe noted the basic problem:

After a month, occupied in foraging around, I returned to Ireland with only forty pounds, which disappointed all our friends. I told Stephens not to depend on America for further assistance. "The Irish-Americans," I said, "will not subscribe until they are obliged to. They, have been humbugged so often they have lost confidence, and at present have no faith in attempts for the regeneration of Ireland."[11]

Denieffe may have been proven wrong about the willingness of Irish Americans to support Irish nationalist movements, but he was generally correct about the willingness to provide funding. This remained a continuing source of tension between Stephens and the American Fenians. According to O'Leary, Stephens told him that the IRB during the first six years (from 1858 to 1864), received "a little less than £1500; from 1864 to Stephens' third visit to New York in 1866, about £28,500; and during Stephens' stay in the US in 1866, about £2500; total, £32,500. Of this, nearly £7000 was seized by the British when trying to bring it into Ireland."[12] It probably did not help Stephens's confidence in the Americans that he was much more successful in personal fundraising when he visited the US than in relying on indirect American remittances.

These themes certainly were present in Stephens's first visit to America in 1858–1859. Much of his diary during this trip is concerned with almost constant problems in raising appreciable funds; he notes difficulties in raising even small sums from individual subscriptions. As an indicator of larger financial issues, Stephens continually had to borrow money while in America just to pay his travel expenses.[13] Although he was able to collect about 600 pounds, he noted that he failed to get "men of means and influence."[14] In particular, two major names in Irish nationalism and heroes of earlier uprisings, T.F. Meagher and John Mitchel, toyed with the idea of supporting the Fenians and IRB. John Mitchel in particular was considered a major prize. Mitchel was a veteran of the 1848 rebellion who had been transported to Australia, escaped from there, and reached the US in late 1853. He founded a newspaper, *The Citizen*, which took both an Irish nationalist and anti-Papal (not anti-Catholic) stance. As the Civil War approached, Mitchel became somewhat alienated from the mainstream of the nationalist movement because he advocated both proslavery and secessionist positions. Nevertheless, he was somewhat a senior statesman in Irish nationalism, and the Fenians certainly were interested in his support. Although Mitchel later became associated with the Fenians for a brief time, he initially turned down Stephens's advances. This clearly came as a major setback in Stephens's mind.[15]

Stephens paid several visits to the US. Beyond the initial visit in 1858–1859, he returned in 1864 and 1866. These trips were in addition to the time he had to spend in France following his prison escape in 1865. In one form or another, the visits were considered critical in fund raising for the Irish branch, and generally did result in some money being raised. The 1864 trip was particularly important in this regard. Stephens was able to visit the Chicago Fenian fair, where Stephens proved to be a success. He also was able to receive a military pass to visit federal army units; again, he received considerable support from Irish American officers and soldiers. However essential these visits might have been, they raise one question. Stephens authorized other leaders, most notably Thomas Clarke Luby, to act in his stead while he was gone, but given Stephens's autocratic leadership style, it is far from clear how much actual authority these other IRB leaders had. As such, when Stephens was abroad, the IRB may have faced some "dead time" in developing its strategic capabilities.

One issue that began to weigh on relations between the American Fenians and the IRB was the personality of Stephens himself. Stephens demanded dictatorial power, and this was reflected in what could be described as either his self-assurance or arrogance. Many of Stephens's statements, whether private or public, certainly reflected this. In his private diary on January 7, 1859, he noted that ". . . if they are false to me they must be false to Ireland. . . ." Elsewhere, he wrote that, "I have no hesitation in saying that I think very highly of myself. I have grasped more of the truth than almost any other man."[16] From all reports, Stephens was not shy about sharing similar sentiments with others around him.

However much Stephens tended to the autocratic, one contemporary author argued that this was a necessity:

> He was on the field where the action was to take place; he was to assume the responsibility of the movement . . . [his] life would surely be forfeited if he fell into the hands of the British government . . . his action should not be hampered by the dictation of men whose absence from the scene placed them in a position where they were incapable of judging of the necessities of the hour.[17]

As is rather common, personal relationships among the respective leaders had a major impact on the two groups. All reports suggest that Stephens and O'Mahony became close comrades during their mutual exile in Paris following the collapse of the 1848 uprising. Stephens appeared to have considerable admiration for O'Mahony, at least in the period when the Brotherhood and the IRB were being established. According to Stephen's private diary entry of January 7, 1859, "for in him alone I had implicit trust, and to him alone would I wholly unburden myself. . . . O'Mahony, I say it absolutely, is far and away the first patriot of the Irish race."[18]

Even at this point, however, Stephens had established the relative pecking order in his mind:

> . . . should I perish, the cause is lost. For I fear that even he [O'Mahony] lacks many of the essentials of a leader. This fear has been eating into my soul for some time . . . O'Mahony I must *swear* to remain here till we are up at home; and I must also *swear* him not to allow any man to force him to give up his position. The supreme control over the Organisation in America I have already given him. An active man by his side would enable him to make this effective.[19]

One reflection of how Stephens viewed the relative power between him and O'Mahony was reflected in a letter to O'Mahony on April 6, 1859. In this lengthy letter, Stephens gave him extremely detailed and rather imperious instructions on how O'Mahony should conduct his business, including on how to dress when conducting Brotherhood business.[20] All this clearly began to prove a major irritant to O'Mahony who wrote to another IRB leader in 1859:

> I am discontented with Stephens' [sic] treatment of myself. Having long used my name and my person as a shield against his private enemies and the enemies of the organization, he has been for sometime [sic] past making a scapegoat of me among his partizans [sic] and blaming me for shortcomings that were inevitable consequences of his own desertion of me. . . . To this interference with my functions I can no longer submit. Neither can I submit to dictatorial arrogance on his part. . . .[21]

According to O'Leary, who seems to have tried to put the best face on things, Stephen and O'Mahony were almost inevitably due to clash both because of their respective leadership positions and their different personalities. O'Leary considered Stephens as by "far the more active-minded and resourceful man . . . while O'Mahony was more slow, methodic, and cautious."[22]

Denieffe, who was present at a meeting of Stephens and O'Mahony, provided a lengthy but very candid picture of the dynamics between the two:

> In the early part of 1860, John O'Mahony arrived from New York and stopped with his friend James Cantwell at the Star and Garter. His coming had been announced in advance, and he met the captain (James Stephens) by appointment at Langan's. That meeting of the leaders is historic, and I was present and shall never forget it. I was requested to escort O'Mahony to Langan's, as he did not know the way, neither was he prepared for the reception which he received from Stephens when he got there. Stephens, after the formal greetings were over, asked a number of questions; wanted to know why the organization in America had not been kept together, a unit; he wanted to know why O'Mahony and his colleagues had not kept their promise to the men in Ireland and had not furnished the funds necessary to defray the cost of spreading the organization, etc.

To all of those questions O'Mahony failed to give satisfactory answers, whereupon Stephens reproached him in words of the most cutting sarcasm, telling him of his shortcomings, feebleness and insincerity and wound up by reminding him how he, Stephens, had dragged him out of obscurity and put him in a position he never dreamed of.[23]

Stephens and O'Mahony met privately the next day, and apparently some level of reconciliation was reached, but it is hard to believe that after such a public dressing-down O'Mahony bore kindly feelings toward Stephens. This is particularly true because in many ways the American Fenians were the stronger group. Relations reached such a nadir that Stephens sent Thomas Clarke Luby to New York in 1863 with the power to remove O'Mahony. If such an effort had, in fact, been tried, in a real sense it would have pitted Stephens's ideological standing in the Fenians versus O'Mahony's practical power position (at least at that time). In the event, Luby thought better of this, and no action was taken. Even then, however, O'Mahony clearly understood the dynamics of the relationship: ". . . I feel he would supersede me, if possible. He wants a money-feeder for the IRB here, not a directing mind."[24] As part of the power struggle in 1863, a secret resolution was passed by the American Fenian Brotherhood leadership naming O'Mahony as the undisputed leader in the US and relegating Stephens to leadership of only the Irish wing.

However great the tensions between O'Mahony and the leaders of the Irish Fenians, the Senate Wing seemed to be held in even lower esteem. In the words of O'Leary: "O'Mahony was not, indeed, an ideal leader, but he was an ideal Irishman, while Colonel Roberts (president of the Senate) and most of the senators were men of whom we knew little and for whom we cared less. Nor am I aware that any of these gentlemen have done anything since which ought to place them, in the estimation of their own or another generation of Irishmen, on any higher level than they then stood."[25]

Stephens's failure to prop up O'Mahony also could be seen as a reflection of the emerging weakening of Stephens's status in the Fenian network. It might, in fact, be argued that both the leaders somewhat fell together, albeit for different reasons

Despite these differences, the Irish and American branches of the Fenians established rather close relations, particularly during the early days. A key early sign of this alliance was the funeral of Terence Bellew McManus, which might be viewed as the "coming-out party" for the American Fenians and the IRB. McManus had been a veteran of the 1848 rebellion. After his capture by the British, he was tried and sentenced to transportation to Australia. He managed to escape from there in 1851 and he made his way to San Francisco, where he became a well-known, albeit unsuccessful, businessman. He also remained active in Irish nationalist affairs until his death on January 15, 1861. The San Francisco Fenian Circle proposed that his body be moved to Ireland for burial on his native soil. James Stephens reportedly initially opposed this, but his voice became somewhat buried by the groundswell of support for the idea in the US.

The transport of McManus's body became a media circus. When the funeral escort reached New York City on September 18 after the corpse had been shipped via Panama, it was escorted to the Cathedral by a band, police detachment, and troops from the 69th New York Volunteers. The funeral cortege then sailed for Ireland, arriving on October 30. While all this was going on, several Irish groups battled over which one would control the burial in Ireland, but Stephens and the IRB won out.

Once in Ireland, the ceremonies became major affairs. The funeral procession and spectators in Cork reportedly numbered 80,000 to 100,000, and there were reportedly 30,000 marchers in Dublin. Even allowing for the usual hyperbole of the period, everywhere there were massive crowds. The body finally was laid to rest on December 10, with the body lying in state at the Mechanics Institute because the Catholic hierarchy would not permit it at any of the churches. One of the interesting sidelights of the proceedings—which may have been an indicator of later developments—was that there were several reports that members of the IRB and other militant groups wanted to use the environment to launch a fresh rebellion, but these intentions were squelched by Stephens.[26]

Even without immediate actions, however, McManus's funeral provided immense media and public attention to the Fenians, and almost certainly aided in recruiting and fund raising. Just as important, it enabled the IRB to outmaneuver the other Irish nationalist groups for control of the nationalist movement. One problem in many accounts of the Fenians in general and the IRB in particular is that they ignore the fissiparous nature of Irish nationalism. There never really was one "movement," but a plethora of groups, individuals, and organizations with varying approaches and strategies. This was as true after the rise of the Fenians as before. Nevertheless, the Fenians began owning the media message for mid-nineteenth-century Ireland.

As the IRB became more established, the American Fenians sent a number of its members to Ireland to assist the IRB there. These representatives typically were former soldiers or officers in the US military or state militia forces. Their role was rather amorphous, particularly in the early days. The total number of these representatives during the course of the Fenians' existence is difficult to accurately assess, but likely was rather significant. British security services estimated in February 1866 that there were about 500 Irish Americans in Ireland. Most of them were viewed as either actual or potential Fenian activists. One complicating factor in determining numbers is that the British government would arrest Irish Americans entering Ireland whom the authorities suspected as being Fenians, when, in fact, they were innocent businessmen or tourists. At times, the British would detain any American males in Ireland who were wearing felt hats and square-toed boots because these were viewed as being military and therefore probable signs of Fenianism. Whenever the British did a roundup of suspects in Ireland, Americans were well represented. For example, when London suspended habeas corpus on February 16, 1866, and rounded up ninety-eight persons, thirty-eight immediately claimed American citizenship.[27] In fairness to the British, however, most of the Americans arrested did, in fact, have connections to the Fenians.

At times even the Irish Fenians were unsure as to what the precise purpose of some visitors might be. There were several complaints of some Americans who in theory were representatives of the Fenian Brotherhood, but spent their time more as tourists than providing any particular value. Nevertheless, the IRB rather quickly found uses for the American volunteers. In the early stage of these visits by Americans, they were intended primarily as trainers and "drill masters" to improve the military capabilities of the Irish. From all indications, there was no fixed term for their deployments to Ireland, and they could come and go as they pleased. A particular problem was finding the funds to maintain their stays. O'Leary noted the impact of this:

> The upshot of the unfortunate business was that all these men, having first gone to their various places of birth, sometimes finding an organization there and sometimes not, gradually exhausting their funds, and finding mostly no means of replacing them, finally found their way back to America, bringing with them more or less discontent and doubt, and most likely spreading disbelief and discouragement within the range of their influence.[28]

A continuing issue for the American Fenians—and in many ways for analysts ever since—was how much credence to put into IRB claims as to its strength and capabilities. This obviously was not limited to the Irish branch: many similar claims by the American Fenian Brotherhood were equally exaggerated. Nevertheless, decisions on support required and the likelihood of success typically were based on aspirations rather than reality. John Devoy noted that the man who swore him in to the IRB "had a great talent for exaggeration" and probably multiplied the number of members by five.[29] More significant and more telling was a conversation he related between Stephens and Con O'Mahony (a representative to the US) in which Stephens claimed that the IRB was due to immediately receive 100,000 rifles and "a good supply of artillery" from the US. The Americans also were to send several general officers and a large number of colonels to provide leadership, with at least 3,000 officers from the Chicago area alone.[30]

This type of exaggeration and viewing aspirations as capabilities had two corrosive results. From the standpoint of IRB members who believed these types of claims, they had a legitimate reason to ask why they were not seeing the results of such immense American power. From the American perspective, claims of a powerful IRB meant that they questioned why the Irish did not seem to be accomplishing anything visible. O'Mahony evidently was not comfortable with the optimistic reports he began receiving from Ireland, and sent at least two teams of American Fenians to Ireland to conduct independent assessments of just how capable the IRB actually was. In the words of the letter of instructions he sent to the leader of one team:

> When arrived in the latter city you will report immediately to [Stephens] and . . . you will place yourself completely under his orders for the period of three months . . . and you will perform faithfully such duties as he may assign you. At the end of three months, you will, as the resolution of the C. C. F. B. points out, render a full report in writing of the state of the I. R. B., specifying in the said report its constitution, mode of government, the manner of persons whereof said government is composed, its military strength, its financial resources and expenditure, and its general availability for successful action within the present year, taking in account the means at the actual disposal of its Executive aided by such assistance as can be furnished it from America within that time according to your own experience of both organizations up to the time of making your said report, and using your own military knowledge as your sole guide in

forming your opinion. In making the said report you will state nothing but what you shall yourself have acquired an actual knowledge of. You will set down no fact from hearsay or upon reports furnished you by others, judging in all cases from such surroundings as you shall be brought in contact with while performing your duties under the C. E. If in your unbiased judgment there should be no probability of successful action this year (1865) you will in that case return to these Head Quarters after the expiration of the three months. . . .[31]

There is no record of just how well the IRB responded to these inspection visits, but it is hard to believe that they could be well pleased. They certainly provided "minders" to the American visitors to monitor what they were up to. Perhaps fortunately for relations between the two branches, all the inspectors provided positive reports.[32] Given the setbacks suffered by the IRB in 1865 and 1867, the judgment of the assessors might well be subject to question.

One other note should be added about the Fenians as a transnational group. This is the existence of the group in countries other than Ireland and the US. There were Fenian circles and supporters in other countries. The first, as noted earlier, were the cells in England itself. Under the Fenians, these small conspiratorial groups were not terribly significant until the 1870s, but their existence created significant problems for British security services and considerable public concern. The second area was Canada. There certainly were Fenian circles within the province of Canada and the other North American provinces. Although the American Fenians made much of the Canadian circles and invited their representatives to all the conventions, the number of Canadian Fenians was relatively low. According to one estimate, the number of members and supporters in Quebec City was 200; Montreal, 355; and Toronto, 800.[33] Smaller towns and rural areas likely added some numbers of sympathizers, but they would almost inevitably be disorganized.[34] Finally, given that British courts sentenced a number of Fenians to transportation to Australia, there were some Fenian groups there. Although there certainly were Fenians in a number of areas outside the US and Ireland, the key point was that they never came close to reaching critical mass. The group's future rested on the Americans and the Irish.

Chapter 3

The Fenians, American Society, and the American Government

Nearly all Irish officers with scarcely an exception are members of the [Fenian Brotherhood]; and it is no secret that many United States Senators and government officials are its avowed friends.

—*The Crisis*, October 25, 1865

The status of the Irish in the US during this period was not particularly high. Particularly in the mid-nineteenth century, with the rise of various nativist groups and the Know Nothing Party, the Irish generally were toward the bottom of the social structure in the US, with many non–Irish Americans viewing them as only slightly above African Americans, whether slaves or Freedmen. In part, this was associated with the Catholicism of most Irish immigrants, and the Irish Protestants generally had an easier time with assimilation and acceptance as "true Americans." By the mid-nineteenth century, most Irish Protestants typically were not as subject to active prejudice as were the Catholics.

Despite their low social status, there was one fact about the Irish that caught the attention of American politicians. This was that they made up a significant voting bloc available for capture. Particularly in the cities of the Northeast and upper Midwest, Irish immigrants and second-generation Irish constituted enough votes to decide elections if they voted as a group, which typically was the case. This applied not only to local elections, but also nationally. As such, many political leaders made a point not only of showing support for the Irish overall, but to the Fenian movement to a greater or lesser extent. In some ways the Irish somewhat wasted their electoral power by being a solid Democratic Party bloc until the 1870s, but few Whig Party or successor Republican Party politicians saw any reason to unnecessarily create motivations to alienate the Irish vote.

Some indication of the level and types of support for the Fenians can be displayed by the various statements of support and monetary contributions during the Fenian fair held in Chicago in March 1864. Fernando Wood, who served both as New York City Mayor and as a US Congressman, sent a message of support and a contribution of 100 dollars. Michigan Governor Austin Blair issued a statement approving the goals of Irish independence. Postmaster General Montgomery Blair sent 25 dollars, together with the message:

> I have always sympathized warmly with Ireland, and rejoice in the conviction, which daily grows stronger, that the days of her oppressors—the haughty and heartless British aristocracy—are numbered. To the cold-blooded, calculating policy of this odious class we owe the planting of Slavery on this continent, and consequently all the horrors we have witnessed in the war which now shakes the continent. Let us triumph in this struggle, and there will soon be an end put to the sway of the oppressors of Ireland, and both parties so understand it.[1]

Several other national and state politicians also sent statements of varying degrees of support, together with lesser sums of money. Likewise, a number of military officers of various ranks (including several general officers) contributed, along with contributions issued under the name of particular regiments, usually with messages of strong political support.[2]

Key members of the American national government also appeared to at least tolerate if not publicly support the movement. Many members of Congress—obviously particularly those from districts in which there was a large Irish population—were openly supportive of the Fenians. For example, Fenian President William Roberts received an invitation to visit the House of Representatives, where he was escorted to the floor and introduced around. *The London Times* of October 3, 1865, however acerbic, was very correct: "The Irish vote has become a matter of consequence, and American newspapers and American politicians have not been slow to pander to the weaknesses and delusions of those who dispose of it."[3]

Irish block vote. Politicians
i.e. support Fenians -

The Fenians, American Society, and the American Government   31

These overt signs of support extended to the Presidential administrations during the existence of the Fenians. William Seward, the US Secretary of State under both Lincoln and Johnson, provided at least some relatively quiet support for the Fenians.[4] One reflection of Seward's attitude at the diplomatic level came when Colonel Gleason of the Army of the Potomac spoke at a Fenian meeting and the attorney general of Louisiana presided at the Fenian Convention in Cincinnati. When Britain protested, Seward reportedly answered that the colonel was on furlough and that the attorney general was responsible to his own state.

This attitude also seemed to be the case within the White House itself, albeit even more quietly. The Fenians obviously became a significant movement under President Lincoln, but with more pressing issues on his hands, there are few indications that he thought about them much either way. As long as the Union forces were successfully recruiting the Irish (among others), he appeared to have an attitude of laissez faire. There was some question as to the stance that President Andrew Johnson took toward the Fenians. The earlier common perception was that Johnson was an active although somewhat quiet Fenian supporter. In large measure, this was a result of a meeting held between Johnson and the Fenians. A delegation of Fenians visited Johnson at the White House not long before the 1866 invasion. The Fenian Secretary of the Treasury Bernard Doran Killian asked President Johnson what position the US government would take toward a Fenian operation in Canada. Johnson reportedly stated that he and the administration would "acknowledge accomplished facts." There would be two ways to interpret this response. The first would be that it was essentially noncommittal, and might be viewed as political-speak. The second way would be that it was the equivalent of a wink and a nod approving any Fenian actions without a formal commitment to this position. This certainly was the way the Fenian leadership took the remark.

First, merely receiving a White House invitation was a telling sign. Second, when the Fenians did actually move into Canada it took Johnson six days to finally issue a presidential proclamation condemning the attack (this despite that federal authorities at the local level had been responding for several days); in part this reportedly was because Seward actively opposed the idea of issuing such a proclamation. Finally, there was an interesting conversation reported a few years later. In 1868, Fenian President O'Neill went to White House to meet with President Johnson. O'Neill had been friends with Johnson from 1862, when Johnson had been military governor in Tennessee. According to Henri le Caron, who was present and who was a senior Fenian official (and British spy), O'Neill received a cordial welcome. According to le Caron, Johnson said:

> General, your people unfairly blame me a good deal for the part I took in stopping your first movement. Now I want you to understand that my sympathies are entirely with you, and anything which lies in my power I am willing to do to assist you. But you must remember that I gave you five full days before issuing any proclamation stopping you. What, in God's name, more did you want? If you could not get there in five days, by God, you could never get there; and then, as President, I was compelled to enforce the Neutrality Laws, or be denounced on every side.[5]

More recent research by Peter Vronsky has cast significant doubts on the standard narratives on Johnson's supportive stance.[6] Even while the administration was paying lip service to the Fenians, it was actively exchanging information with the British government in efforts to foil Fenian operations. The US and the British, through their envoy Sir Frederick Bruce, maintained extensive channels on passing their best analysis on Fenian activities that could create instability. As noted later, there certainly were significant areas of tension between the US and Britain, but the Johnson (and later Grant) administration ultimately seemed to find quiet areas of cooperation with Britain to be less objectionable than active support of the Fenians.

Why then the perception by the Fenians at the time and many analysts since of high-level government support for the movement? However much Johnson did or did not agree with Fenian goals, political realities were much more important. This particularly was the case during the 1866 congressional elections. At that point, Johnson was fighting for his political survival. The political dynamics were very complex. Although Johnson was a "Union" Democrat, Lincoln had selected Johnson as his 1864 running mate in an apparent effort to form something akin to a national unity government. After Lincoln's assassination, Johnson found himself to be increasingly isolated politically. He was being battered by the radical wing of the Republican Party, mainly over Reconstruction. He was forced to rely on Democrats both for support for his policies, and as impeachment loomed, simply to stay in office. During this period, the Democratic Party essentially owned the Irish vote. Johnson was desperate to keep Democratic congressmen in office and this almost certainly shaped his decision making both over more general Irish American issues and the Fenians in particular. Johnson said he "frankly admitted that the Government, surrounded by difficulties in its internal policy, and anxious to obtain support from any quarter against the violent party in the North were desirous of avoiding, if possible, any collision with the popular sentiments of the Irish masses."[7] The sad irony for Johnson was that despite these efforts, his preferred candidates fared poorly in the 1866 elections, especially in New York State, and he lost virtually all his political credibility.

When Ulysses S. Grant succeeded Johnson, the atmospherics and practical actions changed significantly. Grant certainly was no friend of the British, but he also showed little patience with the Fenians. The administration reportedly began employing private detectives to actively collect intelligence on the Fenians. According to private British dispatch on June 15, 1868: "[The government] learned from other quarters that the Secretary of War receives daily telegrams from officers employed by him on the frontier and that, besides these, a special officer, General Sharp, is employed by the State Department to watch the movements of the Fenians in the direction of St. Albans, whence there seems the greatest possibility of an expedition being despatched.[sic]"[8] The general attitude of the Grant administration seemed to be that it would not go out of its way to break the Fenians, but that it would scrupulously enforce the neutrality laws. This attitude certainly was evident in the reaction surrounding the 1870 Fenian operations.

The Role of Diplomacy

Beyond domestic politics, larger diplomatic issues also played a key role in events. The diplomatic relations of the US with Canada certainly played a significant role in the relative lack of concern within the US government about the rise of the Fenians. Direct US–Canadian relations, however, were only a relatively minor part of the story. As John Bartlet Brebner noted, this was better described as the "North Atlantic Triangle," with the Canadian colonial government being only one leg of the triangle. In many ways, in fact, this was the shortest leg in terms of importance for most of the nineteenth century, with the relations between the US and Britain being more significant, both in general and in regard to the Fenians in particular. Canadian authorities typically were either ignored or minimized in talks between London and Washington. In some ways, this actually was a logical and diplomatically correct situation. Although the Canadian provinces were in proximity to the US, they were not independent entities, but were colonies of the United Kingdom. This was particularly pronounced before the 1867 Confederation. As Secretary of State Seward noted, ". . . [T]he government of the United States holds no correspondence directly, upon any subject, with the Canadian authorities mentioned in the said resolution, or with the authorities of any colony, province, or dependency of any other sovereign state."[9]

The nineteenth-century concept of Manifest Destiny within both US governmental circles and many (if certainly not all) American political thinkers and ideologues certainly played an important role in relations with Canada. Many argued that Canada inevitably would almost by osmosis become part of the United States. Even as late as 1867, Secretary of State William Seward would tell a Boston audience that "I know . . . that Nature designs that this whole continent, not merely these thirty-six states, shall be, sooner or later, within the magic circle of the American Union."[10] Other American politicians were more direct. A bill (H.R. 754) for the "admission of the States of Nova Scotia, New Brunswick, Canada East, and Canada West, and for the organization of the Territories of Selkirk, Saskatchewan, and Columbia" was introduced in the House of Representatives on July 2, 1866. This bill was very detailed, with provisions on how the Canadian debts would be resolved, and the US electoral districts that would be established. It reportedly received particularly strong support among Irish Americans. Although not passed by the Congress, even the consideration of such a measure was unlikely to assuage Canadian sensibilities. Likewise, when US reparations claims were made against Britain for its tilt toward the Confederacy during the Civil War, one of the proposals reportedly taken seriously both within the American administration and Congress was for Britain to cede the Canadian provinces to the US in lieu of reparations.[11]

In a sense, the US attitude may have been driven in part by the British attitude toward Canada and the other North American provinces. London certainly had no interest in ceding its possessions in North America, while at the same time concerned as to the economics of such colonies. The British tried to rule Canada on the cheap. By the time of the Fenian era, there were significant movements within successive British governments to economize on colonies, particularly within North America. This was reflected particularly in terms of the military forces that London was prepared to support within the colonies. In a letter from Benjamin Disraeli, Chancellor of the Exchequer, to Lord Derby, September 30, 1866, he stated that, "It can never be our pretence [sic] or our policy to defend the Canadian frontier against the United States. If the colonists can't, as a general rule, defend themselves against the Fenians, they can do nothing . . . what is the use of these colonial deadweights which we do not govern?"[12]

The Civil War brought US-British-Canadian relations to a dangerous new low. Although it might be assumed that Britain would support the Northern side in this conflict—particularly because of the issue of slavery, which had been abolished in the colonies by Parliament in 1833—a number of issues quickly emerged that led to sharp tensions between the US federal government and Britain, with US-Canadian relations as somewhat collateral damage. At the start of the war, Britain declared "strict and impartial neutrality," but (perhaps more by omission than commission) appeared to recognize the Confederate States as legitimate combatants, which did not sit well with Washington.

There were increasingly hostile official communications between US federal and state officials and British officials in Canada concerning issues such as weapons purchases, recruitment by the US of Canadian subjects, and myriad of other issues.[13] Canada refused to sell arms to either side during the Civil War, citing strict neutrality. In effect, however, this largely impacted the northern states, including New York, who were in a geographical position more likely to be able to actually buy and receive the weapons. Although this became an inconsequential issue as the war progressed, American states were relatively desperate to arm their forces as the war began, and this refusal created some very ill feelings.[14] Likewise, as the Union forces required ever-increasing numbers of troops to replenish the huge losses they suffered during the course of the war, there were frequent complaints from the Canadian government about illegal recruiting of Canadian subjects. One example from the Canadian Consul General in Buffalo may be used to represent the tenor of these protests:

> I regret to state that from the lists of substitutes which are now published in this city, and from information derived from various sources, I perceive that the number of British subjects, many of them boys under eighteen, enlisting into the United States service is very much upon the increase. How many of these are drugged in Canada and brought over to this side it is impossible to say; but that a regular system is now organized by which men are passed over the frontier and kept in durance and stupified with liquor until they enlist into the United States service, I have no doubt whatever.[15]

Despite a string of official protests by the Canadian and British governments, the US government largely ignored them beyond promising to look into things some day. Internal Canadian documents that later were released indicated continuing frustrations and unhappiness by their senior leader as to relations with Washington.

Such Canadian governmental unhappiness seemed to seep into Canadian public attitudes. However much Canada and other North American provinces may have been the last step in the Underground Railroad and however much war aims of the American North were philosophically akin to Canadian attitudes, a series of large and small actions soured Canadian public opinion. An anecdote by Brebner likely illustrates sentiments in Canada over the course of the war: "Perhaps the children of western Canada summarized public opinion pretty accurately. At the beginning of the war when they played "North and South," it was hard to get enough on the southern side. As the war went on and on and Anglo-American relations grew worse, fewer and fewer youngsters would consent to play Northerners."[16]

During the war, there were concerns by the North that Confederate insurgents would use Canada as a base from which to raid the northern states.[17] On at least one occasion, Major General John Dix, commander of the Department of East, sent a detective from Buffalo into Canada to gather intelligence on Confederate intentions.[18] Dispatches in 1864 indicated that "an unusually larger number of disloyal citizens of the United States" were in the Halifax area for several months.[19] Likewise, rumors were reported of operations to be conducted in the Niagara region. According to one dispatch, "There are about forty rebels in Marysburgh, Prince Edward's County, Canada, on the North side of Lake Ontario, and North-west of Oswego. They drill regularly about three times a week, and are armed with revolvers. They board with the farmers in the neighborhood. . . ."[20] Although none of these particular operations actually came off, they continued to create local tensions.

The so-called Trent Affair came close to leading to outright war between Washington and London. On November 8, 1861, Union Captain Charles Wilkes, commanding the USS *San Jacinto*, stopped and boarded the British ship *Trent*. He then seized and removed as contraband of war two Confederate diplomats, James Mason and John Slidell, who were traveling to Europe in an effort to seek diplomatic relations between the Confederacy and Britain and France. The British public and political leadership erupted over what they saw as something akin to governmentally directed piracy against one of their merchant vessels. British Prime Minister Lord

Palmerston declared, "I don't know whether you will stand it, but I'll be damned if I do," and reinforced the Canadian provinces that might become embroiled in a war with the US.[21] After a period of sharp tension, President Lincoln backed down, removing the threat of imminent hostilities through disavowing the actions of Captain Wilkes and releasing the two envoys. He refused to issue a formal apology, but these two practical actions were sufficient to end the immediate crisis, although some unhappiness clearly remained on the British side.

One step taken by Lincoln that represented a significant step forward was the issuance of the Emancipation Proclamation on September 22, 1862, which put the North on "the right side of history." Beyond the morality of this act, it also represented a major propaganda coup for the North, especially in dealings with most Western European countries. The British government in particular found itself almost inevitably having to support Northern war aims. Nevertheless, tensions continued between the sides. While not auguring actual conflict, several incidents helped keep relations on the boil for the rest of the war.

A number of stresses were created by British acquiescence (and some US government officials at the time would argue complicity) in the operations of Confederate raiding ships against Northern merchant shipping. The most notorious of these Confederate vessels was the CSS *Alabama*, launched in 1862. This actually was built in a private British shipbuilding yard outside Liverpool at Birkenhead, England. Under British neutrality laws at the time, it was possible to build warships as long as they were not actually armed until after reaching international waters. This was the case with the *Alabama*, and there were absolutely no suggestions at the time that the shipbuilders did not know that it was intended as a warship, especially as its construction was arranged by a Confederate navy officer. The *Alabama* case was a particular bête noir for the US government due to the success of the ship, which captured or burned about sixty-five Northern ships before being sunk itself in 1864. Two other Confederate commerce raiders of lesser success also were launched in Britain. More directly involving the Canadian provinces, Halifax provided ship repair facilities to Confederate vessels, and there was an incident involving the seizure of the Northern vessel USS *Chesapeake* off Massachusetts and its sailing to Halifax.

Finally, there was a small raid by a Confederate group of about twenty-five members against St. Albans, Vermont on October 19, 1864, launched from Canada. The Confederate force, commanded by Lieutenant Bennet H. Young, robbed the three banks in the town, holding the townspeople hostage and killing one, and then unsuccessfully tried to burn down the buildings in the town. They then escaped to Canada with more than 200,000 dollars in bank loot. About half the group was arrested in Canada, and somewhat less than half the money was recovered and returned to the US. The legal process in Canada then created fresh turmoil in cross-border relations. The judge handling the case ruled that the Confederates were soldiers acting under orders. As a result, Canada both refused to extradite the accused, and then the judge released them. They were re-arrested for violation of the neutrality laws, before being released again after a time. The ongoing legal complications created an uproar in the US and very stern (for diplomatic-speak) warnings from the US government as to the impact on relations.[22]

The government of Canada, in response to these activities, established a special police force to patrol the border and a call-up of militia along the border. Orders authorizing the call-up of fifteen militia companies were issued on December 19, 1864, with these units released from duty in the summer of 1865. Following the St. Albans raid, the American authorities reported that a vigilante group intended to raid Kingston, Canada in retaliation, which the US government reported to the Canadian government. There also were reports that some small Confederate vessels intended for raiding were hidden on Lake Erie. Due to treaty restrictions on the number of US and British vessels on the Great Lakes, there were only limited governmental forces available, but both sides increased their strength on the lakes. Two American boats were in fact attacked. In February 1865, the province of Canada passed the "Act for the prevention and repression of outrages in violation of the Peace on the frontier of the Province and for other purposes" formally criminalizing violations of order by "aliens"; this somewhat assuaged US sensibilities, but certainly was not taken at face value by Americans along the border.

One diplomatic assignment by the British government helped resolve many of the day-to-day tensions between London and Washington toward the end of the Civil War. Sir Frederick Bruce was appointed British ambassador at the end of February 1865. Bruce got along very well with most American government officials, and reportedly became friends with Seward. Bruce's approach generally was to use informal approaches to the Americans, particularly over issues with the Fenians, and to avoid formal protests. Even when the Canadian colonial government wanted official protests to be lodged, Bruce normally managed to dodge these demands. His overall approach seemed to reduce a number of diplomatic flash points and helped facilitate some reasonably coordinated (certainly never perfect) diplomatic approaches toward the Fenians.[23]

A current scholar of the Fenians, Peter Vronsky, in fact has argued that "A review of the diplomatic despatches of Frederick Bruce, the British envoy in Washington at the time, reveals a conspiracy indeed; not between the United States and the Fenians to invade Canada but one between Britain and the United States to secretly contain the Fenians without Irish American voters finding out."[24] He persuasively argues that quiet US-British diplomatic cooperation against the Fenians was significantly greater than commonly noted. He also notes that the Canadians largely were left out of these informal agreements. This approach to the US-British diplomatic minuet over the Fenians has considerable validity. At the same time, however, the actions of the American administration equally may have represented the equivalent of triangulation between competing domestic and foreign interests. At the very least, the Fenians themselves viewed the US political system as generally favorable to their cause, and this may have been the critical component of developments.

Canada, Fenians, and American Public Sentiment

Given the four years of stresses along the border during the Civil War, the general attitude of American border residents toward the prospects of cross-border operations—as long as they went the other way—was rather blasé. Many seemed to view it as just payback. There is no known public opinion survey as to the majority opinion, but two newspaper commentaries from the area likely were representative of the majority of their readers. The first was from the *Daily Journal*, Ogdensburg, New York, March 29, 1864, page 3, and the second is from *The Buffalo Express* of June 12, 1865:

> As our neighbours have been chuckling over our domestic troubles for the past three years, we may be pardoned for feeling a grim satisfaction at seeing them quaking at a spectre in their own midst. Evil days may come upon them sooner than they think. They have long been politically and financially bankrupt; who knows how soon they may be compelled to confront armed sedition at their own doors?
>
> A new excitement has broken out in Canada, in relation to the Fenian Brotherhood. It is said that our government has

furnished the Canadian authorities information that the Fenians on this side meditate an attack or raid on Canada. We don't believe our government has done any such thing, neither do we believe the Fenians meditate any attack. From all we have been able to learn of the brotherhood, we believe them to be peaceably disposed, law abiding men. We think, however, that a little raiding by British subjects from this side upon Canada would open the eyes of those Canadians who seem to consider that kind of performance upon us all right.

In short, given the domestic political realities in the US and the string of public and diplomatic stresses between America, Britain, and Canada, the Fenians had every right to expect at least acquiescence by the American government if not passive support. This environment was close to a green light for Fenian violence.

Chapter 4

"The Great Schism"

Instead of harmony and unity of action, they were blackguarding and vilifying each other in the most scandalous way, flying at each other's throats in a more vicious and vindictive manner than the Kilkenny cats.[1]

—*Blackwood's Magazine,* September 1911

As has been somewhat a pattern with Irish nationalist groups over time, the Fenian Brotherhood faced a major schism at the end of 1865. A convention was held in Philadelphia beginning on October 16. A group of Fenians calling themselves "men of action" assailed O'Mahony over what they viewed as his unwillingness to start operations against Britain. A new constitution was adopted, stripping O'Mahony of much of his power, and establishing a strong senate to oversee the president.[2] O'Mahony was reelected president, but this almost certainly was of small comfort to someone who had previously faced little open opposition among his membership.

In December, charges and counter charges exploded among the leadership, particularly over how an estimated one million-dollar treasury was being managed. There were allegations of fraud, elaborate and unnecessary spending, and general mismanagement. One of the targets was the Fenian headquarters on Union Square in New York City, which was rather luxurious. As the *Brooklyn Eagle* (a newspaper normally sympathetic to both O'Mahony and the Fenians) described the mansion, it included a "central parlor of the mansion, which is fitted in a manner to satisfy the caprice of an Eastern despot, with luxurious carpets, ebony and rosewood desks, carved folding doors, with gorgeously tinted stained glass windows, sofas, divans, and inviting looking arm-chairs, all comfortably upholstered with national colors, green and gold."[3] O'Mahony's stated rationale for the expenses associated with the mansion was that the Brotherhood needed a substantial headquarters for the public to take it seriously.

O'Mahony drew a salary of 2,000 dollars a year as president of the Brotherhood, and this also was assailed by Senator Roberts and his supporters. Roberts insisted that the presidency should be unpaid. This, of course, was relatively easy for Roberts, because he was a fairly wealthy businessman. O'Mahony on the other hand had basically no financial assets. As the public charges and debates became increasingly hostile, they reinforced already existing public perception problems for the Fenians. Opponents of the Fenians had long argued that the movement was a fraud with its primary victims usually identified as "poor Irish servant girls" who were giving up their paltry wages to the Brotherhood. A flavor of the rhetoric surrounding this attitude was provided by the *New York Times*:

> We have it from high authority that the President of the Irish Republic in America and Head Centre of the Fenian Brotherhood broadly charges that some of his brethren of the Cabinet have been concerned in stupendous frauds upon the treasury, and that to these frauds the origin of the secession movement in the Brotherhood may be traced. On the other hand, the ten "malcontents" who have given so much trouble to the dwellers in the Union-square palace, allege that of those lavish contributions which the frugal and industrious Irish servant-girls in the United States have contributed with the expectation of liberating their native isle, no insignificant share has been squandered if not embezzled by the salaried officials who utter their edicts from the headquarters of the Fenian President in New-York.[4]

The Fenian senate (of ten members) brought charges against President John O'Mahony and Bernard Doran Killian, the Secretary of the Treasury for various acts of "malfeasance." Beyond the charges directly relating to cash flow, the issue of "Fenian bonds" loomed large. These bonds, "redeemable six months after the acknowledgement of the Independence of the Irish Nation with interest from the date hereof inclusive at six percent annum payable on presentation of this bond at the Treasury of the Irish Republic," became a battlefield for the leaders when O'Mahony insisted on signing them and personally controlling their issue.

When O'Mahony essentially ignored the charges by the dissident wing, he and Killian were deposed, and William R. Roberts, the Secretary of War, was named president. Roberts had emigrated to the US from Ireland in 1849. In contrast to O'Mahony, Roberts was relatively uneducated, with a background as a merchant. He was very successful in his business and reportedly was a millionaire. Parenthetically, it should be noted that despite Roberts's arrest for participation in the 1866 Fenian raid into Canada, he later was elected twice to the US House of Representatives from 1871 to 1875 as a Democrat from New York. This was followed by service as a member of the board of aldermen of New York City in 1877 and then appointment under the Grover Cleveland administration as Envoy Extraordinary and Minister Plenipotentiary to Chile from 1885 to 1889.

The other significant figure to emerge during this split was Thomas W. Sweeny (also spelled as Sweeney), who was confirmed as the Fenian Secretary of War. Born in County Cork Ireland in 1822, he immigrated to the US with his mother in 1827 after the death of his father, and grew up in New York City.[5] At the beginning of the Mexican War in 1846, he was elected as a second lieutenant in the 1st Regiment of New York Volunteers, and he saw considerable action in the war, earning the nickname of "Fighting Tom." He was wounded twice, losing his right arm. Based on his record as a volunteer officer, he was offered a commission in the regular army. During the Civil War, he served in the Missouri and Pittsburgh Landing campaigns, where he was wounded twice more. By the end of the Civil War, he was a Brevet Major General of Volunteers and a major in the regular army.

In its official statement of December 7 naming Roberts, the senate declared, "[T]he Secretary of War, a tried and experienced soldier, whose ability and gallantry have stood the test of eighteen years, has been impeded in the perfection of his plans for immediate action by the imbecility and the dishonesty of men in whom we had, unfortunately, reposed our confidence." In this official circular, the senate ensured that it gave the post office box in New York where funds could be sent to its faction. It also rented a new headquarters in New York City, the Moffatt Mansion, at a rent of 18,000 dollars for eighteen months, together with a 6,000 dollar security deposit.[6]

O'Mahony struck back against his ouster. He counter-charged the senators involved with making unsecured loans of the Fenian treasury and other forms of financial irregularities and refusing to open the books. He also accused the senators of bribing a reporter to support their cause. Some Fenian circles (particularly in New York City) expressed support for O'Mahony rather than the so-called Senate Wing and putatively expelled the senators who ousted O'Mahony from the Brotherhood. The first official communique from his wing was laconic, but very straightforward: "GENERAL ORDER, NEW SERIES. —Orders on military affairs of the Brotherhood will be disregarded, if not approved by the undersigned. Brothers, beware! JOHN O'MAHONEY [sic], President F. B."

Although O'Mahony's ouster was couched in terms of financial shenanigans, there certainly was more to it than that. There had been increasing tensions surrounding the immediate strategy of the Fenians. O'Mahony seemed to focus on longer-term militant operations and particularly on its support for the nationalist movement in Ireland. In a speech by him at the Cincinnati conference, he laid out the Fenian strategy:

> The Fenian Brotherhood is founded upon the conviction that a military organization at home is absolutely essential to the liberation of Ireland. . . . Our countrymen, and all those who love Ireland, must be organized in these United States. Here a never-failing base of supplies must be created and secured, the Irishmen of the British colonies aiding in the work. Our Brothers in Ireland and Great Britain must be thoroughly organized for insurrection and that organization must be liberally subsidized as well as armed and supplied with military officers by the Fenian Brotherhood. . . . It is evident that our brothers in Ireland need military leaders and competent line officers to act under them. Hence I recommend the immediate formation of a military branch of the Fenian Brotherhood. . . . [They] should hold themselves constantly in readiness to go to Ireland. . . . New York should have its Fenian Brigade, Philadelphia, Cincinnati, Boston, Chicago, their Fenian Regiments.[7]

Although there was a whiff of an attitude that "Yankee pluck and ingenuity" could overcome inherent weaknesses among the rebel movement in Ireland, this remained the official strategy under O'Mahony. Based on other reports at the time, O'Mahony clearly believed that a war between the US and Britain was inevitable. As part of this war, the Fenians would be essential in liberating Ireland. The realism of this analysis was open to considerable question, but it seemed to undergird much of the initial Fenian planning at least under O'Mahony. Also, this strategy seemed to call for some patience in waiting for both the US government to act and for the strategic environment to be optimal: "Our fellow-citizens will not forget that this

Brotherhood is virtually at war with the Oligarchy of Great Britain, and that while there is no Fenian army as yet openly in the field—such an army nevertheless actually exists, preparing and disciplining itself for freedom's battle, ambushed in the midst of it enemies, watching steadily its opportunity and biding its time."[8] Importantly for later developments, O'Mahony seemed to explicitly rule out operations against Canada: "I must here refer to the late terror caused in Canada by the fear of our organization. . . . Let them set their hearts at ease with regard to the Fenian Circles of the Canadas. These are not organized for the purpose of making a revolution in these provinces. Their object has relation to Ireland alone."[9] In private letters for internal Fenian use, O'Mahony was a bit more nuanced. Even there, however, he clearly viewed Canada at best a (rather small) means to an end. He argued that a "revolutionary organization in Ireland to be absolutely essential," and that a "Canadian raid . . . a mere diversion."[10]

The split between the "Irish first" and "immediate action" had been a recurring theme among the Fenian leadership. Nevertheless, particularly in the early period of the American Fenian Brotherhood, there was considerable interest in operations from the US directly against the British in Ireland. For example, during an organizational meeting in Brooklyn, a Fenian speaker suggested, "If 400,000 Fenians should land in Ireland would it not surprise all England. Strike but one blow and the invader would fly before the Macs and O's as chaff before the wind. Let the O'Briens take the right, the McMahans the left and the O'Neills pierce the center."[11] One somewhat overlapping issue was the preparation of the Brotherhood for military operations. In many ways, both factions were intent on forming a credible, if not overwhelming, military offensive capability. Whether this was for operations in Canada or for an invasion of Ireland seemed almost immaterial in terms of building up a Fenian army.

In October 1865, the Fenian Brotherhood issued a circular under John O'Mahony's signature to improve the professionalism of the military wing. Under provisions of these instructions, any appointment of officers had to be after an examination of their qualifications by a three-member board. Parenthetically, the commissions for these officers were in the "Army of the Irish Republic." In practice, this title morphed into the "Irish Republican Army," which may have been the first usage of this title, even if it fell out of favor until the emergence of the "new" IRA. Also, an assistant inspector general would be appointed for each state to vet candidates before their nomination. In a copy of federal procedures for commissioning officers, all these processes would be "with the consent and advice of the Senate."

Likewise, "The Revised Army Regulations of the U.S., so far as the same can be made applicable, is hereby adopted for the government of the military organization of the F.B. in America," and "[t]hat the rank and pay of all officers in the military service of the F.B. of America, be based upon the system adopted for the Regulations of the U.S.A., and shall be determined by the Senate."[12] For those officers sent to Ireland, they would be provided with transportation, along with six month's salary, although only three months would be in dollars, with the remainder in Irish Republic bonds, these payments in advance. For those in Ireland longer than that, "the officers to be paid as regularly, as the nature of the service will permit, monthly thereafter by the financial agent abroad."[13] This same circular established staff sections consisting of the adjutant general, ordnance, inspectors generals, engineers, quartermaster, medical and subsistence, and pay department.

In a follow-up secret circular, the Brotherhood ordered that, "[e]ach Centre of Circle will forward to this Department on the 10th, 20th and last day of every month a roll of fighting men ready at a week's notice to take the field for the cause of Ireland."[14] Each circle was to regularly drill its members at the company level, and where possible at battalion. The circles were also to report the quantity of weapons they held, with the War Department making up any shortages. Inspectors general were required to inspect the condition of all weapons and to report on their condition to headquarters.

As is described in more detail elsewhere, one issue driving the Irish First versus Canadian Invasion debate was the realism of each approach. Beyond the bureaucratic politics and struggle for Fenian leadership, this strategic conceptual conflict was very real and very legitimate. Many of the O'Mahony supporters found the concept of an invasion of Canada to be both unlikely to succeed and to be strategically pointless. The opponents, on the other hand, viewed American Fenian direct operations in Ireland as unlikely to provide much practical value to the larger nationalist struggle.

The Senate Wing seemed much more intent on immediate military operations. Roberts, the new president, wasted no time in stressing the militant aims of the Fenians. In his inaugural address, he stated:

> It is therefore useless—nay, it is criminal—to waste precious time now in idle discussion. Action must be the order of the day. Our means, our energies, our whole thought, must be directed toward the military arm of the Fenian Brotherhood, through which alone we can accomplish the freedom of Ireland. Every

energy must now be given to aid the veteran soldier who directs the military affairs of the Brotherhood. He has great faith in leaden bullets, and very little in paper ones; and as I am entirely of his way of thinking, you may rely upon my placing all the means at my disposal under his control and direction. Time, circumstances and the Almighty seem to favor the movement for the overthrow of that despotic and brutal Power which has left desolation in the track of her friendships and misery as the legacy of her slaves. . . . England must meet privateers on every ocean, and Irish foes in every clime. We will strike at her wherever she is most vulnerable, and where we can best assist our brothers at home, and let those who lead or follow in this movement sacrifice something of feeling, time, or personal pride.

This "immediate action" approach was undergirded by a thorough skepticism of the Irish Fenians. Roberts expressed this lack of faith in the Irish in an address to the Brotherhood in which he asserted that according to his information "the representations of Stephens, when in America, about the strength of the I. R. B. were absolutely false; and that there was no organized body of men in Ireland powerful enough to commence a revolution with the slightest hope of success, at the time named by Stephens, when he promised that he would commence the light by a certain date, provided he received a certain sum of money."[15]

As the split became complete, both leaders, O'Mahony and Roberts, held separate "dueling" conventions within a month of each other in an effort to show who actually was in charge. O'Mahony held a convention in New York City in January 1866 where his delegates reinstated the 1863 Constitution and abolished the Fenian Senate. Sweeny, representing the Roberts faction, actually attended this convention, but he was both outvoted and outshouted. The Roberts convention in Pittsburgh in February concluded that anything decided at the O'Mahony convention was null and void.

Whatever his feelings toward O'Mahony personally, when a split in the American Fenians became increasingly likely, Stephens strongly supported O'Mahony. He sent a letter to all the American Fenian circles that read:

IRISH REPUBLIC.

To the Members of the Fenian Brotherhood, and the friends of Ireland generally in the U. S. of America, Canada, etc.

Dublin, December 23, 1865.

Countrymen and Friends: Aware that certain members of the
Fenian Brotherhood, and notoriously the "Senate" of that as
association. have, madly and traitorously moved to a mad and
traitorous end, raise the cry of "to Canada!" instead of the cry
of "to Ireland!" and aware that John O'Mahony, known as Head
Centre and President of the Fenian Brotherhood, has wisely and
firmly, as in duty bound, opposed this mad and traitorous diversion from the right path—the only path that could possibly save
our country and our race. In consequence I hereby appoint the
said John O'Mahony representative and Financial Agent of the
Irish Republic in the United States of America, Canada, etc.,
with ample and unquestionable authority to enroll men, raise
money, and fit out an expedition to sail for Ireland and reach
Ireland on the earliest possible day, and in all other ways in
which, to the best of his judgment. he can serve Ireland—that
land to which he has devoted life and honor—I hereby authorize
and call on him.

James Stephens.

This letter almost certainly reflects policy preferences rather than personalities. Stephens had to be concerned that a Canadian strategy would lead
to less direct support for Ireland. In any event, it did not prevent a split in
the American Fenian Brotherhood and a severe weakening of O'Mahony's
position. According to John Devoy, a senior IRB leader, the Fenian Brotherhood split (and Stephen's reaction) had a rather immediate impact on the
IRB also. It meant that both American officers and weapons were diverted
from Ireland. It also had significant political effects:

> Its moral effect on Stephens was very bad and it made him
> commit the worst blunder of his whole career. Overrating his
> popularity in America, and throwing all prudence to the winds,
> he wrote a letter to O'Mahony, which he evidently expected
> would leave the Head Centre's opponents without a following,
> but which had the very opposite effect. It widened the breach
> and made it irreparable. The prompt publishing of the letter by
> O'Mahony rendered it morally impossible for the Senate wing

of the American movement to support the Home Organization so long as Stephens remained its leader.[16]

Some attempts were made to heal this rift in 1866. The reconciliation initiative was made by O'Mahony, which is not surprising because he was in the weaker position. There was little prospect for face-to-face meetings between the leaders of the two warring factions, so O'Mahony tried to use General William J. Halpin as an intermediary. Roberts essentially refused to cooperate, and the effort went nowhere. For the remaining time of the Fenian Brotherhood, it was divided into at least two—and for a period, three—feuding factions. A senior Fenian leader probably summed up the organizational environment best:

> differences between the "President" and the "Senate," . . . created a disastrous dismemberment of the body of the organization. In a personal way the differences bred distemper, distemper vilification, vilification subterfuge, and subterfuge found sustainment in dishonor, and culminated in hatred. The American public was disgusted, the Irish cause disgraced by the charges and counter charges that the interested parties too readily rushed into print.[17]

Chapter 5

The Campobello Island Raid

Let them come, if they dare.[1]

—Saint John Morning News

With the split in the Fenian movement and the internal attacks on his position, O'Mahony clearly felt that he had to do something to retrieve his standing. It is far from clear that he actually had changed his thinking about the "Ireland first" strategy, but he was becoming increasingly isolated from the levers of power within the Fenians. Separate conventions and high-level meetings began being held by the Brotherhood, with "dueling" meetings held in January 1866 by the O'Mahony faction in New York City and in February by the Roberts faction in Pittsburgh.

As became somewhat a pattern, events in Ireland also played a role in American Fenian strategic calculus. These events dated from 1863. James Stephens decided to launch a newspaper, the *Irish People*, both as a propaganda outlet and perhaps more importantly as a fund-raising organ for the IRB. The paper was run by Stephens himself, together with John O'Leary as editor, Thomas Clarke Luby and Charles J. Kickham as assistant editors, and Diarmaid (or Jeremiah) O'Donovan Rossa as business manager. In one sense, this was a logical use of available IRB resources: it ensured that the senior members of the IRB had direct control of messaging for the group. On the other hand, it also meant that the senior leadership was further risking exposure by direct involvement in a public newspaper. One other peculiarity of the newspaper was that its offices were located near Dublin Castle, the seat of the British government in Ireland. Whether this was a result of efforts to show defiance to the authorities or it simply was a convenient or cheap piece of real estate is not known, but it represented a possibly dangerous choice.

The first issue of the *Irish People* appeared November 28, 1863. Stephens evidently intended for himself to be the principal writer for the paper, but the reaction—both by readers and by the others working on the newspaper—was not terribly favorable; one letter to an editor described Stephens's lead article as "all dashes, commas, and bosh."[2] Within three issues, Stephens left the writing to others, and O'Leary became the editor, as he explained because of his "being clearly, if not the fittest person for the post, certainly the least unfit."[3]

The paper was published from 1863 to 1865 and proved to be very popular among Irish nationalist circles, although never reaching the circulation levels of the principal Irish newspaper *The Nation*. It began facing two significant problems, however. The first was financial. While having strong circulation, much of this was free, and payment was very hit and miss. Facing a choice between making money or getting the IRB's message circulated as widely as possible, the group rather understandably chose the latter. As a result, however, the *Irish People* became a financial drain rather than a moneymaker. John Devoy described the attitude at the time:

> I got a bundle of 25 every week, which I distributed free. I gave five of them free every Thursday to an old newsdealer who kept a little shop at the corner of the Sallins Road and Main Street, so that he might sell them, and I sent a few by mail to prominent people. Two country school teachers whom I had sworn in and whose salary was only £40 a year I put on the mailing list in the office of the paper, as they lived too far away for me to deliver them, and after a while Con O'Mahony, who was a clerk in the office, sent them bills. When they failed to pay the bills he dropped them, and when I heard of it I told Rossa, who was Business Manager, and he reprimanded O'Mahony sharply. "You know the miserable salaries that country school-masters get," he said to O'Mahony, who had been a teacher himself, "and these men can do a lot of good by handing the paper around." Con pleaded "business reasons," and Rossa said: "To the devil with your business reasons. The organization can't be run on business principles and we must push it in every way we can. Put them back on the list." When I offered him payment for the 25 cop-

ies I was getting, Rossa asked me: "How much salary are you getting, John?" I told him £50 a year and he said: "Oh, trash, man, you have a lot of expenses to bear" (which was true) "and I won't take your money." He then told O'Mahony to send me 50 copies and no bills.[4]

The second issue was that the newspaper offices became a hub for Fenian organizational activities. Visitors from the US reportedly routinely would visit the newspaper to make contact with the IRB leaders, and meetings between IRB leaders and members regularly were held there.

Throughout 1865 and 1866, Stephens continued to insist that the IRB was prepared to launch a major uprising in Ireland. There is every reason to believe, however, that he had to know the dismal state of the Irish nationalists in terms of their readiness. During this time, the IRB had about 2,000 rifles or muskets, many obsolete, a number of sporting shotguns, and some revolvers. Their principal weapon in terms of numbers, in fact, was the pike. Pitting insurgents armed with a pike against British military units was a recipe for massacres of Stephens's own fighters.

The Irish Fenians had two back-to-back disasters in 1865 and 1866. Stephens had declared 1865 as "the year of decision," and it somewhat was, although not in the way he intended. Viewing the actions of the IRB in Ireland as increasingly threatening, the British Parliament suspended the right of habeas corpus in Ireland and began mass arrests of suspected Fenians, including a number of Irish Americans in the country.[5] The British success in tracking down suspects was aided considerably when an American envoy, P.J. Meehan, carrying papers linking the American Fenians and the IRB and a draft for 500 pounds to the IRB lost them at Kingston railway station on July 15, 1865, and they were turned over to the police. According to Donovan Rossa, "he thought it better not to have those papers in any pocket of his, as he told us, [so he pinned them] inside the waist of his drawers. The pin slipped out and the letters slipped away unknown to him."[6] In his memoirs, John Devoy added a further factor: "The truth is that he was a drinking man and was undoubtedly under the influence of liquor when the incident of the 'Lost Documents' occurred."[7] In fairness to Meehan, these papers merely further confirmed intelligence that the British already had on the IRB leaders. The documents did, however, provide the final rationale for a British decision to move against the group.

Further disaster struck on September 15, when the police raided the offices of the *Irish People*. Thomas Clarke Luby, fearing such a raid, had removed a cache of IRB documents from the newspaper offices, intending to destroy them at his home. Unfortunately, he had failed to do so by the time the police arrived at his house. Reportedly, "Luby, apprehending for a long time that the police were likely to pay him a visit, had carefully put this document [laying out the members of the executive committee of the IRB] in one envelope and his love letters in another, and then proceeded to mark the envelopes wrongly."[8] The combination of lost documents led to a major dragnet for Fenian leaders. James Stephens initially was able to hide (somewhat in plain sight), but he eventually was arrested on November 12.

After Stephens's arrest, those of the military council who were still free met in Dublin. The intent was to appoint at least an interim leader for the movement while Stephens was in prison. Virtually all the major civilian leaders were either being held by the British or on the run. Without some form of established leadership, the odds were good that the IRB could implode. The members of the military council included General F.F. Millen, Colonels Michael Kerwin, Denis F. Burke, and William G. Halpin, and Captain Thomas Kelly. All were American Civil War veterans. Kelly generally was viewed as the most capable officer, but he also had held the lowest rank among them during the Civil War. As a result, Millen became the favorite for elevation to power, at least for the military wing. Millen had had a particularly colorful history. Originally born in County Tyrone, Millen eventually became an officer in one of the competing armies during the conflicts racking Mexico in the 1850s and 1860s. While reading an American newspaper in Mexico in 1860, he discovered the existence of the Fenian Brotherhood. Millen continued his war in Mexico, rising to the rank of general. In 1864, he was ordered to travel to the Mexican consulate in New York City for a mission for the government, where he quickly also visited the Fenian headquarters. Millen apparently then completely abandoned his position with the Mexicans and joined the Fenians. By the time of Stephens's arrest, Millen had been operating for the Brotherhood and the IRB in Ireland for several months.

The process to replace Stephens was marked by considerable turmoil. According to John Devoy's account:

> The dissatisfaction over the lack of military preparation found expression in an effort to put a military man temporarily in Stephens' place. Several of the old Centres and practically all the new ones came to me before the formal opening of the meeting and insisted that I propose General Millen, Chairman

of the Military Council, for the position. We knew nothing of
Millen, except that he was Chairman of the Military Council,
and we had been told that he had been a General in the Mexican
Army, and we believed it would be easier to elect him on that
account. If a military man were at the head, we thought, he
would naturally start the necessary military preparations. . . . We
were greatly surprised when, one after the other, all the members
of the Military Council, except Millen himself, spoke against
the motion [to appoint him]. They said nothing against Millen, but it was quite evident that they had no confidence in
him. They pleaded for delay and urged that no hasty action be
taken. . . . At the second meeting called by Col. Kelly, Millen
was not present, but he sent a long letter in reply to one from
Stephens (written in his cell and brought to Kelly by Michael
Breslin), ordering Millen's return to the United States "to take
command of the expedition." . . . Kelly hint[ed] (not to the
whole meeting, but in conversation with individuals) that Millen
intended to abscond with all the available funds, which he had
insisted must be turned over to him. Those who were responsible
for selecting Millen were turned against him . . . and I moved
that the motion I had proposed at the previous meeting be
rescinded and it was done by a unanimous vote. None of us
ever saw Millen in Ireland again.[9]

John Devoy led a group that broke Stephens out of prison on November
24, in a carefully planned and very well-executed operation. Even though
the Fenian movement received a psychological and propaganda boost from
this prison break, the nationalists clearly had received a body blow from the
multiple arrests.[10] After Stephens was arrested in 1865 and was broken out
of prison, he held a council with Fenian leaders. According to Denieffe's
account, all the other leaders argued for immediate armed action, but Stephens overruled them and ordered a delay: "I concluded then and there
that Stephens' work was done, and his usefulness ended on that night of
November 26, 1865."[11] Stephens then fled to the US and subsequently to
France.
    A further blow struck the IRB in early 1866. Even though the Fenians
clearly had been hit hard by the arrests, the British government continued
to receive reports about IRB unrest brewing. These fears almost certainly
were magnified after Stephens's prison break. Despite the informers within

the IRB, British authorities seemed to work under the assumption that with Stephens's freedom, he would be in the position to actually lead the uprising he had long promised. The British could not count on his unwillingness to do so. As a result, the British Parliament, with minimal opposition, passed a bill to suspend habeas corpus in Ireland on February 17, 1866. After passage of the law, the British began a widespread roundup of IRB suspects. Importantly for later developments, the suspension of habeas corpus applied only in Ireland, not in England or Scotland.

With O'Mahony's leadership in peril and the Irish Fenians in disarray, the O'Mahony faction increasingly came under pressure to do something quickly. Bernard Doran Killian, the Fenian Secretary of the Treasury in the O'Mahony faction, reportedly pushed insistently for an effort to capture Campobello Island in New Brunswick, directly across the border with Maine. The strategic calculus reportedly was that the Fenians could then use the island as a base for seaborne operations against British shipping and for further offensive operations. The Brotherhood, in fact, began issuing letters of marque for privateers "to attack, seize, take, and destroy the ships and other vessels belonging to the inhabitants of Great Britain . . . on the high seas, or between high and low water marks, and to bring the same to some convenient port . . . in order that the Courts . . . in our said Republic . . . [to adjudge if they are] lawful prizes."[12] This was despite the fact that the Fenians did not have a fleet. Seizing the island and declaring it an independent entity would—if the United States would recognize it as a legitimate belligerent—make such operations legal acts of war rather than piracy. The Fenians apparently thought that they could turn some of the legal niceties that Britain used in regard to the Confederacy during the Civil War against London. The huge assumption here was that the US government would, in fact, tilt toward such Fenian plans.

As became the pattern of Fenian operations, rumors and exaggerations on both sides began to swirl. Newspaper reports began claiming that several thousand Fenians were prepared to strike. Likewise, local New Brunswick newspapers expressed concerns about the presence of Fenian Circles in New Brunswick; the Orange Order newspaper *Burning Bush* warned that 12,000 "Fenians were prepared to rise on a moment's notice."[13] It appears as though—however exaggerated this figure—the Fenians themselves expected at least significant support from the locals once they crossed the border.

Whether there were, in fact, Fenian members or sympathizers in New Brunswick, once the operation began, there was minimal evidence of any active support for the Fenians. One small group of Toronto Fenians under the leadership of Michael Murphy took a train toward New Brunswick and were arrested by the police. That ended the entire representation of Canadian Fenians. Likewise, the Fenians seemed to expect an even friendlier reception from the Maine residents. There were continuing ill feelings among the Maine population dating back to the Civil War as to perceived (and probably actual) sympathies among the New Brunswickers for the Confederate cause. The *Machias Republican* argued that "The Provincials are terribly frightened, which is pleasant for us to contemplate. They are now reaping what they sowed a little time ago."[14] Unfortunately for the Fenians, however, no matter what bitterness still remained among the people of Maine for the government and people of New Brunswick, they were not particularly ready to sign up for the Fenian cause. In general, the locals maintained an attitude that might best be described as neutral curiosity once the Fenians arrived.

Rumors and a degree of panic in some areas of New Brunswick about a Fenian attack began reaching a boiling point in December 1865. Soldiers and militia units went on alert, the public began runs on banks, and there was considerable pressure on the provincial government. One of the reasons for concern was whether the New Brunswick volunteer militias were up to the task of repelling invaders. Although there were British regular forces in the province, the front line of defense in the event of an invasion was inherently going to be the volunteer militias. As with virtually every government during peacetime, the New Brunswick provincial government was reluctant to "waste" money on defense, and, in fact, in 1852 stopped all funding for defense. This policy, however, changed by 1859, and the province began rebuilding its forces. A number of militia companies were formed, reportedly with considerable public enthusiasm; by 1866, there were more than 2,000 active militiamen (known as "A category"), together with many lesser-trained volunteer units. Most contemporary reports praised the military bearing and snappy appearance of the militias, but this was a far cry from actual combat effectiveness. Many units received basic training from serving or retired British officers or noncommissioned officers, and officers for the companies were appointed by government based on merit rather than the common practice at the time for officers of militia units to be elected by their troops. Nevertheless, there were a number of reports from the period as to organizational issues. As one example from the Saint John *Morning News*:

> . . . veterans to Col. Robertson's Battalion of the City Light
> Infantry were called upon to assemble themselves on the Barrack

Square to answer the roll-call and perform certain other military formalities. . . . Promotions among the officers during the past year seems to have been so great and transfers so extensive, that mostly all the Companies have got new Captains. This, together with the rain, caused a good deal of confusion among the "Rank and File," who kept wandering about in all directions searching eagerly for their missing chief.[15]

These types of reports were important in the Fenian assessments of their chances for success in any operation. Looking at it from the standpoint of Fenian leaders, an ill-prepared New Brunswick militia, the unlikelihood of having to face regular British forces, the prospect of receiving support from sympathizers on both sides of the border, and the prospects of the US government remaining aloof from involvement all could add up to at least a chance for success. Unfortunately for the movement, all these assumptions proved to be false.

After the earlier December scare of a Fenian invasion, there was a fresh round of alarm as Saint Patrick's Day 1866 approached; this concern was not only among the public, but also by the provincial authorities. As a result, early in the year, the British moved a warship, the HMS *Pylades*, closer to the border off Saint John. The province also activated about 14,000 militiamen of various categories. When Saint Patrick's Day passed uneventfully, both the authorities and the public relaxed somewhat, but some planning and preparation for border defense continued.

The Failure of Security

In the meantime, the Fenians continued their preparations under Killian's direction. As typical, they were less than discrete about their plans:

Charles W. Beckwith of Fredericton [in New Brunswick] was attending Harvard University in Boston when a former Frederictonian, Jack O'Brien, a Fenian leader, invited him to a rally. There the proposal to invade Campobello was openly discussed. Without delay, Beckwith forewarned New Brunswick authorities. As usual, British spies were omnipresent and also provided detailed reports.[16]

Although it has been alluded to already, the issue of maintaining security bedeviled the Fenians throughout their existence. The Fenians faced a problem that many such groups have faced before and since: to recruit members and to motivate existing members they had to be somewhat public as to their plans and overall goals. At the same time, however, this provided a wealth of easily available intelligence for governments and police services. The key factors seemed to be whether governments would pay attention to reporting and then whether they would act on it.

Equally significant, the Brotherhood was riddled with spies and informers. The latter typically were relatively low-level, working for whatever money was available, but some such as "Red" Jim McDermott, with close ties to O'Mahony and Rudolph Fitzpatrick, the Fenian assistant secretary, had good access. McDermott, for example, reportedly provided the British with ciphers, documents, and locations of arm caches. He also reportedly was used to disrupt Brotherhood political processes. McDermott continued his operations against other Irish nationalist groups after the fading of the Fenians. He was denounced by several senior FB and IRB leaders beginning as early as 1864, but O'Mahony continued to defend him as a loyal member throughout his regime.

During the Brotherhood's history, leaders certainly understood that there were security problems. Some efforts were made to tighten internal security and to create countermeasures. In some cases, this simply was trying to outwait the authorities. For example, from then-President John O'Neill to a Centre in Buffalo in 1868, he stated that ". . . the government is keeping a close eye on us just now, which is one reason why I am opposed to removing the arms from your city. In a few months we can remove them without being suspected."[17] The group also developed a rather primitive system of codes.[18] Unfortunately, the code they used appears to have been so easily broken that it likely provided a false sense of confidence. Likewise, Fenian leaders couched their letters and other correspondence in ways that they clearly thought disguised their meanings. A good example was from a letter sent from Colonel Kelly to O'Mahony relating the preparedness for an uprising in Ireland. It would take a stupid British police official indeed not to find the contents suspicious:

> Returning to Dublin I made the acquaintance of a large number
> of friends, of all ranks, and on the advice of my doctor I then
> came to this latitude where I find the climate to be exceedingly

healthy. My expectations here and in Dublin were amply realized. Among the workmen at my business, and I have been high
and low, the determination seems to be unanimous that there
must be a strike for wages here this year. Indeed, from what I
have seen I think the union will become defunct if it does not
take place, because fully one-half the best workmen I have met
express a determination to emigrate if they have to live on present rates beyond next harvest. Men fitted to direct movements,
as you are accustomed to have them done in America, are sadly
needed, although much is being done by men versed in the
English style of polishing; yet they are necessarily circumscribed
in their operations by reason of the increasing vigilance of their
employers. A good number of our mechanics, as far as I have
seen them, are competent and skilled to undertake any kind of
contract, if the plans were drawn and they only had the tools
and foremen, and the remainder of those I have seen, if the
proportion in other parts of the country is nearly commensurate,
need but competent instructors and fitting machinery to those of
England. The whole country appears to be of one mind on this
point, with but few exceptions, the opposition and persecution
of the Cullen police to the contrary notwithstanding.[19]

Long-term agents and infiltrators within the Fenians also were very
significant. Some of the agents reached very senior positions within the
Brotherhood. Two of these agents were particularly important. The first was
Fenian General Francis Millen, who as noted earlier for a brief time was
considered for selection as the IRB military leader. It is not clear exactly
when he first started as an informer for the British, but his senior position
certainly gave him extraordinary access to the Irish side of operations. E.M.
Archibald, the British Consul in New York, wrote a secret letter to a British Undersecretary, Sir Thomas Larcom, on March 13, 1866, stating that
Millen "proposes to furnish H.M. Government with the fullest details of all
the information he possesses in reference to the military organisation [sic],
enrolments, arms, &c. &c., in England and Scotland as well as Ireland."[20]
    Among other intelligence reporting, Millen reportedly provided a table
"showing the location of Fenian centres in Ireland," their strength in men
and equipment, and their training level, together with similar information on
the Fenian Brotherhood in the US.[21] It is unclear how long Millen actually
reported to the British, but his information came at a critical time. Although

there clearly were financial reasons for Millen to become a turncoat, there are indications that he was driven as much by his loathing for Stephens as by the remuneration. Whatever his ulterior motives may have been, Millen publicly accused Stephens of misappropriating Fenian funds and of being guilty of "callous heartlessness" and "disgraceful extravagance."[22]

Perhaps the most important of the agents in the American Fenian Brotherhood (and certainly the best known afterward) was Henri le Caron, whose real name was Thomas Beach. Le Caron was born in Britain, but emigrated to the US during the Civil War and enlisted as a private. By the end of the Civil War he had reached the rank of first lieutenant. Shortly after the war, he became a self-recruited agent, objecting to what he saw in the Fenian movement. He rose rapidly in the ranks, and then successively held positions as major and military organizer of the Irish Republican Army, inspector general, colonel and assistant adjutant general, and finally general and adjutant general. He was sufficiently close to General O'Neill (at that time, the President) that when the latter was facing an audit by the Fenian treasurer, and O'Neill had used organizational funds for personal use, le Caron loaned him 364.41 dollars to balance the books.[23] In his later position in the Brotherhood, le Caron had access to virtually every aspect of the Fenian military planning. It got to the point where le Caron both hid Fenian arms caches and almost simultaneously reported their locations to the British. As with many agents both before and since, he clearly exaggerated some of his reporting, but there was virtually nothing that the Fenians did in secret that was not passed on to the police.

Despite having a number of agents and informers inside the Fenians, governments' intelligence operations against the Fenians were marked by a number of problems. The first was the sheer number of agents and informers: there were so many, and with such little coordination, that on occasion they reported on each other. This was exacerbated by the Canadians and British having at least three different services taking reports from agents. Certainly not all of the reporting by agents and informers was particularly accurate. At times, in fact, they likely fell into much the same trap as the Fenian leadership itself, viewing aspirations as actual capabilities. Although there was constant reporting on Fenian plans, the actual response to Fenian operations was not always particularly effective. In large measure, this may have been because with the number of splits and cross currents within the Fenians, there simply was too much confusion within the leadership itself for accurate assessments to be made by outsiders. At the same time, however, it was difficult for the Fenians to do anything without it being known by opposing governments and police. Also important was a consistent issue still experienced: the best intelligence in the world is completely pointless unless it is acted on.

From the Fenian side, there was awareness that they were faced with a large number of spies and police informers. This, in fact, was impossible to ignore if they only looked across the ocean to Ireland. There had been a steady stream of trials of IRB members, with virtually all these trials prominently featuring the testimony of police informers. Likewise, mostly at a somewhat later period, a similar pattern existed in Canada. The American Fenians could not imagine that they were immune from this.[24] In several cases, in fact, Fenians did identify some agents in their midst, but only a very few were actually removed from the group. In general, after such charges key leaders vouched for the accused, having developed strong trust in them. It was much more common for very loyal Fenians who ran afoul of the leadership to be accused of being traitors or police agents; the assumption seemed to be that disagreement equated to disloyalty. O'Donovan Rossa gave a personal example of this:

> I have been three times expelled from the membership in the Irish revolutionary societies of America by the controlling powers of those societies. No charges preferred against me, no trial, or no summons to appear for trial. A simple announcement made that O'Donovan Rossa is "expelled" or suspended. That announcement, virtually declaring me a traitor, is sent to every club of the organization throughout the nation, and to every affiliation it has in foreign lands.[25]

Moving to the Border

Fearing interference by American authorities—with considerable justification after General Grant issued orders to stop cross-border operations—in late March the Fenians began moving members to Maine separate from their weapons. The Fenians chartered the vessel *Ocean Spray* and used it for shipping weapons and ammunition. Despite this precautionary measure, most of the Fenian members who traveled to Maine wore at least partial uniforms, along with knives and pistols, and they made little effort to conceal their membership. The points of concentration for the Fenians were Calais and Eastport, Maine, where General Killian and his staff arrived on April 10.

Apr 1866

i.e. in the

Me.

One suggestion that planning may already have gone awry was that "Killian applied at the Frontier Bank for funds and presented a telegram from New York certifying that his bankers held sixty thousand dollars at his credit. The bank would not advance the money and he is expecting the necessary vouchers by the steamer tomorrow."[26] The members, of course, had not yet received their weapons, so they initially spent their time marching or simply relaxing. As with virtually all Fenian operations, the number of troops they had in place is subject to considerable question. Members came and went as they pleased, so any strength figure was likely to be a moving target. Most estimates are in the 700 to 1,000 range, and these appear to be reasonable. Most probably, the lower figure is the closer to reality.

Almost as quickly as the Fenians arrived, government response on both sides of the border began. On the US side, urgent cables from the Eastport Collector of Customs requested that a senior military officer be assigned to the area. The lieutenant governor of New Brunswick, Arthur Hamilton-Gordon, also cabled Secretary of State Seward to notify him of the impending arrival of the *Ocean Spray* and its arms cargo.[27] The US administration quickly sent law enforcement officials to Maine to enforce neutrality. The US Navy also dispatched a naval squadron of five vessels to patrol the coast. Perhaps most importantly in terms of perceptions, the War Department sent Major General George Meade, well known on both sides of the border as the winning general at Gettysburg, to supervise the security response. This move likely had a major impact on public confidence that the situation would be managed. The presence of General Meade clearly was reassuring to a number of people in New Brunswick. As the *Morning Freeman* on April 24, 1866, reported:

> [In addition to British forces, we now have] the American troops on their side armed to preserve the neutrality of the United States, and placed under the command of General Meade, the hero of Gettysburg, and commander of the Army of the Potomac, and the son of an Irishman, and by the way a Catholic to boot. The fact that General Meade was sent down to the frontier, is conclusive proof that the United States Government is in earnest.

Actual US federal army strength in the area initially was minimal, with only about 135 artillerymen stationed at two posts along the border. When Meade traveled to his post, he traveled with sixty-three more artillerymen as reinforcements. This was a small number of troops, but had symbolic value as showing his seriousness of purpose. In any event, with the naval vessels offshore, Meade was not likely to require a significant presence of soldiers.

One other fortuitous situation made Meade ideal for his role. Major General Sir Charles Hastings Doyle commanded the British forces deployed in response to this crisis.[28] During the Civil War, General Doyle had spent some three months as an observer at the Army of the Potomac under Meade's command, and the two reportedly became close friends. The two visited each other during the weeks of the Campobello incident, and there was every indication of very open communications between the two. This extended to lower levels, with US and British officers socializing on both sides of the border.

Likewise, the colonial government in New Brunswick responded rapidly. Vice Admiral Sir James Hope dispatched at least five combat ships to the area, together with his flagship, the HMS *Duncan*. Together with the normal ship complements totaling more than 1,400 seamen, all of whom could be deployed as landing parties, there were 150 Royal Marines on the *Duncan*. British regular ground forces also were moved toward the border, and "by the third week of April, the strength of British regular infantry in New Brunswick and Halifax had doubled."[29] General Doyle initially was somewhat reluctant to put British regulars directly on the border, fearing desertions by some British troops; the desertion problem was rather endemic to the British army of the day, and in fact some British soldiers did try to desert to the nearby US. Nevertheless, he did deploy a battalion of the 17th Regiment together with supporting elements. Likewise, the militia was activated and deployed to their assigned areas along the border. In short, the Fenians now were outnumbered, outarmed, and outmaneuvered even before getting organized.

The initial "military operations" that the Fenians launched became rather ludicrous, despite creating a series of alarms among the New Brunswickers along the border. On April 13, two boatloads of Fenians landed at Porter's Farm near St. Stephen, firing a few shots in the air, burning some woodpiles, and then withdrawing. On April 14, a steamer carried a Fenian group to Indian Island where they landed and forced the customs collector to hand over his Union Jack. This later was proudly displayed by the Fenians as a war trophy (which may have been the major success they had in this episode). A number of other incidents along the water were reported at the time, but whether these were actual Fenian attempts at operations or simply routine events magnified through a prism of crisis is virtually impossible to determine.

Undoubtedly, to the relief of the Fenians—at least initially—the *Ocean Spray* docked in Eastport on April 17 with the weapons aboard. Unfortunately for their hopes, however, the customs collector, Washington Long, had the ship detained immediately by a US revenue cutter. As an example of some of the complications surrounding the crafting of a legal response, when Long telegraphed the US District Attorney for the region as to further actions, he was told that unless it could be proven that the weapons were intended for foreign territory, he had no legal grounds for seizing the arms. This legal decision typically has been ascribed to political calculations: in an election year in the US, the government did not want to unnecessarily alienate the Irish vote. There likely is considerable validity to this conclusion. In fairness, though, there also was somewhat of a legal minefield for the authorities. Even General Meade, certainly no friend of the Fenians, initially recommended that the arms be returned to the owner of record, a Mr. Kerrigan, providing that he post bond that the weapons would not be used in violation of the neutrality laws.[30] Shortly after, however, Meade decided not to release the weapons. Seizing private property, albeit war material, before any specific crime had been committed rested on very shaky legal grounds, particularly for that era. There was a period at the end of the Civil War during which the government was selling its muskets to soldiers being discharged for six dollars a weapon. Suddenly declaring these weapons as being illegal would require a certain amount of legal gymnastics. Until the Fenians actually violated the neutrality act by crossing the border as an organized group, it was a complicated legal situation with no quick or easy answers.

Fortunately for the stability of the area, the military forces assembling in Maine were less concerned with legal niceties. Commander George Cooper of the USS *Winooski*, a gunboat that had arrived in the area, in the best tradition of "act now, ask permission later," took the initiative and reseized the weapons. Only then did he ask for further guidance from the Navy Department. After considerable bouncing around in the corridors of power in Washington, his actions were approved and the weapons were moved to a government fort, albeit with seven cases of rifles somehow becoming missing.[31] General Meade, who had arrived the day following the seizure, also approved Cooper's action. In practical terms, at this point the Fenians were an army without weapons, and any hopes for practical action had evaporated. Many had already reached this conclusion, and when Meade arrived there may have been as few as 300 Fenians remaining around Eastport.

This did not mean that the Fenians ceased being a major nuisance in the area. The border remained open, with individual or small groups of

Fenians crossing into New Brunswick and militiamen crossing south. Some of the major "fighting" involved small brawls between the two groups. As one example, "A street fight took place yesterday between some British soldiers who came over to Calais, Maine, and some of the Fenians, the citizens are reported to have taken part with the Fenians, and the British were drove [sic] across the bridge with a few cut heads and bloody noses."[32]

There were two more serious incidents. The first was on April 21. This followed Fenian threats against a Maine trader who had been providing information to the US authorities. On the night of the twenty-first, Fenians landed on Indian Island and burned four warehouses to the ground. While Indian Island was on New Brunswick territory, all the warehouses were for property awaiting the payment of customs duties meaning that all the property in them was American-owned, including that of the threatened trader. Following this arson, the British established a small military post on the island, and it was not further bothered by the Fenians.

On April 28, about fifty Fenians boarded the British-owned schooner *Two Friends*, which had been hired by the Fenians to transport troops and supplies. When the captain of the vessel saw that the Fenians were transporting rifles, he evidently had second thoughts and refused to sail. The Fenian leader at gunpoint forced the captain to set off, and when this was discovered by authorities, they began pursuit. Seeing this, the Fenians had the *Two Friends* round a point of land where they could not be seen and found another vessel, the schooner *Wentworth*. They boarded and seized the *Wentworth* and had the *Two Friends* scuttled, then sailed back to Eastport and escaped. This episode of what essentially was piracy was the major incident during the Campobello operation.

It did not take many of the Fenian members terribly long to look at the futility of the situation and to vote with their feet. On April 27, some 200 of them took a steamer to Portland, Maine, and from there railroads to their homes. By May 7, General Doyle reported that the Fenians were "gradually dispersing," and he began to draw down the number of deployed troops. Despite this conclusion, some minor incidents continued. As with some of the earlier episodes along the border, whether such alarms actually were Fenian-inspired or were more the result of jittery troops and sailors is very difficult to determine. In perhaps the most significant of these incidents in terms of public confidence, a very poorly coordinated training drill by HMS *Cordelia* in which it fired blank gun rounds and muskets while berthed near St. Andrews, Canada was mistaken by the residents and the militia as a Fenian attack.[33] Needless to say, a fair degree of pandemonium ensued before a rather chastened ship's captain provided an explanation. Despite this and smaller incidents, things gradually returned to normal in New Brunswick.

Although the "self-withdrawals" of Fenians began as early as late April, small groups of them continued to stay in the Eastport area well into May. In some cases, many of the individual members were in a bad situation. Some could not afford the train tickets to go home, but this also meant that they could not afford the rents and food money to stay. Finally, the US government offered to buy train tickets for anyone willing to take the offer, and this added to the exodus from Maine. Virtually all Fenian presence disappeared in Maine by the beginning of June.

If O'Mahony had calculated that launching a military operation would stabilize his position within the Fenian Brotherhood, he was disastrously mistaken. O'Mahony tried to shift the blame for the botched operation to Killian, but this was not a particularly successful ploy. According to a report of May 10:

> O'Mahoney [sic] has issued a circular stating that he was erroneously informed that the Island of Campobello was neutral ground; that he intended establishing a Fenian camp there; that thence would be sent privateers; that the failure was owing to the undue publicity of the action to the United States and British Governments; that he made a mistake in consenting to the movement, and hereafter will steadily do his duty as a Fenian.[34]

Given the widespread disgruntlement among Fenian members, particularly those who had taken part in the Campobello operation, any apologies were unlikely to be particularly effective, and O'Mahony essentially became a spent force in the movement. He certainly recognized this, and submitted his letter of resignation to Stephens on May 11. In his letter, O'Mahony wrote, "I violated my duty, not alone to the Fenian Brotherhood and the Irish Republic, but to the best interests of the Irish race, as also to my previous unvaried policy."[35] Stephens replied the same day, saying that he "imperatively" felt the need to accept the resignation.

One lesson from the Campobello attempt that should have been taken to heart by the Fenian leadership, whether the O'Mahony or Roberts faction, was that General Meade in particular simply was not going to stand by idly while Fenian forces attacked across the border. However much potential political support by US politicians the Fenians might believe they had, the federal officials on the ground were not willing to allow large groups to breach neutrality treaties. Although with this incident as with later ones, while US authorities might not be able to do much in terms of legal actions against individual Fenian leaders or members—in part due to legal codes themselves, but more often because of domestic political sensitivities—they would respond to major breaches by the Fenians and would take action, whether sanctioned or not. Somehow this did not enter the planning concepts of the Fenian leaders, and they would pay for it in the future.

Chapter 6

Preparing for Invasion

Before the sun of May shines, they [the Fenians] will have conquered a territory, over which the Irish flag will float, and which will serve as a base from which to operate against the British power in Ireland itself.[1]

—Speech by Thomas Sweeny in January 1866 in Buffalo

One advantage might have accrued to the Fenians from the fiasco at Campobello. This was that governments and the public on both sides of the border seemed to view the Brotherhood as a completely spent force. The *Sarnia Observer* of Ontario argued on May 24, 1866, that "so far as any fear of a Fenian invasion is concerned, the whole [frontier] force might be disbanded, for we do not believe the Fenians will venture across the border." Likewise, the *Chicago Tribune* printed an editorial that was republished in the *Toronto Globe* of April 16, 1866, that argued "We only know that the leaders connected with it [Fenian Brotherhood] are without brains, and the followers are very generally without character."[2] Similar sentiments appeared to be prevalent among the respective governments as militia forces were sent home by Canada, and the US redeployed its regular troops.

Other Fenian leaders mooted the possibilities of quick raids, seemingly for lack of any other plans. For example, Sweeny received a letter dated March 3, 1866, from J.W. Bryce, his naval aide, that in "compliance with your instructions" he had examined the chances for capturing Canadian vessels that were iced in.[3] Bryce did not discount the prospects for success, but he noted that it would require 200 to 300 sailors, divided into parties for each ship, with each party "under the command of a reliable and experienced naval officer." He also stated that further intelligence was important. Bryce estimated that the cost of such an operation would be about 12,000 dollars, including the need for bounties for the sailors. He suggested that many of the sailors could be recruited in New York City, but that fitting out such an expedition would be better done in Buffalo or Chicago. Other short-term operations apparently were also under consideration, but Roberts and Sweeny decided to "go big." Sweeney appointed inspector generals for actually assessing the movement's military capabilities.[4] He also stressed the essentiality of more and better training for Fenian soldiers.

The Strategy

Sweeny developed a plan on a full invasion of Canada, based on a multi-pronged advance toward the major cities. In its ultimate form, this became a very complex plan, with many moving parts. Although somewhat lengthy, an abridged version of the strategy is necessary to understand the events of 1866:

> A descent from the Lakes simultaneous with the crossing of the undefined boundary on the line of the St. Lawrence. A column of 3,000 men were to move from Chicago and Milwaukee (24 hours in advance of the movement of Lake Erie), by Lakes Michigan and Huron, seize and advance directly on London by Stratford. This difference in time was given so that the other columns could cross Lake Erie; one concentrating at Port Stanley and moving on London, the other [from Buffalo] concentrating at Port Colbourne, seizing Paris, Guelph and Hamilton. This would compel the enemy to concentrate his forces about the meridian of Toronto, uncovering Montreal.
>
> So soon as this was accomplished, our auxiliaries in Canada were organized and prepared to destroy St. Ann's Bridge, at the junction of the Ottawa and St. Lawrence Rivers, on the Grand Trunk Railroad and the Beauharnois Canal. This would effectually cut off all communication between Upper and Lower Canada. To distract the attention of the enemy while this movement was being made, knowing that wherever I was he would consider the main point of attack, I was advertised [as being] in Erie and in Buffalo and other points along the frontier, the main points of the attack being along the line of the St. Lawrence. In order

to more fully carry out this design, I massed troops at Potsdam Junction and at Malone; threatening Cornwall and Prescott, which had the desired effect. The success of this movement being of vital importance. Brig. Gen. Murphy, commanding the cavalry, was ordered to move on both sides of the Richeleau River and seize the garrisons of Isle aux Nois, St. Johns and Fort Chambley. or cut them off; occupy La Prairie and threaten Montreal by the Victoria Bridge, holding it if possible until the infantry came up; if forced to retire, they would fall back, destroying the bridge and placing all possible obstacles in the way of the enemy.

Simultaneously with this movement a detachment of cavalry was to be sent forward along the line of the Grand Trunk Railroad in the direction of Quebec, seizing Point Levi, if not too strongly garrisoned. Should the enemy move across the river in force, they were to fall back on Richmond, destroying the bridges and giving timely notice of the enemy's movements and holding that point. Should the enemy attempt to concentrate his force from Montreal and Quebec, the forces were to be drawn in between the Richelieu and the St. Francis Rivers and that country held at all hazards, making Sherbrooke the Headquarters. This position can be seen at a glance to be one of the strongest in Canada for defense.

Other accounts indicate that the Fenian leadership also considered operations along the West Coast, the use of a naval force for privateer operations, and the expectation of a simultaneous or near-simultaneous rising in Ireland to be supported by Americans. Sweeny stated that "the minimum force with which I would consent to Invade Canada should be 10,000 men."[5] He also wanted three batteries of artillery—typically about eighteen guns in total during that period. The intent was for each soldier to be provided with 200 rounds of ammunition. He estimated that the cost of such an expedition would be 450,000 dollars. He initially insisted that the attack take place during winter "when the lakes and rivers are bridged with ice. Otherwise, double that force would be necessary." A winter invasion made some sense because many waterways between the US and Canada could be crossed without the need for boats. This timing also would be a surprise both to Canada and to US authorities; nineteenth-century militaries still were accustomed to go into winter camps. The downside was trying to actually operate in Canada during the winter. How Sweeny hoped to support his

forces in a season both where food would be short and his troops subject
to bitter weather was not determined.

Several points can be made about the Fenian strategy. The first is its
sheer ambition. Even very well-trained and experienced armies have found
multipronged offensives to be very difficult to coordinate and control. A
more or less thrown-together force such as the Fenians, who were unable
to drill together beyond company-level at best, would be unlikely to have
any greater luck in coordination. The key element required for any success
in this type of offensive would be communications among the independent
columns and between them and the overall commander. In the nineteenth
century, virtually the only practical means of communications for large
formations would be via rail, mounted couriers, and the telegraph. Based
on the Fenian strategy, all three were problematic.

The strategy called for the destruction of rail lines in Canada. This
certainly would be required to stop or slow Canadian and British reinforcements moving toward the Fenian advances. At the same time, however,
unless the Fenians had the capability to repair rail lines once they had seized
them—a capability nowhere in evidence—they had no way of using them.
Unless mounted couriers traveled back to the US and then traveled north
again to link up with the other columns, they would be traveling through
largely hostile country, with considerable prospect of failure.

For armies of the time, the key communications means was the
telegraph. This was the only means of quick and secure coordination of
multiple forces that were separated. Exactly how the Fenians expected to
be able to use the telegraph system effectively is subject to question. As the
independent columns advanced, they would have to rely on the Canadian
system. Why the Canadians would leave the lines intact in between the
columns is unclear; the normal response to finding foreign forces using the
national system would be simply to cut the lines. The only other option for
the Fenians would be to send couriers back to the US; use the American
telegraph system; and then use couriers to carry the messages to the forward
columns. This would become increasingly slow as the columns advanced
farther into Canada. It also presupposed that the US government would
permit the Fenian forces to use the American telegraph system for these
purposes; as it turned out, this was not the case.

Many of the same issues surrounded the logistics of the Sweeny's plan.
It focused on acquiring weapons and supporting gear, but seemed to pay
little attention to the more prosaic elements of food, shelter, and the like.
During the preparations for the invasion, there is no evidence of attempts

Hope is not a plan.

to purchase major quantities of cargo wagons, dray horses, or oxen to transport supplies. "Living off the land" may have sounded romantic, but was not terribly practical for large numbers of forces, and was unlikely to endear the Fenians to the Canadians who were subject to confiscations for food or shelter. There is an old military adage that "amateurs talk strategy, professionals talk logistics." Given the wealth of experience among the Fenian military leaders, the apparent gaps in planning for communications and logistics remain rather surprising.

One other note should be made. Many reports from the time and most analysts since have described the Fenian operations of 1866 as "raids." This implies an intent to attack specific areas and then to withdraw. This decidedly was not the intent. The strategy was to seize and hold territory, either permanently or at least for an extended period. Without understanding this strategic intent, many aspects of the subsequent developments cannot make sense.

In any event, Sweeny simply could not find sufficient funding for his ambitious plans; he stated in his official report that he had only about one-quarter of the money he thought necessary for the invasion. Nevertheless, he proceeded because—according to him—he was pressured into going ahead by several circles and ". . . I reluctantly yielded, preferring the chances of an honorable failure in the field, to the disintegration of the organization. . . ." He had to cut back on the purchase of weapons and as for artillery, "I had none whatever, but trusted to the gallantry of my soldiers to capture it." Of course, unless the horse teams and caissons for the guns were also captured, there would be no practical way to move them for further operations.

Acquiring the Means

A major push began in early 1866 to acquire more weapons and supplies for a major operation and to distribute them to the various circles.[6] Likewise, the Fenians increased their intelligence collection across the Canadian border.[7] A Fenian named John Canty bought a house near Fort Erie on the Canadian side of the border and reportedly provided a significant amount of intelligence to the Fenians on the Niagara area. Peter Vronsky in his recent history of the battle of Ridgeway argues for the criticality of Canty in particular in providing intelligence on the terrain in the Niagara Region and on key facilities in the area.[8]

In reality, much of this information could just as easily been collected by American tourists or business travelers routinely crossing the border.

Also, in his after-action report, General O'Neill stated that "I received no written instructions, and had no map of the country."[9] Basic information on the terrain in the area of operations certainly would be useful, but not necessarily critical. Skilled and experienced military leaders, which O'Neill certainly was, have always tended to develop a keen eye for terrain and how to make the best use of it. This certainly was the case with O'Neill and his use of terrain during the Ridgeway battle.

As the date for invasion moved closer, the Fenians also made efforts to coordinate the movement and support of their forces. One letter from Buffalo provides some interesting insights into the processes involved, and it deserves quoting at length:

New York, May 13, 1866.

Major-General T. W. Sweeny, Sec'y of War, F. B.

General:—In obedience to your instructions I proceeded at once to Buffalo and as far as possible placed myself in correspondence with the parties named in said instructions. Mr. O' Day and Colonel Hoy had already opened negotiations with Messrs. Dole and Rice of the New York Central Railroad, and a few hours after my arrival in Buffalo we had an interview with them, and after discussing the matter thoroughly, they decided they could not aid us directly, as they were rather peculiarly situated, but offered to lend us the use of their warehouses for the storage of our merchandise. We subsequently visited two other parties with like result. At last, Mr. Frank Gallagher and myself visited another gentleman named John S. Mundabac, a large owner of canal boats, and he has agreed to furnish us with all the boats necessary and also a sufficient number of tugs to bring the expedition to its destination.

I have this day received a dispatch from Mr. O' Day, telling me that the contract is drawn out in a legal manner by a lawyer in the following manner: That boats are chartered to go to Canada for cargoes of ashes, so that there will be no suspicion of their going over the river. None of our men appear in the business at all, so there can be no suspicion aroused by their being seen around the boats. We are to pay $25 per day for the use of the boats and the tugs are to be paid what they demand. I could not learn the price, but believe it will be moderate. The boats will be ready at our call. Our merchandise is to be packed securely in boxes and disguised as much as possible and marked to some fictitious party on Lake Superior. When our goods leave here a man is to proceed to Buffalo to claim and reship them. Mr. Mundabac will recognize him and then have the goods placed in a boat where they will remain until you are ready. . . .

A. L. MORRISON, Senator, F. B.

The letter then goes on to provide the best intelligence the writer had on the Canadian defenses in the Niagara region.[10]

On May 10, Sweeny as Secretary of War issued General Orders No. 3 directing the commanders of all regiments to pack their equipment and to be ready for transportation to their assigned sectors, with "orders to move [to] be communicated by telegraph in a few days." He established the following rendezvous points: The troops from New York and New Jersey to Buffalo; troops from Massachusetts, Rhode Island, and Connecticut lo Dunkirk (New York); troops from Pennsylvania to Erie (Pennsylvania); troops from Indiana and Tennessee to Sandusky City; troops from Ohio, Maryland. North Carolina and Virginia to Cleveland; troops from Kentucky and Missouri to Toledo; troops from Illinois to Chicago; troops from Iowa and Wisconsin to Milwaukee; and troops from Michigan to Port Huron.

The actual movement of troops became somewhat of a public spectacle as the trains became more and more crowded with Fenians moving to the jump-off points. At least some of the Fenian soldiers tried to maintain some level of secrecy about their intent, but at times this effort was less than convincing: "When questioned, they replied that they were going to Canada to work on rail roads; or, in some cases, that they were former soldiers, bound for California—hardly a convincing answer, when they arrived here [Buffalo], as many did, from Cleveland, Cincinnati, even from Indiana and Illinois."[11] More often than not, however, the soldiers engaged in singing Fenian fight songs, bragging about who they were, and generally being careless about security. Their overall conduct while moving to their jump-off points reportedly was less than stellar: "The Fenians from Cleveland arrived here [Buffalo] this morning. Several fights occurred on the train, and out of three hundred and forty-two that started, quite a number

Comical lack of discipline

left by the way, badly hurt. One at Ashtobula will die. They left the train a mile outside Buffalo, separated, and are now scattered through the worst places in the city, and are very disorderly. . . ."[12]

Buffalo showed the largest build-up of Fenians, but Fenians began pouring in all along the eastern and Great Lakes borders with Canada. Establishing figures for how many Fenians actually were staged for deployment is next to impossible; it is probable that the Fenian leadership itself at the time did not have exact figures. Some evidence can provide clues, however. After the failure of the invasion, the US government issued paroles to the Fenian rank-and-file. There reportedly were some 7,000 paroles given; these were required to be signed before the government would pay for rail transport to the soldiers' homes. Many of the Fenians living in the border cities such as Buffalo and Chicago likely never found any reason to sign the paroles. These cities had considerable Fenian membership. As such, it is fair to estimate that somewhere around 8,000 Fenian troops were present along the border, theoretically available for the invasion.

Fenians seemed on the move throughout New York State during late May and the first few days of June. This could be illustrated by one day's edition of the *New York Tribune* of June 4, 1866:

> Syracuse: "On the afternoon train going west yesterday, there were six car loads of Fenians. One company of 120 were uniformed, and carried several Fenian flags. They got off in Rome. This morning there arrived here 74 more from Binghamton, with five cases of arms, bound east." Worcester, Massachusetts: "A company of 80 Fenians . . . left here this evening by the Northern Railroad for the front." Erie, Pennsylvania: Three hundred Fenians embarked near this place for some point in Canada this morning. A fleet of seven large fishing boats has also left Barcelona for Long Point with Fenians and supplies." Poughkeepsie: "A squad of Fenians left Matteawan yesterday; a squad left Newburgh on Friday, and a squad will leave here on Tuesday or Wednesday for the Canada border." Burlington, Vermont: About 150 Fenians passed through here last night bound for St. Albans, which makes about 450 who have arrived since 6 p.m., yesterday." Baltimore: "It is reported that a party of 60 or 70 Fenians arrived here to-night [sic] from Washington, and were joined here by about 100 more, supposed to be bound to Canada."

Movement of Fenians to border reported in N.Y.

Cavalry w/o horses.
Red legs without guns.

As a minor but rather curious sideline, Irish Americans reportedly were not the only volunteers for operations against Canada. The *Buffalo Express* on June 5 reported that in New York City: "During the afternoon [probably 3 June] a delegation of colored men called upon Head-Center Roberts and offered their services, with a detachment to back them, to march on Canada in order to fight for Irish liberty in the Fenian army. They stated that in fighting for Celtic independence they would be enabled to avenge the foul outrages perpetrated on their colored brethren recently in the Island of Jamaica." There reportedly were similar offers made in Philadelphia. Why African Americans would choose to support Irish Americans given the long-standing tensions between the two groups, especially after the New York City draft riots, is somewhat a mystery, but at least some were willing. Likewise, the *New York Times* on June 14, 1866, reported from Buffalo that "Two companies of Indians have come here to aid the Fenians." None of these offers of direct support ever came to fruition, but somewhat muddy the historical picture.

On May 10, the Fenian War Department formally mobilized the army. It was not until three weeks later that the commanders of the three wings were formally appointed: Brigadier General C.C. Tevis for the approach from Chicago and Milwaukee to London, Ontario; Brigadier General W.F. Lynch to be headquartered in Cleveland to attack the Lake Erie and Ontario region; and Brigadier General S.P. Spear to attack from Ogdensburg, New York and St. Albans, Vermont. The forces at that point reportedly had about 10,000 rifles and 2.5 million rounds of ammunition, but as noted no artillery.

Importantly, it also had no actual cavalry. There was in theory a cavalry brigade of five regiments under the command of Brigadier General M.C. Murphy, to be attached to General Spear. Although some troops reportedly were intended as cavalry, they had no horses. This appeared to be the same logic as with artillery: the troops could form units once they seized horses in Canada. A problem with this logic was that not all horses are created equal. The qualities desired in a cavalry horse normally are far different than those in a good farm horse, which likely was going to be the majority of the horses the Fenians would find at hand. Also, training horses to work together as a unit always takes time and effort. Both these factors would almost certainly limit mounted Fenian efforts to small-scale tactics.

Although many of the Fenian weapons were war surplus and had been purchased legally, the group also was very active in acquiring other weapons, either quasi-legally or illegally. In some ways, what became almost a contest between the government and the Fenians began over control of these arms. For example, on May 30 the US Marshal in New York seized fifty Remington revolvers and 8,000 rounds of ammunition from the steamer *General Sedgwick*, which had arrived from Galveston. The shipment was addressed to "D. O'Sullivan, No. 700 Broadway, New York." A number of documents also were seized, including letters addressed to the Adjutant General, Fenian Brotherhood. A letter dated May 13, 1866, that was seized provided a very useful example of some of the illegal sources for the Fenians in their quest for weapons and equipment and how they garnered support from individual soldiers and officers:

> I also telegraphed from Warrington Junction to my friend here at Galveston, and stated to him that we had plenty of "pipes" but not a sufficient quantity of "tobacco" and begged him, for God's sake, to obtain all be could of 58 calibre [musket ammunition] . . . [Weapons and ammunition were apparently provided by a sympathetic sergeant at the military base in Galveston; whether winked at by the commander or outright theft is not clear.] [We] "took away as much as the Government wagon could carry." [Material boxed up, but then] "lo! A messenger came and told us that the things were missed, and that they were after us. Col. Ellis, of the Seventeenth Regulars, and Lieut Smith of the Seventeenth approached us, and told me, that they knew it was a good cause, but nevertheless they should do their duty. We saved, however, from the whole, the following amount: Eight thousand rounds and fifty Remington revolvers. We lost Burnside rifles, revolvers, &c. in abundance, and any quantity of ammunition. We invited the officers and gave them a champagne supper. They expressed their sympathy with us, and, under the circumstances, we did as well as we could hope to do. They also released the giver from arrest."[13]

As the Fenian forces moved into their deployment areas, arrangements had to be made to house and equip them. As the Fenian units arrived in Buffalo, they convinced the train conductors to stop the train about a mile outside the city. They then broke up into groups of about fifty and then further dispersed into their quarters. Individual troops were spread throughout the city wherever they could find housing. Unsurprisingly, most of the housing was in the Irish section of the city in the First Ward. All this seemed to be well organized, with little indication of major problems in either quarters or

Much support for same things but not sufficient aid deeply insufficient support in critical areas. (handwritten annotation)

food for the troops. From all indications, most room and board was provided gratis by "loyal" Irish Americans. The process clearly needed a rather large and effective support structure. Some indication of the amount of support in Buffalo was the long list of Buffalonians whom O'Neill thanked in his later official report on his operations. Townshend Hall in Buffalo was used as the main rendezvous point for the troops, with Fenians arriving in Buffalo holding nightly meetings there. A reporter for the *Buffalo Express* offered a delightful account of his efforts to find out what was occurring inside:

> [The Fenian troops] were marched to Townsend Hell, at the corner of Main and Swan streets, reaching it about midnight, and disappeared up the stairway leading to its interior. Our reporter attempted to elicit some information concerning the strangers, but his questioning entirely failed to awaken confidential impulses in the stern bosoms of those to whom they were addressed. He was informed that a citizens meeting was being held in the hall—perhaps he would like to go up—nothing to hinder—by all means he should go up and see; and the invitation was accompanied with such grim, sarcastic smiles that the unfortunate reporter has not yet recovered from the chill shudders into which a lively imagination thereupon threw him.[14]

Once the troops arrived in Buffalo, they needed to be equipped. Despite a significantly large number of Fenians in the city, the leaders tried to be relatively discreet about the next step in their plans. Patrick O'Day was the Fenian coordinator in Buffalo. On May 30 the *Buffalo Courier* published the following advertisement that served to alert incoming units where the arms and equipment were available:

> Peremptory sale of muskets, rifles and commissary stores by P. O'Day, at his auction and commission house, Nos. 20 and 22 Pearl Street. Friday, June 1, at 10:00 A.M., will be sold on account of whom it may concern without reserve—muskets, rifles, carbines, swords, knapsacks, habbersacks [sic], tents, caldrons, frockcoats, navy white blankets, U.S. grey blankets, 23 halters, bridles, 50 horse collars, wrappers and drawers, 400 overcoats. Terms cash.[15]

The *Buffalo Express* picked up the story from there on May 31 and June 1:

Our reporters visited Mr. O'Day's establishment yesterday . . . but were assured that the boxes of muskets, pistols, etc., had not been opened—would not be opened until Friday, and that the consignee knew nothing whatever yet as to the quality, manufacture, pattern, or value of his weapons—not even sufficient to recommend them to a purchaser. One side of Mr. O'Day's establishment seemed to be filled with formidable boxes. . . .

[On 1 June] We announced yesterday, most of the large cases of muskets had disappeared from O'Day's auction rooms, how or when no one was able to say. Nevertheless the advertised [sale] came off. . . . Some new muskets were put up first, and although only some thirty or forty were to be seen the crowd were informed that the weapons would be sold by the case, and that the purchaser could either take one case or the whole lot. The lot was knocked down to Mr. F. B. Gallagher [almost certainly Frank Gallagher, a Fenian Senator in Buffalo] at $3.80 for each musket. . . . [Details are then provided about the sale of haversacks and other equipment without any inspection, all to buyers with very Irish-sounding names.] Some persons in the crowd were foolish enough to think that the purchasers intended the munitions for the Fenians, but we were *assured* by others that such was not the case. . . .

Mr. O'Day was asked how it happened that so few muskets were offered for sale, when it was known that 48 hours before one side of his large establishment had been entirely occupied with cases of arms, & c. . . . He replied that on Thursday night, when his place of business was closed, there were a large quantity of munitions of war ready for sale, but when he arrived yesterday morning a great portion had disappeared, and he suspected that those rascals, the Fenians, had carried them away. The explanation was regarded as entirely satisfactory.

As a final note to this story, a *Buffalo Express* reporter who visited the Fenian landing area in Canada after the operation actually had been launched reported that he saw "a number of boxes" of what almost certainly were muskets marked "P. O'Day." It might also be noted that O'Day was on the platform for a rally supporting the Fenians on June 1.

John O'Neill and the Buffalo Troops

John O'Neill emigrated to the US in 1848, and settled in Elizabeth, New Jersey. After failing in business, he enlisted in the Regular Army in 1857 and served as a cavalryman in the West, most notably during the Mormon War. Shortly after, he deserted and moved to California where he joined the 1st Cavalry and was promoted to sergeant. He initially served with this regiment in the Civil War until he received a commission in the 5th Indiana Cavalry in December 1862. He established an outstanding combat record particularly in battles against the Morgan's Raiders, a Confederate quasi-guerrilla group in Kentucky, but began to resent his lack of further promotion. As a result, he transferred to the 17th United States Colored Infantry in the rank of captain, but left the service before the war ended. After his resignation, he became a land agent in Tennessee. He also was very active with the Fenians, rising to the rank of colonel in the Fenian Brotherhood and commander of the 13th Tennessee regiment.

As per the original orders, O'Neill arrived in Cleveland on 28 May. There he—and the Fenian high command—faced a dilemma: General Lynch, who was supposed to command that Fenian wing, was nowhere to be found. Some have since argued that he was very ill, but the exact causes for his absence remain unclear. With the command situation in total disarray, O'Neill was ordered to move to Buffalo, and, as senior officer, to command the attack across the Niagara. He received his written orders mid-day on May 31.

On paper, O'Neill had more than four regiments for his offensive. This included the 13th Tennessee regiment (which had been his command); 17th Kentucky regiment under the command of Colonel Owen Starr; 18th Ohio Regiment under Colonel John Grace; and the 7th New York Regiment under Colonel John Hoey. Some reports have indicated that the first three regiments were somewhat composite, with Fenian troops from a number of areas comprising them. The 7th Regiment reportedly was almost exclusively from the Buffalo area. In addition to these regiments, he also had two Indiana companies under the command of Captain Hagerty.

The reason for the phrase "on paper" is that none of these units were anywhere close to being a what would be viewed as normal strength for a regiment at the time. As with all Fenian operations, the actual number of troops who crossed the border with O'Neill has been subject to debate, both at the time and by later writers. Leaving aside grossly inflated and

Last minute change in command at Buffalo

alarmist figures from the immediate reports, the proposed numbers typically have ranged from 800 to 1,500. Compiling the number of prisoners taken by the US and Canada, casualties, and the few who simply escaped at the end of the operation, a figure of somewhere between 900 and 1,000 would seem to be reasonable.[16] Most authors have agreed that there probably were about 800 Fenians actually involved in the Battle of Ridgeway. O'Neill stated (several years after the fact) that he had about 800 men available, but only 600 actually made the crossing. Moreover, "Many of the men who crossed over with me the night before managed to leave the command during the day—some recrossed to Buffalo, and others remained in houses around Fort Erie."[17] Certainly, in the aftermath of the Fenian withdrawal after the battles, the Canadians arrested a number of Fenians who for one reason or another were no longer with their units.

Even taking the highest credible figure of 1,500 Fenians crossing the border out of Buffalo and the few hundred crossing in the East (to be described later), it is clear that only a minority of Fenian troops actually engaged in the invasion. At best, somewhere between a quarter and a third of the soldiers entered Canada. Most remained on the American side of the border. In part, this can be ascribed to problems in coordination; other difficulties resulted from transportation bottlenecks. Some troops arrived late, and some made it only partway. The US government was partly responsible by interfering with some travel, and the Fenians had some separate issues with contracting for vessels and the like. Even when all this is taken into account, a number of troops and officers simply decided not to cross. It is very likely that some of the troops and officers determined that the "great adventure" began to pale as they got closer to the prospects of actual combat.

Discounting the Fenians

Despite numerous warnings and the physical evidence of a Fenian buildup along the border, neither the US nor the Canadian government seemed to take the Brotherhood's preparations particularly seriously. Some US government officials became engaged in preemptive actions against a Fenian attack across the border, but these activities were scattered, uncoordinated, and not notably effective. Some weapons shipments were seized, some Fenians were detained, and other low-level actions were taken.

While these activities were going on south of the border, the British and Canadian authorities seemed to cycle through extreme alarm to complacency and back again. Overall, however, they made virtually no practical preparations. After a series of false alarms, the Canadians likely were suffering from "alert fatigue." Every time the militia was activated, men had to leave their jobs, their farms, and their families. This created very real economic and social costs. Even with these issues, however, the Canadian government seemed to be very ill-prepared. As Lieutenant Colonel George T. Denison, a Canadian cavalry militia commander noted:

> During all this time no preparation of any kind for campaigning was made, no organizing done, no staff officers appointed, no stores or equipments [sic] prepared and practically everything neglected. The rifle companies all over the country were scattered and had no connection with each other. They were not told off into battalions, nor officers carefully picked out to command the battalions; and during all March, April and May in the face of constant and alarming indications of danger, nothing was done.[18]

The Fenians were on the border without practical preparations to deal with them. The stage was set for their invasion.

Authorities slow to act.

John O'Mahony, first President of the Fenian Brotherhood. Courtesy of Project Gutenberg.

JAMES STEPHENS

James Stephens, leader of the Irish Republican Brotherhood. Courtesy of the
National Archives, NARAL 530230.

HEAD-QUARTERS OF THE FENIAN BROTHERHOOD, UNION SQUARE, NEW YORK.

Fenian Brotherhood Headquarters, New York City. Courtesy of the New York Public Library Art and Picture Collection. "Head-quarters of the Fenian Brotherhood, Union Square, New York." New York Public Library Digital Collections. Accessed April 28, 2016. http://digitalcollections.nypl.org/items/510d47e1-10dd-a3d9-e040-e00a18064a99.

MEETING OF THE FENIAN CONGRESS IN THE ASSEMBLY BUILDING, PHILADELPHIA.—[SEE PAGE 694.]

Fenian convention in Philadelphia in October 1865. *Harper's Weekly,* November 4, 1865.

James Stephens speech at Jones's Wood, New York City, April 15, 1866. *Harper's Weekly,* June 2, 1866. From the author's collection.

An early print of the Battle of Ridgeway. The depiction is highly inaccurate, reflecting how a 19th Century battle 'should' be fought, rather than what actually occurred. Courtesy of the Library of Congress, LC-DIG-pga-01485 (digital file from original print).

Townsend Hall in Buffalo, New York, circa 1890. This served as the primary assembly point for the Fenians who invaded the Niagara. Courtesy of the Buffalo History Museum.

General John O'Neill, leader of Fenian forces at Ridgeway. Courtesy of the National Archives, NARA 526300.

General George Meade, who led the US reaction to Fenian operations in 1866 and 1870. Courtesy of the Library of Congress.

FUNERAL OF CANADIAN VOLUNTEERS KILLED IN A SKIRMISH WITH THE FENIANS: SCENE IN THE CEMETERY AT TORONTO.—SEE PAGE 663.

Funeral in Toronto of Canadian volunteers killed at the battle of Ridgeway. The Illustrated London News, June 30, 1866. From the author's collection.

The USS Michigan, whose crew seized the Fenians as they tried to cross from Old Fort Erie to Buffalo. Courtesy of the Library of Congress.

The Canadian General Service Medal with Clasp Fenian Raid 1866 awarded to Private Pierre Proulx, 9th Battalion Voltiguers de Quebec. Similar medals with Clasp Fenian Raid 1870 were awarded for those operations. These medals were not authorized until 1899 after Canadian veterans petitioned Queen Victoria. From the author's collection.

William Roberts, President Fenian Brotherhood. From the author's collection.

"Fighting Tom" Sweeny, Fenian Minister of War. Courtesy of the Library of Congress.

THE TABLES TURNED—JOHN BULL CAPTIVE TO THE FENIANS.

FITZ-JONES ("*a thramplin' Saxon*"), while attempting to cross Broadway on St. Patrick's Day, became entangled in that "dreadful procession," and was forced to grace the triumph of his enemies for at least three blocks. "Devilish annoying, you know."

Political cartoon of *Harper's Weekly*, April 4, 1868. Caption reads: The Tables Turned – John Bull Captive to the Fenians. Fitz-Jones ("a tramplin' Saxon") while attempting to cross Broadway on St. Patrick's Day, became entangled in that "dreadful procession," and was forced to grace the triumph of his enemies for at least three blocks. "Devilish annoying, you know." Although somewhat pro-Irish (or at least anti-English), this cartoon typifies the non-Irish press coverage of the Irish, almost inevitably depicting them with quasi-simian features. From the author's collection.

Irish American Fenian prisoners in England: "Dennis F. Burke, late Colonel, 88th New York Vols ; John Dunn, late of the American Service ; Francis Nugent Kavanagh, late a lieutenant in the American Service ; Frank Leslie, late an officer in the American Service." Courtesy of the the New York Public Library, Manuscripts and Archives Division. "Dennis F. Burke, late Colonel, 88th New York Vols ; John Dunn, late of the American Service ; Francis Nugent Kavanagh, late a lieutenant in the American Service ; Frank Leslie, late an officer in the American Service." New York Public Library Digital Collections. Accessed May 17, 2016. http://digitalcollections.nypl.org/items/510d47dc-9681-a3d9-e040-e00a18064a99.

Canadian militiamen standing over the body of a dead Fenian after the battle of Eccles Hill in 1870. Courtesy of the Missisquoi Historical Society/Musée Missisquoi Museum.

The "Cuba Five" after their arrival in the US from English prison. They offered the potential for a resurgence of the Fenian movement. John Devoy (far left), standing, Charles Underwood O'Connell, (second from left) seated, Harry Mulleda (center), standing, Jeremiah O'Donovan Rossa, (second from right) seated, and John McClure (far right) standing. Lithographed by Robison & Mooney, 112 Nassau Street. Courtesy of the Library of Congress, LC-DIG-pga-08083 (digital file from original item).

Fenian Banner. Courtesy of the Library of Congress, LC-USZ62-38607.

Chapter 7

The Invasion in the Niagara

Let cowards bend in abject prayer,
Let tyrants frown and threat,
Be ours the duty to prepare
With sword and bayonet.

—Michael Scanlon

About midnight on June 1, 1866, Colonel Starr led the advance party to Black Rock (then a small village about two miles north of Buffalo, now a part of the city) where they used a canal boat to cross the Niagara River and to land about a mile north of Fort Erie. The force landed about 3:30 A.M. and raised the Fenian flag of the 17th Kentucky Regiment. The main body crossed on four canal boats about three hours later. As the troops were crossing, they were issued their Springfield rifled muskets, ammunition, and bayonets.[1] Before daybreak, the main Fenian forces were on Canadian soil.

There was some confusion among outside observers at the time—and possibly among the Fenian rank and file themselves—as to the actual strategic logic surrounding the attack on Ridgeway. Newspaper reports from the time suggested that it might be a feint, preceding a major Fenian operation elsewhere. Others called it in the terminology of the time as a "forlorn hope," or a deliberate sacrifice of troops to enable larger follow-up forces to break through. At least in part, these theories probably were created by the sheer number of purportedly combat-ready Fenians who, in fact, never made it across the border. As the *Buffalo Express* noted on June 5, "While we had assuredly in this city some two or three regiments of Fenians, well armed, equipped and drilled, and while liberal detachments have been reaching here from abroad during the past week, amounting to more than another thousand, the whole augmented army in the field only amounted to about 1,000 men." Likewise, there were considerable numbers of Fenian troops in Ogdensburg, and in Malone, about 300 Fenians were "walking about the town" "apparently without design or object."[2]

Beyond the purely military aspects of the operation, the earlier (and continued) splits within the movement appeared to add to the inability of the Fenian leaders to deploy all their potentially available forces. The *Buffalo Express* of June 5 reported that supporters of Fenians were split among factions as to whether the invasion was wise or even if it was authorized. Although some clearly were fully supportive and willing to participate, "Others, less confident, or less bold, deprecated this attack of the Sweeney party; affirming that it was totally unauthorized and without the sanction or consent of the Chief Organizer of the Irish Republic, James Stephens, without whose orders, nothing for the disenthrallment of Ireland could be done."

The Movements of the Opposing Forces

After establishing their beachhead, the Fenians moved into Fort Erie. A distinction probably should be made here. There were, in fact, two "Fort Eries." The first was the actual fort. This dated from the War of 1812 and became thoroughly derelict afterward. In 1866 it had virtually no military significance other than its location at a critical point on the Niagara River. The second Fort Erie was a village that was then (as it is now) a very bustling town and a worthwhile military objective as a logistics hub; it also for a time was called Waterloo, but to avoid confusion, it will continue to be called Fort Erie in this account. O'Neill moved one of his units to the north along Niagara Road to guard the approaches from that direction and to cut telegraph lines and to sever rail links between Fort Erie and Port Colborne, which was the logical route for any forces counterattacking the Fenians. His troops had become scattered in foraging expeditions and some probably in personal sightseeing trips, so O'Neill had to consolidate his forces, which he did at Frenchman's Creek, about three miles north of Lake Erie. His troops began to dig in at Newwbiggin's farm. After waiting there for reinforcements and not receiving any in quantity, he then moved toward Lime Ridge Road. Shortly before beginning the march, the Fenians destroyed a significant quantity of weapons and ammunition. Although some analysts have claimed that these initially were intended to provide arms to Canadian Fenians, it is more probable that they were meant for Fenian reinforcements from the US who never came. O'Neill himself said that the reason for destroying weapons was that he had weapons for 800 and had only 500 men actually with his column.[3]

O'Neill took several measures that were unlikely to endear him to the local Canadians. None of his troops had had breakfast, so he ordered the local civilians to provide meals for 1,000 troops. He offered to pay in Fenian bonds, but unsurprisingly this offer was refused.[4] He also put adult males under house arrest, but this seemed to be more pro forma than rigidly enforced. One result of the Fenian presence, however, was to create a significant number of Canadian civilian refugees. Exact numbers are impossible to determine; but many Canadians found it prudent to leave what clearly was becoming a combat zone. Interestingly, many chose to flee south to the US rather than farther into Canada. One contemporary diarist described the movement to the US as being a "swarm."[5] His troops also began seizing horses from farmers in the area, with a reported forty to fifty horses impressed into service.[6] Reportedly, none of the horses had saddles or stirrups, and the troops had to ride them bareback, obviously limiting their usefulness. There certainly were no indications that the Fenians tried to create a true cavalry unit, no matter how miniscule, out of the horses they now had. The Fenians also confiscated a large number of shovels, pickaxes, and saws, obviously expecting the need to create breastworks and entrenchments during the campaign. In some ways, these tools may, in fact, have been the most important confiscations the Fenians took.

Even as early as June 1, O'Neill began to be concerned as to how isolated his forces were. He recognized that his was not the primary column; without some other efforts within Canada, his troops were in a very hazardous position. According to Sweeny's official report, he received a telegram from Captain Hynes the night of June 1. The exchange read: "Our men isolated. Enemy marching in force from Toronto. What shall we do? When do you move?" He sent the following answer: "Reinforce O'Neill at all hazards; if he cannot hold his position let him fall back; send him and his men to Malone as rapidly as possible by the Rome and Watertown roads." Finding that there simply was no means of transportation, Sweeny claimed that he then ordered the commander of the Fenians in Detroit to advance from Port Hudson to Sarnia in an effort to distract the British and Canadians and possibly to give O'Neill's troops an escape route. Sweeny's orders, however, were essentially ignored. O'Neill and his troops were alone.

As the British and Canadian government finally recognized the reality of the invasion, they quickly called out the militia forces. Critically, however, the only units called up initially were the infantry. Neither of the militia artillery batteries near the Niagara frontier were able to deploy—one, in fact, had had its guns withdrawn for security reasons.[7] Why the cavalry militia was not called up immediately—the first cavalry troop was not activated until about eighteen hours later—remains a mystery. The commander of the cavalry unit that eventually was used along the Niagara, the Governor General's Body Guard for Upper Canada, later expressed his attitude at the time:

> The idea never entered my head that the authorities would send infantry without any cavalry whatever. I should have known that infantry officers would probably forget all about the cavalry, but I must confess I never thought of such a thing. I do not blame myself for not foreseeing this, for I was still a young man, only twenty-six, and I had not then that confidence in the average stupidity of officials which, through long experience, I have since acquired. I went to town as quickly as possible, still no orders for the cavalry, although everyone else seemed to be ordered out. I had made up my mind to go over as a volunteer on my own account when, late in the afternoon, I received my orders.[8]

Viewed from an operational perspective, a logical objective for the Fenians was the Welland Canal, running from Port Colborne, about nineteen miles from Fort Erie, on Lake Erie to St. Catharines on Lake Ontario, a distance of about twenty-six miles. Beyond being an important water transport link, a major rail line ran along the canal. Major General George Napier, British commander of all the forces in Ontario ordered Colonel George Peacocke, a British Regular, to deploy a mixed force of British regulars and Canadian militia at St. Catharines, with a purely militia force at Port Colborne. The Port Colborne force was comprised of the Second Battalion, Queen's Own Rifles from Toronto, 13th Battalion of Hamilton, and the Caledonia Rifles and York Rifles companies. These units totaled about 861 officers and troops, and were the ones involved in the upcoming battles. The fighting at Ridgeway and Fort Erie was completely a Fenian versus militia struggle.

Even if the Fenians had significant logistics problems, the Canadian militia may have fared even worse. The militia battalions started their deploy-

[handwritten: But Can forces as unready as the Fenians.]

ments miserably equipped and supported. Most of the troops did not have packs, and many did not have canteens. Shovels and axes were not carried, nor was cooking gear. There was no immediate medical support. The Queen's Own troops were deployed from Toronto without any ammunition for their weapons. Despite knowing this, Major General Napier told the troops in two addresses that they ". . . were likely to be engaged with the enemy within twenty-four hours, (his first speech), or within twelve hours (his second version of the first speech). . . ."[9] Although seemingly not receiving the same amount of attention by analysts, even basic tools for weapons maintenance were missing: "They had not a wrench in the battalion to unscrew looks, nor a worm-screw, of which every man should have one wherewith to draw charges from rifles. The nipples of some were, after the action, plugged with dirt and could not be fired off. There was no battalion armourer. They had no oil for springs, or to protect burnished steel from rust."[10]

This was an endemic problem. Units that were not immediately deployed suffered from the same logistics issues. Even with the delay in activating the cavalry:

> The want of organization or preparation in view of the long threatenings seems almost incredible. I had to take my corps on a campaign without the carbines I had asked for, but with revolvers for which we had only some four or five ten-year-old paper cartridges for each. We did not know whether they would go off or not. We had no haversacks, no water bottles, no nose bags. Some of us had small tin cups fastened on our saddles. We had no canteens or knives or forks, or cooking utensils of any kind, or valises. We had no clothes except those on our backs (I had an extra flannel shirt and one pair of socks in the small wallets in front of my saddle). We had no tents and no blankets. The militia infantry were almost as badly off.[11]

Most of the Canadian militia were armed with fairly old rifled muskets. Their actual training with those weapons, beyond drill and ceremonies, was rather limited. Estimates were that only about half the troops had actually fired live rounds during training. One company out of the entire force was equipped with the modern Spencer repeater rifle. The Spencer was a good weapon, but less accurate than the rifled muskets and required different ammunition than the other weapons. Also, soldiers who were not accustomed to fire discipline tended to fire off ammunition at a very rapid pace, necessitating an ample issue of ammunition. The militia unit with Spencers was only issued twenty-eight rounds per man.[12] Even more importantly, most of those armed with Spencers had never handled them until deployed for this operation. As one ensign whose company was issued the Spencer argued, "We knew our Enfield Rifles, but knew nothing about these others, and a very poor thing they turned out to be at any distance over two hundred yards."[13]

One other problem for the Canadians and British was the quality of their senior military leadership. Although much of the criticism was after the fact, few of the key leaders emerged from 1866 with terribly impressive reputations. Major General George Napier, British commander of all the forces in Ontario (Canada West) was described by then-Colonel and later to be Field Marshal Wolseley as ". . . not a shining light. . . . In private life a charming man, he was quite useless at all times as a commander."[14] Likewise, at somewhat lower levels, the Canadian and British commanders displayed an interesting set of issues, as will be seen. In general, however, the commanders showed a woeful lack of preparation for field operations in general. This was as true of the commanders of the British regular forces, who in theory were the professionals, as it was of the militia commanders. As one example, "The British commander of the operation, Lieutenant Colonel George Peacocke, had only a postal map torn from an almanac, on a scale of ten miles to the inch and showing mail delivery routes but no roads or topographical features."[15]

The command system for the Queen's Own Rifles and 13th Battalion became rather snarled. Obviously, a single commander for the entire column was necessary. Lieutenant Colonel Alfred Booker of the 13th Battalion was (barely) the senior officer in the field, so he logically took overall command. Although this was the proper choice based on military protocol, it was not necessarily particularly popular, forcing many of the troops to serve under an unknown commander. Booker possessed what was called a "first class certificate," meaning that he was considered a fully trained militia officer. He had not, however, ever commanded a unit in the field. One reflection of how well Booker was prepared for field command was that he deployed "without a map or even a pencil and paper with which to issue orders, and without his horse."[16] The other senior commander with this column (at least initially) was Lieutenant Colonel J.S. Dennis of the Queen's Own Regiment, who likewise held a first-class certificate and had no field experience. A contemporary officer had the following observation on Dennis: "Lieut.-Colonel J. Stoughton Dennis, Brigade-Major of the 5th District, was a very good office man in time of peace, the exact type of man to be dear to the official heart, a good red tape courtier, but useless as a soldier."[17]

The Queen's Own Rifles (QOR) left Toronto about 6:30 A.M. on June 1 in the steamer *City of Toronto*. The troops landed at Port Dalhousie and used the railroad to move to Port Colborne by 12:00. Scouts from the QOR reported that there were Fenians around Fort Erie. The QOR stayed at Port Colborne. Booker's 13th Battalion left by train about 9:30 A.M. and traveled to Dunnville and disembarked there. Booker then received orders from Colonel Peacocke to move to Port Colborne; the battalion then reboarded the train and arrived there about 11:00 P.M.

In the meantime, Peacocke was assembling his forces. He began with elements of the 16th Foot and two companies of 47th Foot (British regulars) and a battery of Royal Artillery. He moved from Toronto to Hamilton, linked up with about 200 other regulars and militia, and moved to St. Catharines. Peacocke believed O'Neill was moving toward Chippawa, and he called for more regular and militia forces to deploy there. Eventually, he assembled about 1,700 troops. He then moved his forces to Chippawa. By that night, he received word that O'Neill had remained at Newbiggin's farm.

Peacocke decided to join all units at Stevensville. This small village was located about fifteen miles by road from Chippawa and about five miles from Ridgeway railroad station. This was a logical choice tactically because it was on the rail line between Port Colborne and Fort Erie, making troop and equipment movement easier. Peacocke announced that he planned to start his march at 6:00 A.M. and to arrive by 11:00 A.M. He also sent Captain C.S. Akers to coordinate planning with Lieutenant Colonels Booker and Dennis. Captain Akers was a British regular officer in the Royal Engineers. As a regular officer and a member of the Royal Engineers—which during that period were generally considered to be the quintessential military professionals—his advice would be taken very seriously by militia officers, even if they were technically senior in rank to him. At same time, Peacocke telegraphed Booker to arm a ferry boat to protect the Niagara River and to be available to provide a communications link along the river. Although Peacocke clearly intended this as a rather minor part of the overall tactical scheme, it was to have major consequences.

Captain Akers arrived at Port Colborne at about 1:30 A.M., and he relayed orders from Peacocke for Booker's and Dennis's forces not to advance on Fort Erie on their own. They were to join with Peacocke at Stevensville. Booker and Dennis fought the orders, arguing that they were more current on Fenian movements and that an advance on Fort Erie should be made. Captain Akers essentially unilaterally approved the change and then telegraphed Peacocke for his approval. Booker sent a telegram to Peacocke requesting permission to use rail to Fort Erie and suggesting that Peacocke move down the river road to trap O'Neill. Akers then joined Dennis in going off to find a vessel for the Fort Erie mission. It is hard to escape the belief that Dennis found such a mission to be much more to his liking because it gave him the opportunity for an independent command. In response to the telegram sent by Akers, Peacocke ordered that there would be no change to his plans, but Akers and Dennis had already gone.

Dennis and Akers linked up at Port Colborne with the commander of the *W.T. Robb*, with a crew of three officers and nineteen men. The background of the *Robb* was rather interesting. A local businessman, Lachlan McCallum, formed the Dunnville Naval Brigade as a local militia unit. In 1864, he built a steam-powered tug named *W.T. Robb*, named after his friend Walter Tyrie Robb, who was made captain. Members of the Dunnville Naval Militia used this vessel to practice shore landings during 1864 and 1865. When Lieutenant Colonel Dennis arrived, he took direct command and reinforced this crew by loading the members of the Welland Artillery Battery, which consisted of three officers and fifty-one men under the command of Captain Richard King.[18] Although labeled an artillery battery, this militia unit had had its cannons removed much earlier because it could not secure them properly. As a result, its officers had been training its members as infantrymen. At this point, two very distinct and very separate battles developed and have to be covered in turn.

The Battle of Ridgeway or Limestone Ridge

On the morning of June 2, O'Neill marched to meet the weaker force, Booker's. O'Neill began his movement at dawn. He marched troops along a back road that intercepted Lime Ridge Road. This ran along a ridge known as Lime Ridge or Limestone Ridge, which was thirty to forty feet high and about half-mile wide at the battle site. Both fields of observation and fields of fire were excellent from this position. With O'Neill's combat experience, he almost certainly was seeking an area of high ground to use as the backbone for his battle plan. The roads around the area were forested on each side. O'Neill's mounted scouts notified him of the Canadian column approaching. He established defensive positions at the intersection of Stevensville Road and Lime Ridge Road. He sent out an advance guard and pickets of about

150 troops to occupy orchards in front of his position. The Fenian forward troops moved to Bertie Road and made barricades from local fences. These barricades extended for several hundred yards along Bertie Road.[19]

Booker's troops had not spent a comfortable time in moving forward for the operation. With a lack of canteens, many had to rely on streams or cooperative locals for whatever water they could find. Only some had been able to find food for breakfast on June 2. Many who had, in fact, eaten had been provided only salted herring, not exactly an ideal prebattle meal. Even fewer militiamen had found adequate shelter. As a result, many of the troops entered the morning of battle tired, hungry, and thirsty. Nevertheless, Booker began his forward march about 7:00 A.M. As with many aspects of the battle of Ridgeway, his movement to battle remains controversial. Lieutenant Colonel Peacocke sent a telegram that morning, ordering Booker not to engage the Fenians.[20] Exactly when Booker received this is debated. Peter Vronsky makes a persuasive argument that Booker received it before the battle.[21] In this case, Booker may well have ignored the order and entered battle in an effort to gain unit and personal glory. Other Canadian analysts, including some contemporary with the battle, have stated that the telegram arrived after the engagement began. In either event, the militia forces fought without the support of Peacocke's forces.

At the same time, Peacocke seemed to take a somewhat leisurely approach toward the movement of his column. The initial movement on June 1 by rail had been marked by frequent stops, meaning that the troops did not arrive at their initial camp until about 8:00 P.M. His march the next morning started about two hours late. Once the troops got started, they moved rather quickly. The day's heat began to take its toll of the troops rather quickly, however. This was particularly the case with the British soldiers; in contrast to the Canadian militia, the British soldiers may have been overequipped, and they carried heavy loads of individual equipment. One British soldier, in fact, died of heat stroke; he was the only British regular soldier to die during the day's operations. Due to the heat, Peacocke ordered a halt and initially considered remaining overnight. He eventually changed his mind and ordered his troops to resume the march after about a five-hour delay. One possible positive for this halt was that it enabled a small body of about fifty-five cavalrymen to join the column. This cavalry unit was the Governor General's Body Guard for Upper Canada, later to be called the Governor General's Horse Guard. All these delays were exacerbated by the route Peacocke chose to use. He very much "took the long way around." As with many other key issues surrounding Ridgeway, this engendered controversy both during the time and since. Some have claimed that Peacocke was deliberately sabotaged by local guides; some have argued that Peacocke ignored locals who knew the best way; others have said that he deliberately chose the particular route because he believed it to be better for marching troops. Whatever the reasons, Peacocke was still three miles short of Fort Erie when he ordered a stop as dusk fell.

Booker marched his troops in columns toward Ridgeway, with Queen's Own Rifles at the head of column, followed by York Rifles, then 13th Battalion, then Caledonia Rifles. Because there were no wagons available, spare ammunition and supplies were sent back to the railhead. There was only one horse with the force, belonging to one of Booker's officers; Booker confiscated this for his use. Some locals informed Booker that there were Fenians nearby, but he dismissed these warnings. Booker did have an advance guard for the column, but did not have scouts in front of them.

First contact with the Fenians began about 8:00 A.M. After a few shots were fired, Booker halted the column and sent out advance companies, which came under ineffective sporadic fire at a range of about 200 yards. Canadian Queen's Own Rifles troops deployed by companies through farmers' fields and began pushing back the forward Fenian elements located in adjoining orchards. From contemporary accounts at the tactical level, the inexperienced Canadian militiamen seemed to believe that they were gaining a major victory as they pushed back the Fenians they initially encountered. These Fenian elements were intended for early warning and to wear down any advancing forces before they hit the main position. Their role was to fire and withdraw in good order back to the main lines, but inexperienced troops (and commanders) were unlikely to understand this and believe that they were gaining a major victory.

The forward Canadian units began running low on ammunition, and the company armed with Spencers completely spent their ammunition. Booker ordered the 13th Battalion and the York Rifles to relieve the Queen's Own Rifles, and the QOC fell back for relief. As the shift was taking place, some advanced elements received fire from their rear by their own side, but apparently no casualties resulted from friendly fire. At about this time, however, the militia lost its first casualty, Ensign Malcolm McEachren, who was killed. The Canadians continued advancing, and they pushed initial elements of the Fenians as far as Bertie Road, and O'Neill pulled his troops back to the main body. At one point, in fact, advance militia elements on the left began to flank the Fenian positions on their right flank.

Up to this point, the battle had gone well for the Canadians. They had not dislodged the main Fenian position, but with the exception of the units that had passed beyond the point of being supported by other troops, the situation seemed to be reasonably well in hand. Some analysts since then have, in fact, argued that the Fenians were about to retreat.[22] This seems to be speculative, but the situation was not promising for O'Neill and his troops. At about 9:30 A.M., however, things began to go very, very sour for the Canadian militia.

Controversy continues to surround the next few moments of the fighting, with multiple competing narratives as far as the sequence of events, who knew and did what, and even if some things later reported actually happened. Although an official court of inquiry later was held, it produced more smoke than light.[23] The two main points of contention involve a series of orders transmitted by bugles (which was how tactical battlefield orders were being transmitted) and shouts of "cavalry."

Some—but not all—of the forward-deployed militia skirmishers reported hearing a bugle call to retire. According to official testimony, in fact, one of the most forward units heard the bugle for "retire," then "advance," then "retire on the double." Others, depending on their location, reporting hearing a single signal to retire or no signals at all. Enough troops, however, heard the signal to retire that a large number began retreating to join the main column. This in itself was not critical or necessarily unusual; massing troops for an assault on an enemy's main body would have been a very straightforward battlefield tactic. Again, however, this assumed that the subordinate commanders and troops understood the intention of the orders.

At about the same time (although the chronology never actually has been fully agreed upon), someone in the main body of troops called out "Cavalry! Watch out for cavalry!" Again, it has never been conclusively determined who started this. Lieutenant Colonel Booker denied shouting such a warning, and no other officers stepped forward to claim responsibility. It is quite possible that it was a militiaman who was simply spooked by seeing a Fenian on horseback and magnified that to a horde of cavalrymen. One participant in the battle claimed (long after) that it was, in fact, a herd of farm horses feeding in a meadow.[24] It appears that the warning quickly was spread by other troops. The concern as to the likelihood of a mass cavalry charge was handled well by the conclusions of the Booker court of inquiry (whose president was in fact a cavalryman):

> The Court, with respect to this part of the affair, are of opinion that to adopt the idle rumor that the enemy's force was partly composed of cavalry in a country where such an arm could be of scarcely any value in attack, or to assume, even for a moment,

that a mounted corps which he could not see was advancing at such a rate to render it necessary to give the words of caution which he used, was ill-judged, and was the first act which gave rise to the disorganization of his force, which then followed.[25]

However, the fear of facing a cavalry charge originated, Lieutenant Colonel Booker's response turned into a disaster. He ordered his troops to form a square. The square was the standard formation of the nineteenth-century British army for infantrymen facing a cavalry attack. The square was simply that: the infantry troops moved into a tight shoulder-to-shoulder formation with one-fourth of the unit facing each direction, providing 360-degree protection. The officers and the unit colors would remain inside the hollow area of the square. Cavalry charging such a formation would face a wall of bayonets in whatever direction they attacked, and it was rare for a British square to be "broken." Well-trained and experienced soldiers could form square, then move back into column formation, and then back to square if necessary, quickly and efficiently. Unfortunately, the Canadian militiamen were not up to this level. Captain Gardner, one of those falling back from the woods observed: "the column in the road [was] standing in the form of three sides of a square and a number of men standing loosely around. Some of the men had their bayonets fixed and some not."[26]

Booker ordered the square to be formed in the middle of the road where the militiamen were very exposed. Seeing such a tempting target, the Fenians shifted their tactical focus and opened fire on the formation; apparently most of the Canadian casualties were suffered at this point. Booker tried reforming his troops into columns once he recognized that there was, in fact, no cavalry charge. The withdrawing elements collided with the half-formed formation. Total chaos resulted among the troops. At this point Booker seemed to have totally lost control. He ordered all units to retire, when the Fenians launched a counterattack. Accounts from the time suggest that the Fenians charged with fixed bayonets, with some shouting Gaelic war cries and others the Confederate yell. The confusion among the militiamen quickly changed to panic. A total rout resulted.

The Canadian militiamen fled for their lives. Their officers tried to restore some order, but this proved futile. One officer noted that Booker ". . . got the bugler to sound the "halt" several times, and I heard the bugler say he was tired sounding the "halt."[27] One officer, in fact, reportedly was trampled by his own troops, and had to be carried off the field by other militiamen. Only two companies—the York Rifles and the 10th Highland Company of the Queen's Own Rifles—retreated in good order. O'Neill later noted that the route of the Canadian retreat was littered with abandoned weapons and other equipment. After the battle, an indication of how other militia units viewed the outcome and the behavior of the troops involved were the sobriquets given in rough soldier humor to the two units involved: the Queen's Own Rifles as "Quick outta Ridgeway" and the 13th Battalion, who wore red uniform jackets, as the "Scarlet Runners." Both units later established distinguished combat records in numerous subsequent campaigns and very much overcame this reputation, but they clearly had significant issues in this battle.[28]

The Fenians chased the militiamen through Ridgeway, then stopped the pursuit about a mile past the village. The Canadian units regrouped around the railhead at Port Colborne. Once they were disengaged, the officers restored order reasonably quickly, and, in fact, a number of the troops later were deployed for mopping up operations against Fenian stragglers. Booker himself did not fare as well. By his later account, he requested that a regular officer be appointed to replace him as the overall commander of the forces, but instead he was relieved of both that command and command of his battalion. According to some accounts, this definitely was a good decision because his behavior in the wake of the battle was at best eccentric.[29]

The Canadians lost nine killed on the battlefield, with four dying of their wounds within a few days of the battle, and twenty-two dying of wounds or disease later. There were thirty-seven wounded, some with wounds requiring amputation. There is some question as to the number of Fenian casualties, but they lost about six killed and probably about twenty wounded. These casualty figures were very light in terms of Civil War battles, frequently expressed in terms of thousands, but they had a major impact on Canadian society, which had not had to face any significant warfare for a generation.

After he halted his pursuit, O'Neill began moving his force back to Fort Erie. At this point in the battle, he recognized that considerable numbers of British and Canadian troops were approaching. O'Neill could not know exact numbers, but he likely overestimated the forces maneuvering toward him; for example, even in his official report written some time later, he claimed that he faced about 1,400 militiamen at Ridgeway. The movement to Fort Erie made tactical sense in that it gave him time to regroup and to assess what to do next. He also needed to provide for his troops, many of whom had not eaten anything that day and almost certainly needed some rest.

The Skirmish at Fort Erie

This led to the next battle, in this case with Lieutenant Colonel Dennis as the Canadian commander. The *Robb* had docked at Fort Erie that morning at about 8:30 or 9:00. Crewmembers and the troops of the Welland Battery had cleared through the town, with initial arrests of about eleven Fenian suspects. Further searches around the perimeter of the town resulted in a number of other detentions. Ultimately some eighty-nine Fenian prisoners and suspects were held by the militiamen. By mid-afternoon, the Canadians began receiving reports of a large number of Fenians approaching Fort Erie. Captain King of the Welland Artillery ordered his troops back on the *Robb*, but he was overruled by Lieutenant Colonel Dennis, who ordered the troops back on shore. Captain King reportedly strongly protested this decision, but had no option but to obey orders.

Dennis marched the troops in formation to a point in the town where the Fenians easily were able to outflank them. A Fenian charge broke up the Canadians, but there was some initial heavy fighting and strong resistance by the grossly outnumbered militiamen. Captain King was severely wounded in the battle, in which he lost his leg, but remarkably there were not Canadian fatalities. Casualties among the Fenians were much higher. The overall casualty toll for both sides was nine Fenians killed and fourteen wounded, with the Canadians suffering five wounded and thirty-seven captured. Eighteen Canadians were able to make their way to the *Robb* and were evacuated. Other militiamen were able to sneak away inland. Lieutenant Colonel Dennis disappeared at some point during the fighting. His later account was that seeing the large number of Fenians, he ordered the militia forces to disperse and to try to exfiltrate out of the town to Canadian forces. Vronsky argues that Dennis may well have disappeared after the first shots were fired.[30] The court of inquiry after the battle seemed to try to avoid passing judgment on this issue. What is certain is that Dennis appeared at Peacocke's headquarters about 3:00 A.M. with his luxuriant whiskers shaved off and dressed in rough workingman's clothes.[31]

Although commonly described as a rather major battle, the fighting at Fort Erie may better be viewed as at best a skirmish, which is how O'Neill later characterized it. He said that the fighting lasted only about fifteen minutes. This might be somewhat shorter than the actual time elapsed, but it clearly was over rather quickly. The first spurt of fighting was intense, with the Canadians battling hard, but there was no way they could overcome the odds facing them. As the results became clear, the *Robb* pulled out from shore and withdrew with its cargo of Fenian prisoners. As with the early battles in the Civil War, the Fenian attack became somewhat of a spectator sport: "Crowds of people have come on the eastern trains to see the fighting. The station at Lockport alone sold 400 tickets to this place [Buffalo] and Niagara Falls."[32]

The Fenian "Way of War"

A good snapshot of the members of the Fenian forces that entered Canada along the Niagara was provided by the *Buffalo Express* on June 6, 1866. Likely working from booking records, it listed the names, age, religion, and country of birth of the Fenian prisoners being detained at the Brantford Jail in Ontario. Of the ninety-eight prisoners examined for this book, twenty-five were Protestant, reinforcing the earlier discussion as to the participation of non-Catholics in the movement. The soldiers were fairly evenly mixed between US-born and Irish-born, with forty-four of the former and forty-seven of the latter. There also were six who had been born in Canada, but almost certainly had earlier emigrated to the US, and one lone soldier who had been born in Germany (and whose now-lost story would probably have been interesting).

Breaking their ages down in age bands, there were thirty prisoners who were fourteen to nineteen years old; thirty-eight who were twenty to thirty years old; nineteen who were thirty to forty years old, and eleven who were forty years old or older. There were two fourteen year olds and two fifteen year olds in the population. The oldest prisoner was fifty-one. The relative ages of the prisoners actually were rather high for a military force of the time, most of which relied on very young recruits, but the high portion of "twentysomethings" would suggest (as was the assumption at the time) a significant number of Civil War veterans.

The rank-and-file Fenians were dressed in a wide variety of clothing. A few wore green uniform jackets, specially made for the Fenians.[33] Others were in mixed uniforms, others in civilian clothes. Observers noted that very many of them continued to wear the "US'" or "CSA" buckles on their belts if no other uniforms. Some of the soldiers from the south wore the remnants of Confederate gray uniforms. Virtually all of them wore at least some green, if nothing else green ribbons tied or sewn to their clothing. Many of the officers wore their full uniforms from the Civil War. The number of officers who continued to wear their Union uniforms from the

Civil War likely led to the fear expressed by one Canadian veteran that "[we] imagined the possibilities of the entire victorious Union Army coming over to help the Irishmen."[34] Whatever their clothing, all Fenians had their full combat kit of weapon and accoutrements.

The Fenians maintained rather good military discipline and overall proper conduct while engaged in their operations in Canada. There was some early reporting of widespread looting, but in general this seems to have been much exaggerated.[35] Much of this would be in the eyes of the beholder. Nineteenth-century militaries were very accustomed to foraging or "living off the land" for food and the like based on the alibi of military necessity. Given the Fenians' lack of supplies, this certainly occurred. What would be a normal military practice for their veteran soldiers would be viewed as looting by all the Canadians who had to give up their food or horses. Even Somerville, who spent every opportunity to excoriate the Fenians, noted the overall good behavior of the Fenian forces. He argued that there was some "spoliation" by Fenian soldiers, but this was stopped by their officers.[36]

There did seem to be some initial issues with the Fenian troops and pubs or grog houses. Several reports noted their fondness for occupying these targets. Again, however, the Fenian officers responded rather quickly. This was likely to have been the result of trying to maintain basic military discipline:

> When the invaders had filled themselves, and drank all the liquor in the village they still demanded more. One hundred and fifty or two hundred continued about that hotel, singing, and dancing several hours. At last O'Neil and other officers with drawn Swords came, supported by armed pickets and drove them away, using such reproaches as, "You blackguards! do you think we brought you to Canada to get drunk, and make sport? You came here to fight. The army of red coats will soon be on you! Are you in a state to meet the red coats? For shame! Soldiers of the Fenian brotherhood! Shame!" And the officers drove out the plunderers before them.[37]

One other example of the desire by the Fenian officers to fight "a gentleman's war" might be given, directly involving O'Neill. This was a letter dated June 5, 1866, sent to Buffalo newspapers while he was a prisoner on board the US steamer *Michigan*:

To the Editor,-You will please make known through the news columns of your paper, that have in my possession a gold mourning ring, engraved with the following inscriptions: on the outside in black ground the word, "in memory of," on the inside "Lucretia Wrigly, ob't 6th Feb., 1829, Act' 6," and under that, "Mary Wrigly, ob't 6th Feb. 1830, Act 45," besides some other rather indistinct characters, that the claimant will have to describe. Also a lady's gold pencil and mounted gold eye-glass, with chain attached made of fine beads. These articles were found on the person of one of the men in the scow; and I wish to say, to the credit of the men, that loud and earnest threats of lynching the fellow were made, such was the indignation at an act calculated to throw discredit on all, and so contrary to discipline and the wishes of our body. And I wish to say farther that were it not for our present circumstances and relations, such an act would, as it ever will be by me and my associate officers, have been punished with all the rigor of army discipline. You will oblige us all by the publication of this communication, both to set us right, and that the property may be restored to its owner. (Signed) JOHN O'NEILL Colonel.[38]

However much the Fenians were viewed by the Canadians as desperados, the treatment of prisoners and Canadian wounded by the Fenians was generally proper. Again, what few abuses took place were quickly corrected by the Fenian commanders. Fenian officers provided safe conduct passes to several Canadian doctors and helpful civilians to treat the wounded, and in most cases Fenian troops provided aid and comfort to wounded militiamen. General O'Neill in particular seemed intent on treating prisoners and wounded in a gentlemanly fashion. One account noted that O'Neill made a special point of ensuring that a Canadian wounded officer whom he visited was comfortable and then refused the wounded officer's offer to surrender his sword, saying "No, I will not take it; its possession may be a solace to you. I will leave it by your side."[39]

Several of the Canadian officers also established a very informal modus vivendi when it came to the wounded and their treatment. For example, Major Denison recounted one incident:

Shortly after I arrived Dr. Kempson, the reeve of the village [Fort Erie] came to me and introduced himself, and later on he brought a man up and introduced him to me as Dr. Donelly, a physician from Buffalo who had come over to assist him in attending to the wounded; for there were a number about the place. As the reeve introduced him to me he winked at me with his off eye, and I knew at once that Donelly was the Fenian doctor. I knew it would not be fair to arrest a surgeon and we could not recognize the Fenians as having any rights, so I took the cue and thanked Dr. Donelly very politely for his humanity and kindness, and as soon as possible Dr. Kempson put him in a skiff and sent him over to Buffalo.[40]

Both sides actually on the battlefield along the Niagara seemed intent on maintaining what they could of the concept of "proper" nineteenth-century warfare. Inevitably, this was not completely possible, especially given the Fenians' complete lack of legal standing. The Canadian and British governments had every legal right to brand them as criminals. This may, however, have even further pushed the Fenian commanders into stressing the military code of conduct of the time for their troops in an effort to demonstrate that they were not "pirates" or "plunderers," but rather a proper army under discipline.

The Night of June Second

The Fenians had won one battle and one skirmish in a single day. This, however, did not equate to a strategic victory. O'Neill and his troops were now isolated at Old Fort Erie, with little prospect of succor and knowing that more forces were advancing toward them, even if slowly. There clearly were some major decisions to be made by O'Neill and his commanders on what to do next. In some ways, the fate of the Fenians in the Niagara would be driven by what the other columns of the multipronged invasion were doing and how successful they were. It is necessary to look at the eastern and western wings of the invasion before returning to the Fenians at Old Fort Erie.

Chapter 8

The Other Fenian Invasion Wings

We are here as the Irish army of liberation; the friends of liberty against despotism, of democracy against aristocracy, of the people against their oppressors.

—General Sweeny

There were two other approaches into Canada as part of the Fenian invasion strategy. The western axis of advance can be dealt with rather quickly. The plan was for 3,000 Fenians to assemble around Chicago and to cross the border under the command of Brigadier General Charles Tevis. In the event, very few Fenians actually showed up, Tevis was unable to find or pay for vessels to transport the troops, and one of his generals (with his troops) necessary for the operation had resigned without telling anyone. This was General Malloy, and afterward Sweeny learned that he had "retired" from the Fenians to accept a commission as a second lieutenant in the US Army. This wing collapsed before beginning.

The Eastern "Invasion"

Sweeny considered this the most important wing of the invasion, and he personally commanded it, arriving in Malone, New York via train on June 4, a Monday. It might be noted that General Meade, commander of the federal forces intended to stop Sweeny's advance actually was on the same train, although Meade decided to detrain at Ogdensburg, New York.[1] The operational plan for the Fenians was to cross the border in two columns, one from St. Albans, Vermont, and the other from Malone, New York. The two columns were separated by the Richelieu river, and were intended to converge on St. Jean, Quebec. Because in this part of New York and Vermont there was only a land border, no water transport—problems with which had plagued both the other wings—would be required. The plan was to have more than 16,000 Fenian troops for the advance on Montreal, including five regiments of cavalry. When Sweeny arrived in the area on June 4, however, there were only about 1,000 Fenians present. While some "cavalrymen" did arrive, they were all on foot, with the intention of seizing horses in Canada. Many of them came with at least some bridles, bits, and the like, but apparently only a few had cavalry saddles.

One question might be raised about the timing of this operation. Launching it within a day or so after O'Neill's advance would have created problems for both the Canadian and British military forces and the US authorities as they tried to respond to two near-simultaneous attacks. The greater the time gap between the two Fenian advances, the easier it would be for sequential rather than simultaneous reactions by the governments. It is quite possible, however, that the date chosen for the attack in the east had little to do with some larger strategic calculus, but was based on more practical issues. One journalist who traveled to St. Albans on a train with the Fenians argued that in his talks with them, "the majority preferring to close up their labors on a Saturday afternoon, and begin their filibustering enterprise with a new week."[2] It is easy to overlook prosaic factors in the Fenian problems with assembling forces such as simply issues for some of the troops in getting time off from work.

The same journalist noted that on the train with the Fenians, "The most surprising element in their manner to my mind, was the general reticence, and absence of that flurry and tendency to braggadocio, so common among new recruits."[3] This description is in contrast with reports issued from other Fenian movements of troops, where considerable uproar was described. Such variations were entirely plausible, based on differing levels of experience and discipline with the various units. The journalist also observed, in common with most descriptions, that the Fenians wore a mix of uniform items.

Sweeny had prepared a long manifesto to be read to the people in Canada where the Fenians were operating. Chalking in at more than 1,000 words, it is unlikely that even supporters would want to go through the entire document. The full proclamation is at appendix 3, but a sample to give a flavor of it includes:

June 5

General Sweeney to the people of Canada:

We come among you as the foes of British rule in Ireland. Exiled from that native land of ours by the oppression of British aristocracy and legislation, our people hunted down to the emigrant ships, or worse, to that charnel of Government institutions, the poor-house; our countrymen torn from their families and friends and hurried in droves into the prison pens of England and Ireland; our country subjected to a foreign tyranny, which disenfranchises the mass of the Irish people and makes poverty and misery the sad rule of their condition, covering our fair land with paupers' graves and wretched hovels, eliciting from the liberal minds of England herself expressions of shame for the Government and indignation for the people.

We have taken up the sword to strike down the oppressors red, to deliver Ireland from the tyrant, the despoiler, the robber. We have registered our oaths upon the altar of our country in the full view of Heaven, and sent up our vows to the throne of Him who inspired them. Then, looking about us for the enemy, we find him *here* [italics in original]—here in your midst where he is most vulnerable and convenient to our strength; and have sworn to stretch forth the armed hand of Ireland and grapple with him. The battle has commenced, and we pledge ourselves to all the sacred memories of struggling liberty, to follow it up at any cost to either of two alternatives—the absolute political independence and liberty of Ireland or the demolition of our armies.

Weapons had been moving into eastern New York for some time. A train with two carloads of Fenian arms reached Watertown, New York, and the local US marshal had placed them under a rather weak guard. In an unusually brazen flouting of the US government by the Fenians, they reseized the cars containing the weapons on June 4 and transported them to Malone. In St. Albans, the Fenian leaders reportedly consulted local attorneys in an effort to sue the US government to reclaim their other weapons through legal channels. Overall, however, weapons proved to be in short supply for the Fenians both in eastern New York and Vermont.

Along with the weapons shipments (many of which failed), Fenian officers reportedly had prepared for operations by conducting reconnaissance of the area of operations in Canada.

The Vermont Wing

Fenian forces used St. Albans as their headquarters for the Vermont wing, moving their advance camp to East Highgate, Vermont. Somewhat in contrast to the situation in Buffalo, the local American response to the Fenians was much more mixed. The Fenians reportedly received some support from the inhabitants in St. Albans, but at the village of Franklin nearer the border, the local residents were very resistant to the Fenians: "They said that they were connected by every tie of family, business, and social relationship with their neighbors across the border. . . ."[4]

The operation quickly went astray. Federal authorities arrested Sweeny and his chief of staff in St. Albans on June 6 for violation of neutrality laws. The actual legal basis for these arrests may have been a bit shaky because they had not actually crossed the border at that point, but such legal niceties were ignored for larger goals. Unable to come up with the 20,000 dollar bail required for his release, Sweeny had to remain in jail for several days before being released on condition that he remain in St. Albans. General Samuel Spear, who had escaped the federal marshals searching for the Fenian leaders because he was away buying supplies, continued to believe in the prospects of the invasion plans.[5] He was determined to launch at least some form of offensive operation.

As a result, on June 7 he ordered the remnants of his forces to cross the border near the Canadian village of Pigeon Hill. There reportedly were torrential rains as the advance began, which likely did not help the morale of the troops. The Fenians dug in on Pigeon Hill, only about a mile inside Canada, with patrols and skirmishers covering about three or four miles around the main position. Small numbers of Fenians provided detachments around the villages of Cook's Corners, St. Armand, Frelighsburg, and Stanbridge. Neidhardt nicely describes the state of the Fenian forces:

> Spear's men had to forage for food and supplies. The Fenian Army's "right wing" now numbered less than 1000 men, and there were guns for only half that number. Ammunition for the muskets was extremely scarce, and the 300 carbines in the camp

had no proper cartridges. And the Fenian war chest contained the paltry sum of $20.15.[6]

Spear issued an optimistic report to the Fenian chief of staff on June 8, arguing that his troops could "live sumptuously off the country."[7] Other reports, however, suggested that the Fenian leadership was having difficulties even in feeding their troops in New York and Vermont, and it is difficult to accept that it would be any easier in Canada. He also said that he had twelve men with horses. This was far different from deploying a true cavalry force. By June 9, however, Spear's optimism had vanished.

The Canadians had had ample warning of the Fenian operation, and given the operation along the Niagara Frontier had occurred days earlier, the government was fully prepared to believe the warnings. They had ample forces deployed in the area. Despite what might seem to be an impossible situation, Spear decided to hold his position. The Fenians in the area had a small skirmish with the local militia, albeit with no casualties on either side, and the Fenians dug in their positions. Their initial operations were aided by the decision making of Captain W.W. Carter, a British regular officer in command of Canadian militia forces, who decided to withdraw rather than fight. This withdrawal, although relatively short, was rough on untrained troops, for whom an organized withdrawal can be one of the most difficult movements. More importantly, it was intensely unpopular with his local militiamen, who basically were being told to leave their property at the mercy of the Fenians. As one member noted: "The men . . . who were leaving their homes and wives and children unprotected and besides did not believe in the expediency or necessity of the movement [the retreat] were furious. Some of them threw away greatcoats and knapsacks, some gave up from sheer exhaustion and had to be carried away."[8] On June 8, however, the Canadians finally moved forces into the area. Perhaps most importantly, there were cavalry forces leading the Canadian column.

In contrast to the relatively good behavior of O'Neill's forces, the troops under Spear created problems for civilians on both sides of the border. On June 6, General Murphy of the Fenians issued an order noting that he had received a report that there had been disorderly conduct and rioting in Malone and banned such actions in the future. Fenians who had crossed into Canada engaged in widespread looting. Three factors probably led to this. The first was geographical: the Fenians were dug in very close to the US border, so it was very easy for them to loot and then to return with their plunder to the US. The second was that virtually all Canadian civilians had fled (either farther north in Canada or south into the US) once their militia withdrew. It probably was psychologically easier for Fenian soldiers to loot empty homes and barns rather than to loot in front of their occupants. Most importantly, however, likely it was sheer necessity. Given the severe supply difficulties, many of the troops probably were close to starving. Although the Fenian troops engaged in looting, their officers did try to maintain some military niceties, including ensuring the free movement of doctors in areas in which the Fenian forces were operating.

As the day passed and essentially nothing happened, the Fenian troops began to show signs of severe disaffection. Entire units began to go south back across the US border. The desertions reached such an extent that General Spear and his senior commanders recognized that simply sitting a mile inside Canada was totally pointless. On the morning of June 9, he marched his troops back across the border. In the withdrawal, most of the Fenian troops simply threw away their weapons; the arms that were still being carried were confiscated by US troops who had arrived at the border. General Spear and his staff surrendered to the senior US officer present.

The only actual military action seen by the forces with the Spear column resulted when about 200 Fenians around Pigeon Hill were rather slow in joining in the retreat. This group initially stood their ground behind a barricade, and the Canadians prepared to assault the position. Once the Fenian troops saw the Canadian cavalry, they broke and ran toward the US boundary. Some Fenians were injured during the cavalry charge despite the Canadians using the flats of their swords rather than trying for lethal cuts. One cavalryman described the final outcome: "In this running fight we soon reached the boundary line. There a company of United States regulars was stationed, and as fast as a Fenian tumbled over the line he was seized and disarmed."[9] There were no serious casualties on either side—except perhaps for severe embarrassment among the Fenians—but the Canadians captured sixteen Fenians. The only casualty in this operation was the accidental killing of a Canadian woman loyalist by the Canadian forces when she panicked and refused to stop after being challenged by soldiers on guard duty after dark.

The Malone, New York Wing

There were other Fenian troops around Malone and Ogdensburg, New York, but none of these forces ever managed to cross the border. There were few federal authorities in the area initially, and the Fenians certainly had little to worry about over the State authorities. Governor Reuben Fenton of New York refused to take any action, arguing that the Fenians might be violating federal neutrality laws, but New York State had no such laws on the books.[10] His conclusion was that there was no statutory basis for state involvement. As US officers and small bodies of US troops arrived in the area, they quickly took control of the situation, with minimal resistance from the Fenians. Officers were arrested and their troops essentially decided to quit.

Even as the operation was falling apart, Fenian officers promised further developments. After General Murphy's capture, on June 11 he reportedly told his forces that another 5,000 Fenian troops were on the way. Given the chaos of Fenian movements at that point, he may, in fact, have sincerely believed this. It is probable that Fenians continued to move toward the area long after they would have made a difference; these troops probably simply turned around and went home. The "great invasion" was over.

Chapter 9

The Aftermath

The only thing to be dreaded, in his opinion, is the interference of the United States authorities.

—Colonel Roberts of the Fenians[1]

When O'Neill assembled his forces at the old fort, he was faced with an almost impossible decision. His troops had won two skirmishes, driving the Canadian militia from the field. He knew, however, that fresh Canadian and British columns were approaching, no matter how belatedly. They both significantly outnumbered his force, and the British regular forces were more likely to be formidable opponents. Fenian supplies, such as food, were scarce. He had received few if any reinforcements. By the night of June 2, O'Neill likely had received reports that the Americans were patrolling the border and at least interfering with—if not actually completely stopping—troops and supplies from reaching him. Communications with other Fenian wings and the senior Fenian commanders probably were nonexistent. O'Neill's back was to the river, and there was little room to maneuver.

O'Neill held a council of war to get input from his officers. He later claimed that he was willing to do an "Alamo scenario" in which he fought to the last man as a symbol of Fenian resistance. It is far from clear that any of his officers or troops were particularly fond of this approach. Fenian troops already were abandoning the fight individually or in small groups and "borrowing" boats along the Niagara River or simply making improvised rafts to cross back into the US. The actual number of Fenians who deserted at this point cannot be estimated with any confidence, but appeared to be steadily increasing as the night wore on.

O'Neill then received word that there was a scow that had been chartered to transport about 500 reinforcements from Buffalo to his position. Given the border controls being implemented by the US federal authorities, there certainly was no guarantee that these troops would, in fact, successfully make the crossing, and the odds were against this. Also, unless the troops received weapons and ammunition prior to crossing, which again had become considerably more unlikely, the Fenians at old Fort Erie would simply have more mouths to feed without any additional combat effectiveness. O'Neill made the decision to withdraw. Using cross-river light signals, he ordered the scow to be moved to his position without any of the proposed troops, and loaded his remaining forces onboard to return to Buffalo.

To understand what happened next, it is necessary to return to the eve of the Fenian invasion and the actions of US federal and local officials. As it became increasingly clear that the Fenians were, in fact, preparing to cross the border, officials began to take action, if initially somewhat tentative and with minimal coordination. For example, on May 31, the U.S. attorney in Buffalo, William A. Dart, alerted the navy gunboat USS *Michigan* at Buffalo and ordered the closing of the port to outbound traffic between 4:00 P.M. and 9:00 A.M. The order also prohibited any outbound traffic at any hour without the vessel being first inspected by U.S. Customs. The mayor of Buffalo reportedly privately informed the Toronto and Hamilton mayors of an influx of Fenians.

One other issue surrounding attempts to craft a response was simply trying to understand what situation was developing. Policy makers and security officials seemed to be very confused as to what actually was happening on the ground, both at a strategic and tactical standpoint. Some reflection of this might be provided by newspaper coverage at the time. Then (and now) officials commonly relied on newspaper accounts to inform them of ongoing developments. The Fenian invasion unsurprisingly was page one news in most New York newspapers. The subheadings for the headlines in the *New York Times* of June 1 and 2 reflect the initial bewilderment: "All Sorts of Stories from All Sorts of Sources, Several Dozen Unarmed Men gone Somewhere, Madame Rumor Says it is All Up with Canada, The British Lion is to be Slaughtered This Very Night, A Bewildering Maze of Conflicting Rumors, Dispatches from Everywhere Telling All Sorts of Stories, Dispatches from Everywhere Contradicting All Those Previously Sent, The Situation Peculiarly Hibernian and as Clear as Mud." In an editorial aside on page one, the *New York Times* noted that: "There is scarcely an assertion that is not speedily contradicted by another equally positive, so that the bewildered reader must be left in a state of dazed dubiousness little short of insanity."[2]

Once the Fenians actually entered Canada, the earlier reluctance among US government officials on the ground to oppose the Fenians seemed to evaporate. Whatever residual possible support remained in the national government, federal forces responded relatively quickly and decisively to the Fenian operations in Canada, especially once the situation became clearer. General Ulysses S. Grant, at the time the commander of the US Army, probably visited Buffalo on June 2.[3] He then issued the following order to General Meade: "Gen. Barry is here. Assign him to general command from Buffalo to the mouth of the Niagara River. The State authorities should call out the militia on the frontier, to prevent hostile expeditions leaving the United States and to save private property from destruction by mobs."[4] In response, General Meade issued orders to Brevet Major General Barry on June 3:

> Orders will be sent you from Headquarters, Department of the East, assigning you to the command of the District of Ontario, extending from Erie, Pa., to Oswego, N.Y., both places inclusive, headquarters at Buffalo.
>
> In advance of the orders and accompanying instruction, I direct you to use the force at your command to preserve the neutrality by preventing the crossing in armed bodies, by cutting off reinforcements or supplies, by seizing all arms munitions, &c., which you have reason to believe are destined to be used unlawfully; in fine [sic], taking all measures, precautionary and otherwise, to prevent violation of law.
>
> For this purpose you will move the forces under your command to such points as are threatened, and you will employ vessels, tugs, &c., such as can be procured for watching the river and lake more [sic], and taking all such measures as in your judgment the emergency requires.
>
> Very respectfully,
>
> George G. Meade, Major-Gen. Commanding

In response to these orders, General Barry deployed troops and issued instructions that prohibited unauthorized communications across the border with Canada. In Buffalo, the army posted a guard at the telegraph office to prevent any communications to or from the Fenians. Quick implementation inevitably was going to be difficult. According to one analyst, in early April 1866, only 357 US Army officers and troops were stationed on the entire New York-Canada border.[5] Nevertheless, these troops were deployed to provide the best control they could of the Fenians. Initially, only one company of the US 4th Infantry Regiment—some 100 troops at most—was available, and they arrived in Buffalo on June 2. Drawing reinforcements from farther afield, General Barry finally was able to muster about 800 troops for his mission.

Local American justice officials also took a very hard line. On June 2, William A. Dart, the US District Attorney for the Ogdensburg region issued orders to the collector of the port of Ogdensburg to "put as heavy guns on the revenue cutter as she will bear and arm any other boat in port with cannon from the arsenal and sink any vessels that attempt to cross to Canada with Fenians on board."[6] Likewise, in Buffalo federal law enforcement officials remained active in supporting the federal forces.

It might be noticed that all the aforementioned actions were directed either by local commanders or law enforcement officials. Initially, nothing came out of the attorney general's office or from the White House. This leads to the question of whether this simply was a matter of communications lags and bureaucratic inertia or if it represented waiting to "determine the facts on the ground," as President Johnson reportedly had promised the Fenians. One important point should be noted, however. The White House did not overrule any of the actions by officials on the ground. Likewise, none of the officials or military officers who were most active in acting against the Fenians was punished for their initiative. The only possible exception was US Attorney William A. Dart, who was removed from his office later in 1866 shortly prior to the elections in an evident intent to placate the Irish vote. Even in his case, however, he returned to government service in 1869, serving as the consul general in Montreal before retiring and resuming a successful private law practice. In either event, on June 5, Attorney General James Speed ordered all US district attorneys and federal marshals, "By direction of the President you are hereby instructed to cause the arrest of all prominent, leading or conspicuous persons, called 'Fenians' who you may have probable cause to believe have been or may be guilty of violations of the neutrality laws of the United States."[7]

Finally, on June 6, President Johnson broke his silence and issued a proclamation on the attack. It read:

Against the Fenian Invasion of Canada, June 6, 1866.

Whereas it has become known to me that certain evil-disposed persons have, within the territory and jurisdiction of the United States, begun and set on foot, and have provided and prepared, and are still engaged in providing and preparing, means for a military expedition and enterprise, which expedition and enterprise is to be carried on from the territory and jurisdiction of the United States against colonies, districts, and people of British North America, within the dominions of the United Kingdom of Great Britain and Ireland, with which said colonies, districts, and people, and kingdom the United States are at peace;

And whereas the proceedings aforesaid constitute a high misdemeanor, forbidden by the laws of the United States, as well as by the law of nations:

Now, therefore, for the purpose of preventing the carrying on of the unlawful expedition and enterprise aforesaid, from the territory and jurisdiction of the United States, and to maintain the public peace, as well as the national honor, and enforce obedience and respect to the laws of the United States, I, Andrew Johnson, President of the United States, do admonish and warn all good citizens of the United States against taking part in or in any wise aiding, countenancing, or abetting said unlawful proceedings, and I do exhort all judges, magistrates, marshals, and officers in the service of the United States, to employ all their awful authority and power to prevent and defeat the aforesaid un lawful proceedings, and to arrest and bring to justice all persons who may be engaged therein.

And, pursuant to the act of Congress in such case made and provided, I do furthermore authorize and empower Major General George G. Meade, commander of the Military Division of the Atlantic, to employ the land and naval forces of the United States and the militia thereof, to arrest and prevent the setting on foot and carrying on the expedition and enterprise aforesaid.

In testimony whereof, I have hereunto set my hand, and caused the seal of the United States to be affixed. Done at the city of Washington the sixth day of June, in the year of our Lord one [seal.] thousand eight hundred and sixty-six, and of the Independence of the United States the ninetieth. Andrew Johnson. By the President: William H. Seward, Secretary of State.

President Johnson's proclamation not surprisingly received a chilly reception from a number of Democratic politicians. Sydenham E. Ancona, a Congressman from Pennsylvania representing the so-called Copperhead wing of the Democratic Party, submitted a resolution opposing the use of the neutrality law being used against the Fenians. Although the resolution failed, it received 113 votes in favor.[8] As usual, trying to separate political posturing in an effort to placate the Irish American vote from actual opposition to the administration's efforts is next to impossible. If nothing else, it gave congressmen from heavily Irish districts political cover no matter what happened.

As part of the overall security response by the US, the captain of the USS *Michigan*, Commander Andrew Bryson, was ordered to patrol between Buffalo and the Niagara Frontier. This iron-hulled gunboat—the first in the US Navy—was home-ported in Erie, Pennsylvania. It was armed with an eight-inch pivot gun, a thirty-pounder Parrott rifled gun, six twenty-four-pounder Dahlgren smoothbore howitzers, five twenty-pounder Parrott rifles, and two twelve-pounder Dahlgren boat howitzers. As such, it represented a major combat vessel on the Great Lakes. Earlier in 1866, it had been moved to Buffalo for repairs, which had been completed just before the Fenian invasion. The federal authorities also took control of two civilian tugs through "brevet extemporization," and armed each with a single gun manned by marines from the *Michigan*.[9] These tugs provided additional patrol coverage of areas in which the Fenians might cross.

The *Michigan* was ordered on patrol the night of May 31, but was delayed. According to contemporary reports, this was the result of the ship's second assistant engineer, James P. Kelley, being a Fenian member or supporter and deliberately delaying the pilot required to get the vessel away from the docks. This delay reportedly involved providing a prostitute and considerable whiskey.[10] Kelley was arrested, but the ship was unable to stop the initial Fenian movement into Canada. It did, however, reach station in time to stop any major reinforcements crossing across the Niagara. It also was cruising off old Fort Erie when O'Neill made his decision to withdraw.

At about 2:00 A.M. on June 3, the Fenian forces boarded two barges towed by a tug boat in an effort to return to the US. Some accounts have suggested that O'Neill abandoned outlying pickets and guards during the withdrawal. He later vehemently denied this, but in the confusion of a quick withdrawal, particularly at night, it is quite conceivable that at least some troops were left behind. The Canadian forces mopping up later certainly captured a number of Fenians; some simply were stragglers, but some likely were inadvertently left behind.

The Fenians were intercepted by the Revenue Service tug *Harrison* operating with USS *Michigan*. The scows were towed to the *Michigan*, and all the Fenians were made prisoner. As with most number estimates involving the Fenians, the exact number held on the *Michigan* and the berthed barges remains debated. O'Neill himself later stated that 317 officers and men surrendered to the *Michigan*.[11] Others have estimated that there might have been as many as 600 to 700. Whatever the true number, O'Neill reported that the Fenian officers on board the *Michigan* were well treated, but men on the scow faced very bad conditions.[12] This is not surprising because the troops had to spend the night in an open vessel; beyond this, however, there was no evidence of deliberate mistreatment.

When the lead elements of Peacocke's column arrived at the old fort on June 3 and saw a barge loaded with Fenians offshore, they were understandably nervous. Major Denison of the Canadian cavalry took a boat to the *Michigan* and conferred with Captain Bryson who was able to explain the situation. Later, the newly appointed commander of the Canadian forces, the British consul in Buffalo and the U.S. attorney all met on the *Michigan*. The Canadians and the Americans quickly reached an understanding (at least locally) that the US would be the one to deal with the prisoners onboard the vessels.

It soon became clear that there was a problem with the prisoners held by the *Michigan*. This was what to do with them. The commander of the *Michigan* said that he had "an elephant" on his hands. This likely was a fair assessment. As the *New York Tribune* reported on June 4, "It is considered unsafe to bring them into this city, as an effort might be made by their friends to release them. There is considerable excitement in this city, but the general feeling is that the Government has done its duty, and our people are glad that the Fenians have fallen into American hands, rather than they should have been captured by the British."

The conundrum over the Fenian prisoners extended to the highest level of the government. Secretary of the Navy Gideon Welles provided a telling description of the internal debates:

June 4, Monday. Bryson telegraphed yesterday that he had captured seven hundred Fenians crossing the river at Black Rock.
I sent the telegram to the President and to Seward, and soon
after called on the President. He seemed a little perplexed. Said
we had an elephant on our hands. I asked whether they were
prisoners of war and what was to be done with them. He thought
we must wait and we should soon have inquiries. Shortly after
my return Seward sent his carriage for me. I went to his house.
He and Speed were sitting on the back porch. Speed had a
telegram from Dart, District Attorney, stating the capture and
making inquiries. Seward asked about the prisoners and what
accommodations the Navy had. I told him none whatever and
that these men could hardly be considered prisoners of war,
even if we had accommodations; that they ought, if prisoners
of war, at once to be turned over to the custody of the military.
He said that would not do. Stanton wanted nothing to do with
them,—there was no military force there. I told him there were
officers and they could call on the militia or call out volunteer
companies in Buffalo. This would be necessary, for such a number
could not be retained by the civil authorities without a guard.
He said, "Let them run away." Speed said that would not do.[13]

However, much the federal officers and units were, in fact, active
against the Fenians, the same could not be said of the local or New York
state militia forces. The governor of New York refused to call out additional
militia units in response to the security situation. What militia units were
in place proved to be ineffectual, either deliberately or through "benign
neglect."[14]

By June 6, the federal government seemed to decide to take the path
of least resistance or at least the path of least political fallout. The Fenian
soldiers who were captured were released on their own recognizance and
lower-ranking officers on 500 dollars bail. Six of the senior Fenian officers
were arraigned before US Commissioner Parker on June 7 in Buffalo, with
most of their bails set around 6,000 dollars. All had to agree to appear for
trial and "subscribe that they will not take up arms in American waters."
The next issue was then what to do with the newly released prisoners.
Many of the soldiers had very little if any money, and the local population
around Buffalo and elsewhere along the border certainly had no particular
desire to have large numbers of disgruntled Fenians roaming their streets.

The American government decided to take the easiest way to resolve the situation and to pay train fares home. By June 15, about 7,000 Fenians had been transported away from the frontier at government expense. Each had to give parole that he would avoid any further actions against Canada. All this was complicated by the number of Fenian officers and troops who simply did not seem to get the word that the offensive was over, and who continued to move toward the border. As late as June 8, the US marshal in Buffalo reported that fifteen carloads of Fenians had just arrived.[15]

As these actions were taking place around Buffalo, the Fenians in the eastern columns were facing similar responses by American authorities. Again, some preemptive measures were taken whether they were completely approved by higher authority. In response to reports that Fenians were massing around St. Albans, Vermont, General Hooker, Commander of the Department of the East and the Department of the Lakes, ordered that all armed bodies attempting to cross the border were to be stopped, and the same for unarmed groups if "it is reasonable to suppose that they are Fenians."[16] Likewise, Colonel Vogden of the US forces issued an order that "All trains to be carefully inspected; any weapons/ammo to be seized, any Fenians moving north to be turned around. . . . any prominent Fenian agitators, leaders or agents, or individuals disregarding the recent proclamation, or designed to violate the neutrality laws . . ." were to be arrested. Any rail lines or telegraph offices supporting Fenians were to have their offices closed. The legality of such orders may have been subject to some debate, but seemingly no one was willing to do so in that environment.

After President Johnson issued his proclamation, General Meade had 500 copies made and distributed to the Fenians in Malone and another 500 for Watertown. Beyond simply ensuring that the Fenian soldiers understood their legal status after the proclamation, this probably served as a good propaganda move to dissuade many of them from further action. Parenthetically, it might be noted that General Meade also had a military band with his forces that regularly performed at the St. Albans village green. The band played "Wearing of the Green" on numerous occasions, which reportedly was a smash hit with the Fenians. Beyond whatever musical value it may have had, this likely emphasized that both General Meade himself and a large number of his troops were Irish American and should be viewed as potential friends even while they were enforcing necessary laws. This seemed to have some effect because no significant incidents were reported between Fenian troops and US soldiers even as the troops were shepherding the Fenians away from the border.

[handwritten note at top of page: More (Left coming to border after O'Neill etc withdrew from Canada.)]

According to the *Herkimer Democrat* of June 13, 1866, 1,000 Fenians left St. Albans and an additional "five or six hundred" left Malone. Even while Fenian officers were being arrested and their troops being shipped away from the border, fresh Fenians continued to arrive in the area. As late as June 14, the *New York Times* reported that "Today squads of soldiers are patrolling the town [Malone, NY], picking up all the fag-ends of the Fenian army, escorting them to the depot to see them safely on board the cars and off to their homes." Finally, after about two weeks the US government was able to stand down its troops, and General Meade could view the mission as over.

The Canadian Response

Returning the discussion to the Niagara area, after the Fenians had actually withdrawn, Lieutenant Colonel Peacocke continued his advance toward Fort Erie. The only real mission for his column at this point was to round up Fenian stragglers, with about fifty being captured. Some excitement was caused when his troops saw two armed men evidently trying to escape; when they ignored orders to halt, the troops opened fire. The two were local farmers with no connections to the Fenians; one of the two died of his wounds.

Some American newspapers—not necessarily pro-Fenian—initially reported that the Canadians had executed Fenian prisoners on the battlefield. This caused a firestorm of public protest. As was typical for the period, however, these stories were totally erroneous. Captured Fenians generally were reasonably well treated, although their status was hazy. Their processing was somewhat between prisoners of war and "unlawful enemy combatants" subject to arrest. The only potentially questionable incident, which may have given rise to at least some of the reports, was the death in combat of Fenian Colonel Bailey at the fighting at Fort Erie. Rumors swirled for a number of years that he might have been killed while under a flag of truce, probably by trigger-happy and nervous militiamen. It has to be stressed that the truthfulness of these rumors never was established, and the Fenian leaders never made an issue of this later.

The key issue came later off the battlefield as the Canadian government had to decide what to do with the Fenian prisoners it held. The Canadian government held 117 Fenian prisoners in Toronto. About a third of these prisoners were sent to trial in autumn 1866; the others were considered "dupes" of their leaders and were released. Twenty-one of the defendants were found guilty of serious offenses, with seven sentenced to be hanged in December.[17] The scheduled executions created a fresh series of stresses between the US and the Canadian and British governments, in particular raising once again how naturalized US citizens would be handled in law. Most American newspapers, whether pro- or anti-Fenian, attacked the death sentences, if not the guilty verdicts. This seemed to accurately reflect public opinion, and the US government became increasingly involved diplomatically. How much the death sentences were a matter of law versus playing to the inflamed Canadian public opinion in the wake of the Fenian attacks is hard to determine. Even if the Canadian colonial government was particularly determined to carry out the executions—and there were indications that it was not terribly set on this—the British government had broader diplomatic issues that were not served by further alienating the Americans. None of the death sentences was ever carried out, and all the prisoners were eventually released after what might be considered a decent interval.

Official letters from the Canadian government to the US had a much more positive tenor about US relations with the Fenians after the federal intervention; even internal exchanges between Canadian and British officials were supportive of how the US responded.[18] There clearly were continued tensions, but fewer public spats over the Fenian issue, at least for a few years.

The Fenian Response

The Fenian leaders rather quickly issued a series of proclamations, public statements, and the like, trying to put the best face on their failures and to rally the troops. Two of these bear emphasis:

HEADQUARTERS OF THE I.R.A.

BUFFALO, June 18, 1866

To the Soldiers of Irish liberty:

COUNTRYMEN AND FRIENDS—The proclamation of President Roberts, just issued, calls upon you to stand firm by the cause, that our movement must and will advance. Under these circumstances and the fact that Congress will, in a very few days, either repeal the neutrality law, or extend to us belligerent rights, in the name of Ireland, we beg of you to do your duty. Let no Fenian so disgrace himself as to accept the ignominious conditions attached to the proffer of Government transportation. Never, Irishmen, forswear your rights as American citizens, or your devotion to the cause for which you have sacrificed so much, and for which you are ready to die. Such conduct would be unworthy of your manhood and race. Be patient; a glorious future awaits you, and ere many days the order to march will gladden your hearts. Therefore, stand firm and don't allow the intrigues of officers who are in pay of the British, cause you to swerve from the only paths of duty and honor. Await the orders of your military officers; conduct yourselves as you have in the past while here, and the citizens of this city will not neglect you.

Fraternally,

J. W. Fitzgerald

Michael Scanlon.

Address from William R. Roberts Headquarters Fenian Brotherhood, No. 706 Broadway, NY, June 13 [1866]

To the Officers and Soldiers of the Irish Republican Army:

Soldiers: In view of the unexpected and repressive measures of the United States Executive at Washington to crush the cooperative movement for the liberation of Ireland, I recommend that you return to your respective homes until such time as a fresh campaign can be inaugurated at a not far distant day. Although the campaign just closed has not carried the banner of your native land to the capital of the British Provinces in North America, it has demonstrated to mankind that you had the bravery, patriotism and skill to accomplish it. You have been victors on every field that your hereditary enemies dare contest; you have proved yourselves good citizens and brave soldiers, and are disappointed in your full expectations, not through any efforts of England's armed minions, but because the Administration of a great and free country chose to exercise to its fullest limits, and even beyond it, the odious and tyrannic provisions of an obsolete law, so as to display its magnanimity to a semi-hostile nation, at the expense of your rights as loyal citizens and the high prerogatives and pride of the greatest nation on earth. However, your efforts are not without great and important results which can scarcely be catinated at present – history will record them, however, as the highest proof of patriotism ever exhibited by an exile race, and as the commencement of a struggle which is certain to end in the complete and absolute independence of Ireland.

Retire, then, brothers, to your homes, carrying with you the admiration and respect of all true worshippers of patriotism and liberty; set to work to reorganize on a more thorough and extensive basis; spend your days at your respective callings and your evenings in preparation. We must avoid in the future the publicity which our proceedings have received in the past, and when next we move, it will be with an organized power that England's greatest strength cannot withstand. I have hopes, too, that the voice of the great American nation will be raised in protest against the severity displayed by some of their servants. Already it is heard in rebuke through their representatives in Congress, the guardians of their honor and their liberties.

I desire that you accept no offers of transportation from officials who deprived you of the very food in some cases which was necessary to supply your pressing wants, and who couple their offers of a free passage with conditions, which, to accept, would cast a stain upon your patriotism as Irishmen and as free citizens, who are bound to sympathize with every struggling nationality.

I remain, Brothers, your devoted friend in the cause of Ireland,

WM. R. ROBERTS

A reflection of Sweeny's bitterness was reflected in his official report that he was betrayed by the US government and its representatives. He said that the actions of American civilian officials "has raised suspicion that the benign influence of the British Treasury had extended itself across the frontier." Likewise, "As to the U. S. Army, it was practically placed at the hands of the British generals. . . ." Some Fenian Brotherhood leaders concluded that the Sweeny-Roberts approach was doomed to failure. Others, however, were thirsting for the next round.

Roberts wing

O'Mahony wing

Senate wing

Chapter 10

The Interregnum

We cannot be far wrong in saying that more blood was shed in one street in New York on St. Patrick's Day than has been expended during all the Fenian insurrections of which any account has yet reached us.

—*New York Tribune*, March 25, 1867

Following the failure of the 1866 invasion, the Roberts Wing held a convention in Troy, New York in September 1866. The two major leadership issues resolved were that Roberts was reelected as President, and Sweeny "issued his resignation" as Secretary of War. Given the normal choreography of such conventions, this probably was, in fact, a firing rather than a resignation. At the same time, however, Sweeny was appointed as the commander of the Irish Republican Army, although this appeared to be more of a pro forma appointment than a substantive one. Despite this new appointment, Sweeny severed his connections with the Fenian Brotherhood. The convention extolled General O'Neill's leadership at the battle of Ridgeway, and authorized brevet promotions for all officers involved in that battle.[1] The citizens of Buffalo also received special thanks for their support of the Fenian invasion.

Two other significant resolutions were adopted at the convention. The first was "On motion, a pledge was then administered that inviolable secrecy [sic] be preserved on all matters transacted in convention, except so much thereof as shall be permitted to delegates to impart to their Circles."[2] Compared to the early conventions, this indicated that the Brotherhood was becoming increasingly concerned about maintaining security over its internal communications flow. Given the number of informers and agents who already were present in the movement, this was quite futile, but at least it indicated some increased awareness of the need for security. One newspaper had an interesting (if thoroughly biased) observation about the security surrounding the convention: ". . . there are a large number of Canadian spies in the city at present, and that it is ludicrous to observe how futile are the efforts of these individuals to conceal their nationality. Do all they would they could not manage to look sufficiently like blackguards to pass for Fenians or Yankee sympathisers."[3]

The other important resolution was "that a call of ten dollars, per capita, be levied, upon each and every member of the Fenian Brotherhood, to be transmitted to Headquarters."[4] The earlier operations had cost a massive amount of money, and the Brotherhood began facing significant financial difficulties. This assessment represented a significant sum for the working-class members, and likely was not viewed very favorably by them. There is no available record of how many members actually made this contribution and whether it was enforced with any rigor. Roberts in his address to the convention noted the issue of fundraising. He stated that before the 1866 invasion he had invited fifty prominent (and presumably wealthy) supporters to the Astor House for a funds appeal. Roberts recounted the results: "at the hour appointed, the room was free from visitors; half an hour after two had arrived, one wealthy, the other I believe rather poor. Another half hour elapsed and there were still but two; ten or fifteen minutes more passed, and the numbers not increasing, I concluded that there would be no occasion that day for any patriotic appeals."[5]

By late 1866, outside observers might have argued that following failed military efforts by each wing of the Fenian Brotherhood, some effort to combine forces for future efforts would be the logical answer. Anyone expecting such unity efforts was disabused of this assumption by President Roberts's address at the convention. He spent the majority of it excoriating both O'Mahony and Stephens. Roberts expressed particular vitriol against Stephens. As one brief example, he argued that the Americans had provided Stephens:

> . . . with a host of cheques; who instead of remaining as of old, an humble supplicant for Irish American alms, became, as the amounts with which he was fed increased, first importunate, then domineering: and finally, when he thought the time had

arrived for him to profit by the false fame, which our ignorance of the man had built up for him in America, he assumed the authority of a self-constituted despot, and sought to hurl his puny thunderbolts at the men to whom he was indebted for the undeserved honors he received and the money which he unquestionably squandered.[6]

One historical curiosity emerged in late 1866. Newspapers began reporting rumors that the Brotherhood was considering forming alliances with some leaders in Mexico, which was embroiled in unrest. Exactly what the strategic calculations were in such a move and how accurate the rumors were remain unclear. The only known direct connection was that of General Millen, a Fenian leader, having served in the Mexican forces. There were meetings with General Santa Anna from Mexico, and he spoke at a Fenian picnic at Staten Island on October 8, 1866. In his speech, he noted that the "flower of his army" when he was fighting the Americans were two Irish companies.[7] It is curious exactly what the participants at the Fenian picnic thought about all this because the two companies to which he referred were the San Patricio (Saint Patrick's) Battalion. They did, in fact, establish an estimable reputation. The problem for the Americans was that most of the unit's members were deserters from the US Army; after the Mexican War ended, some fifty of the soldiers captured by the Americans were tried for desertion and hanged.[8] How recently discharged US soldiers from the Civil War who were at the picnic responded to such praise for earlier deserters may have been very uncertain. In any event, nothing discernible arose from these discussions with erstwhile Mexican leaders.

Simultaneously, things were coming to a boil in Ireland. One other name entered the picture about this time. This was General Gustave Cluseret, best described as a soldier of fortune. He had fought in Crimea and Algeria in the French army, in Sicily under Garibaldi, and in the American Civil War. In the last, he had reached the rank of brigadier general in the Volunteers before resigning his commission in 1863. Cluseret had been dismissed from the French army after supplies had gone missing, then fired as an estate manager "when an entire flock of sheep under his charge most mysteriously disappeared."[9]

Cluseret held meetings with Stephens over the prospects for an uprising in 1867. Cluseret was not particularly enamored of Stephens, describing him in later writings as "vain, despotic, and over-bearing beyond any man I ever saw. As regards action, he was worth nothing."[10] Nevertheless, after these discussions, Cluseret reportedly agreed to take command of operations if he were provided 10,000 men with sufficient weaponry. In the meantime, he received authorization papers from the governor of New York to inspect military installations in Britain, and these papers were then countersigned by the American ambassador in London (who apparently was unaware of his Fenian connections), a true gift for a commander intending forthcoming operations.[11] There are two competing narratives as to what happened next. The first is that Cluseret was overheard discussing his plans in a pub and had to flee arrest. The second, and more probable, is that he reviewed the actual status of the IRB fighting capabilities and concluded that there were no prospects for success. In either event, he left for France and did not return. This meant that the 1867 rebellion was left without a field commander at the last minute.

Stephens had been promising action in Ireland for well over a year. Things came to a head during a December 15, 1866, meeting in New York City. There were about thirty Fenian officers present, most notably Stephens's deputy, Colonel Thomas J. Kelly, General Thomas F. Bourke, and General William Halpin. With the exception of Stephens, all were Irish Americans who had been involved in planning the Irish uprising. The argument over Stephens's perceived inability to make a decision became extremely stormy. The situation became so heated that Captain John McCafferty, a former Confederate officer, drew a pistol and threatened to kill Stephens on the spot. He was talked out of this, but it did not help win anyone to Stephens's side. However correct Stephens may have been about the poor prospects for major armed actions in Ireland, none of those who had spent years in preparing for a rebellion were ready to hear calls for more delay. As Devoy wrote later, "While there were undoubtedly important political considerations involved, the chief question was most certainly a military one, and it was decided by a civilian against the judgment and advice of his military advisers."[12] After a very stormy debate, Stephens was removed as Head Centre of the American Fenian Brotherhood. Stephens left the US and returned to France. He became rather extraneous to the nationalist movement for several years until he tried to make a political comeback. Mortimer Moynahan was selected as Head Centre of the Fenian Brotherhood for about a month, then he was replaced by John M. Gleeson. Neither made much of a mark on the Brotherhood or on history.

An uprising finally erupted in Ireland in 1867. Along with the IRB, a significant number of Irish Americans participated, including virtually all who had attended the December meeting with Stephens. Many had arrived much earlier and had served as organizers for the IRB forces. Among the most prominent of these Americans were General Thomas F. Burke, General Halpin, Colonel Thomas Kelly, Captain John McCafferty, and Captain William Mackay. The pattern for many of the armed bands that took part in the rebellion was that they consisted of Irish foot soldiers and Irish American leadership. One issue that particularly frustrated the British government was that many of the Irish American leaders of the rebellion had previously been detained by British security officials. London normally tried to avoid unnecessary diplomatic stresses with Washington. The routine in the earlier 1860s had become for the British to arrest the Americans and then ship them back to the US on condition that they not return to Ireland. This created much less popular outrage among the American public and was considered a rational legal approach by both capitals, even with the ongoing naturalization disputes. Unfortunately for the process, however, many of the same Irish Americans later returned to Ireland and were very active in the 1867 rebellion.[13]

Again, it is important to note the importance of the Irish Americans in the rebellion. One of the Irish Fenians noted that "they [the Americans] found the difficulties in the way almost insurmountable. The people were badly armed or not armed at all. Many of the local leaders were opposed to a rising at that time, and the clergy almost to a man antagonistic. Still they persevered and accomplished wonders in the brief time given them."[14]

If they accomplished "wonders," they were not particularly discernible. One particular issue might be raised. This was the background of the American advisors and commanders. Although all had had military experience of various stripes during the Civil War, virtually all had served in line units in conventional battles. The only major exception was Captain McCafferty, who had been a member of Morgan's Raiders, a Confederate partisan unit (more commonly considered as bushwhackers by the North). John Devoy provides an interesting anecdote about McCafferty's early meetings with Fenian supporters who were members of the British army:

McCafferty's experience was with irregular cavalry, who never charged, and who only fought at close quarters when necessary in their raids, and depended mainly on the revolver. In a few brief words and with a very quiet manner, he told them what could be done by insurgent cavalry under existing circumstances in Ireland. He began by saying: "I believe in a partisan warfare." Probably only O'Reilly and one or two more knew what the word "partisan" meant, but if he had said "guerrilla" warfare, they would have understood him. One of them, Martin Hogan of the Fifth Dragoons, was one of the two or three best swordsmen in the British army and had cut in two at one stroke of his sabre a bar of iron hanging from a barrack room ceiling. "Do you mean, sir," asked Hogan, "that you wouldn't use swords at all?" "Nothing but revolvers," said McCafferty quietly, and the trained swordsmen were all disappointed.[15]

The larger point was that the best—or perhaps the only—hope for an Irish Fenian uprising lay in guerrilla warfare against an exponentially stronger British security presence. Most of the purported experts provided by the American Fenians had experience only with conventional warfare. However much value they could provide in terms of organization and basic military training, their understanding of guerrilla tactics and larger insurgency strategy was probably close to nonexistent. As shown by later developments, the former US and Confederate officers in Ireland were able to learn at least some of the required skills over time, but it was not until after a number of missteps.

The British already had detained some of the senior Irish leaders, and the uprising reflected a vacuum of centralized control. Although Colonel Kelly tried to put the pieces for an operation back together, individual leaders began to hatch their own plans. On February 10 in London, Kelly and his associates formed a "Provisional Government" and named Cluseret as the commander of the Irish army; the latter, however, declared that he would not return to Ireland until the army was actually established and operations had commenced. Kelly's stated intention was that the uprising would begin in March. John McCafferty, the former Confederate officer, and his supporters, however, decided to begin in February with a raid against Chester Castle to seize arms. As was a pattern with Fenian operations on both sides of the Atlantic, the plan was betrayed by an informer and was called off. Unfortunately, the Chester Castle raid was viewed by some of the Irish insurgents as the kickoff for the insurgency, and the Fenians in County Kerry began unsupported attacks, which were quelled with little problem.

Beyond the actual Fenian bands, the IRB clearly also counted on defections by Irish soldiers in the Royal Army. The British had long relied on recruiting Irish for their military, with thousands of Irish troops in British regiments. Two senior IRB members spent much of their time focused on subverting these same Irish soldiers. The first was "Pagan" O'Leary, so-called because of his insistence that the only hope for the Irish people was to return to their pre-Christian roots. The second, arguably more successful, was John Devoy, who argued that there were "thousands" of Irish troops in the British army who were secretly loyal to the Fenians.[16] As with many such claims on both sides, it is rather difficult to establish true figures. There certainly were Fenian supporters in the regular army units, as demonstrated by a number of courts martial of Irish troops for proselytizing for the Fenians or deserting to them.[17] At no point, however, did these numbers reach critical mass, in part because if the British government began suspecting the loyalties of a particular regiment, it simply shipped it overseas. In any event, any internal army "fifth column" played no role in the 1867 rebellion.

The actual rebellion began on March 5, 1867. In some cases, the operations were begun and quelled in less than twenty-four hours in a particular area. Another county might then erupt, but the British were not faced with a coordinated, widespread, and major insurgency throughout Ireland. As a result, security services and the military were enabled to deal with a small series of incidents rather than a mass armed movement. Beyond the British countermeasures, the IRB members were faced with a major blizzard that hit just as they were starting operations; many Fenian bands spent more time trying to survive the weather than in fighting the British. Irish operations largely were limited to cutting telegraph lines and other nuisance activities. A few raids were conducted on police stations and the like with very mixed results, but generally these were not particularly successful. An Irish politician writing some forty years later provided a caustic but generally accurate assessment:

> [T]here never was a conspiracy or an insurrection in any sense which Italians, for instance, or Hungarians would recognize. . . . The organisers were thoroughly unorganized. The regiments missed their marching orders. The Captains and Colonels . . . knew not where to find their soldiers and the soldiers had neither rifles nor any sort of weapons. A few thousands of would-be insurgents wandered aimlessly about the mountainous districts for a few days, carefully avoiding, like gallant soldier, hurting anybody or anything during their excursion, except a few police barracks, which almost invariably proved to be as invincible as Gibraltar's to the toy bombardment.[18]

In practical terms, the uprising was over in forty-eight hours. It took the British a number of weeks to restore full stability, but most of this time involved efforts at tracking down the various Irish insurgents. One indication of the relative ease of British counterinsurgency in this instance was that the government considered imposing martial law, but dropped this plan because the situation never got serious enough; of course, having earlier suspended habeas corpus, martial law may not have added many substantive benefits anyway. The major claims of success by the Irish nationalists were that some insurgent bands managed to escape. One indication of how badly the IRB was hurt during this uprising, an official Fenian Brotherhood report noted that in the first half of 1867, "in nine out of ten [attempts to contact IRB members], those persons who were either in prison, or had fled the country."[19]

One of the recurring IRB complaints had been the lack of practical support from the American Fenians. In one of history's ironies, a significant attempt to actually provide such support failed due to bad timing. On April 12, 1867, the *Erin's Hope* saga began. After receiving a letter from Kelly requesting more American support, the Fenians chartered a cargo vessel named the *Jacknel* (or *Jacmel*) and loaded it with both weapons and Irish Americans, most Civil War veterans, who wanted to support the independence movement. There likely were about 7,000 rifles and other weapons on board, disguised as normal cargo. The commander of the expedition was John F. Kavanagh, a former brigadier general and congressman. The ship set off from Sandy Hook, south of New York City. Once in international waters, they christened the ship *Erin's Hope*. Arriving off the Irish coast on May 18, they were unable to land at Sligo as they had intended, nor were they able to make contact with local Fenian leaders (most of whom were in jail by this time). Their plans in disarray, a dispute broke out between the crew and a Fenian passenger, resulting in gunplay and two wounded.[20] The captain put all three ashore, and they were arrested. The mission finally found an IRB commander who suggested that they try to offload the weapons and men at Cork. The ship did succeed in landing thirty-one or thirty-two Fenians near Cork, with almost all quickly arrested. The ship then sailed up and down the coast, trying to find a secure place to offload the arms. Failing in this effort, it then sailed back to the US. Not long afterward, most of the arrested Fenians were tried and then expelled to the US.

Irish Americans and Fenian Sleeper Cells in England

The Irish also had a number of what would now be called "sleeper cells" in England, with many—and probably the majority—of these being led by

Irish Americans. The IRB also used England as a relatively safe rear area for political and other support activities. Northern English cities, most notably Manchester, Birmingham, and Liverpool, were considered hotbeds of IRB cells. Not coincidently, these same cities had significant Irish populations with a number of economic and social grievances.

The other advantage for the IRB in operating in and out of England was that although habeas corpus had been suspended in Ireland in 1866, this never was the case in England or Scotland. This made these two areas much safer for quiet operations and coordinating cells. Likewise, at least until the 1880s the British police service arguably was not particularly effective against organized groups such as the IRB. The English model of policing simply was not well designed for this purpose. As a result, the British government felt it necessary to deploy a number of British security officers from Ireland to England to provide support to the outmatched police forces.

As noted, Irish Americans predominated in the leadership of these cells. John Devoy provides a good thumbnail sketch of the background of some of these leaders:

> Some officers, who had served in the armies of the United States in various ranks, commissioned and non-commissioned, were in the cities in England. These officers included Timothy Deasy, who was a Captain in Colonel Cass's celebrated Irish Regiment, the 9th Mass. Inf. Vols.; Captain Michael O'Brien, who was a civil employee of the Engineer Corps of the Army of the Potomac in 1863 under Captain (then First Lieutenant) Ricard O'Sullivan Burke, subsequently entering the army and becoming a non-commissioned officer; and Captain O'Meagher Condon, who had served from late in 1862 to June, 1864, a non-commissioned officer, being First Sergeant at latter date in K Company, 164th Regiment, N. Y. Vol. Infantry. Captain Deasy was quite familiar with the conditions in Liverpool, and it was intended to place him in that city; Captain Edward O'Meagher Condon was made Intermediary for Manchester.[21]

Thomas J. Kelly, who appears continually in the Irish American operations in both Ireland and England, may have been one of the most capable Fenian leaders on either side of the Atlantic. Kelly was born in County Galway in 1833 and emigrated to New York in 1851, where he worked as a printer and joined a local militia unit. In 1857, he moved to

Tennessee where he became the publisher of the *Nashville Democrat*. When the Civil War started, he opted for the Northern side and tried to enlist in the 69th New York Regiment. Before actually reaching that regiment, he joined the 10th Ohio Infantry, also a predominantly Irish unit. He rose to first sergeant in that regiment, seeing some action and being wounded, before he was commissioned as an officer. Kelly later was the chief signal officer for the Army of the Cumberland and finished the war as a captain before being mustered out in 1864.

Manchester Martyrs

Kelly held a secret meeting at the end of June 1867 where he was confirmed as the chief executive of the IRB. Likewise, the IRB in Britain was controlled by three Irish Americans. These were Colonel Ricard O'Sullivan Burke, the principal arms buyer; Captain James Murphy, the Scottish Centre; and Captain Edward O'Meagher Condon, the Northern Counties Centre. Kelly could not completely cloak his activities from the British government, and he very much was on the wanted list. On September 10, 1867, Kelly and Captain Timothy Deasy, another Irish American who served as Kelly's aide, aroused a policeman's suspicions in Manchester and they were arrested initially for loitering until the authorities could find out exactly who they were. Once Kelly and Deasy were correctly identified, the British held them for trial on treason charges. The other three leaders quickly learned of their arrest and launched a plan to rescue them.

On September 18, as Kelly and Deasy were being moved from court to prison and not particularly strongly guarded, a group of IRB members surrounded the police van and forced it to stop. They tried to force the lock on the door but failed. They called on Police Sergeant Charles Brett, who was armed only with a sword and who was inside the van with the prisoners, to unlock the door. He refused. The insurgents then tried to shoot open the lock with a revolver. Unfortunately, Brett had chosen that moment to look outside through the lock. The bullet struck him in the face, killing him. One of the other prisoners in the van, a common criminal not associated with the IRB, then took Brett's keys and opened the van. Both Kelly and Deasy then were spirited out of the country and returned to the US.

The killing of a policeman by the IRB resulted in a lynching mentality in Britain. In some ways, this seemed to have been exacerbated by the fact that a number of Americans were involved in one form or another. A widespread roundup began, with twenty-six suspects eventually being brought to trial. Five were convicted (including Edward O'Meagher Condon, who claimed American citizenship) and sentenced to be hanged. Of the five, a Royal marine was pardoned after the evidence fell apart and Condon's sentence was changed to life in prison due to pressure from the American government; he was later pardoned in 1878. Despite widespread calls in the UK for clemency for the other three, they were hanged on November 23, 1867, with the executioner botching the job with two of the condemned, who were strangled slowly. The prison authorities also refused to allow a Christian burial. Their deaths and immortalization as the "Manchester Martyrs" breathed new life into the Fenian propaganda war against the British. This applied not only within Ireland, but also in England and the US. The various socialist and labor groups in particular within England came out in support of the "martyrs." This support included both Karl Marx and Friedrich Engels. Both had written and spoken on "The Irish Question" quite frequently previously, and the Manchester Martyrs created a fresh round of attention by both men.[22]

Unfortunately for the IRB and the Fenians, this was followed by the Clerkenwell incident. Ricard O'Sullivan Burke, an Irish American mentioned earlier as the weapons procurer for the IRB, was born in County Cork. After deserting from the Cork Militia, he fled first to London and then to New York. He then spent several years as a sailor, followed by further extensive travel. He reportedly served for a time in the Chilean cavalry. At the beginning of the Civil War he joined the 5th New York Infantry, followed by the 15th New York. Burke finished the war as a brevet colonel.[23] During the Civil War period he had been active with the Fenian Brotherhood and had been dispatched to Ireland in December 1865. From there, Kelly assigned Burke as the chief procurement officer. Burke established a front business in Birmingham and bought a significant number of weapons that were then stored in Liverpool; unfortunately for the IRB, however, the bulk of the weapons he had procured never made it into Ireland.

Although Burke had managed to avoid being arrested around the time of the 1867 rebellion, he was arrested in London on November 27, 1867. He and a companion were jailed at the Clerkenwell House of Detention, located in a very poor and heavily Irish area of London, to await trial. James Murphy, another Irish American, launched a plan to rescue the prisoners. After one failed attempt, on December 13 Murphy and his accomplices wheeled a barrel of gunpowder to the wall of the prison and lit the fuse. Sadly, Murphy's zeal was not matched by his knowledge of explosives. The explosion did, in fact, blow a hole in the wall; it was sufficiently effective that if Burke had been where he was supposed to be as part of a prearranged rendezvous, he would have been killed. Along with taking down the wall, the blast also created carnage in the houses and tenements surrounding the prison. Six civilians were killed immediately, with a further six deaths later, and there were about 120 seriously injured, many maimed for life.

Just as the Manchester Martyrs had been a propaganda coup for the Fenian movement, the Clerkenwell incident was a public relations disaster. Karl Marx likely did a good job of summarizing the results: "The London masses, who have shown great sympathy toward Ireland, will be made wild and driven into the arms of a reactionary government. One cannot expect the London proletarians to allow themselves to be blown up in honour of Fenian emissaries."[24] The Fenian Brotherhood in the US disavowed the operation. Even the IRB Supreme Council in 1868 condemned the bombing; some, in fact, argued that it was a rogue operation, but given the seniority of the planners of the rescue attempt, it clearly was a Fenian effort gone sour.

The Emergence of John O'Neill

In 1867, a fresh attempt was made to unite the Brotherhood in the US. John Mitchel, the hero of 1848, was invited to take over leadership, with the clear expectation that he would receive support from both wings. He, however, refused the offer. In a letter explaining his decision, Mitchel said,

> I once more decline . . . to participate in the Fenian movement as at present organized, or rather disorganized. I disbelieve in the existence of any fighting in Ireland, and in the possibility of making any fight while England continues at peace. This has been my opinion for many years. I have never yet joined in any appeal to my countrymen in America to contribute their money towards any such premature and impossible attempt. It is but wasting their means and, what is worse, it is wasting and rising up their patriotic enthusiasm and destroying their trust in the faith of man. I do not wish either your branch of the organization or that of Mr. Roberts to use my name in any manner whatever.[25]

Instead, Anthony A. Griffin was elected as the chief organizer of the O'Mahony wing, with the Roberts wing still remaining separate. Rather than appearing very interested in reconciling the two wings in the US, Roberts instead tried to reach agreement with the Irish movement, apparently calculating that this approach would smother the competing Brotherhood wing.

After the failure of the 1867 uprising the IRB itself split, with one wing calling itself the Directory. On July 4, 1867, Roberts pushed through the "Treaty of Paris" with the Directory. Under this agreement, the Roberts wing would focus both on Canadian operations and material support for the Irish uprising. This was predicated on the Roberts wing being recognized as the "true" Fenian Brotherhood by the Irish. On his return, Roberts held a national convention in Cleveland on October 3, announcing his total victory for the Senate wing. In practice, however, little appeared to have changed.

The election of John Savage as president of the O'Mahony wing in August 1867 led to fresh efforts at reuniting the two wings, but these were stillborn. In practical terms the O'Mahony-Stephens-Savage-Gleeson wing became immaterial for several years. One illustration of how impotent this wing had become—and how financially stressed it was—was when this wing offered to sell 2,000 stands of arms "at a bargain" in February 1867.[26]

From the start of his presidency, O'Neill was determined to launch a fresh attack on Canada. His principal—and it might be argued almost exclusive—focus was on reenergizing the military capabilities of the organization for renewed operations. In this, he was supported by what became known as the "Canada-fighting" Fenians, who had held a special convention in Utica, New York in February 1867.[27]

O'Neill directed that Fenian rifled muskets be sent to factories where they were converted from muzzle-loaders to breech-loaders, making them compatible with the more modern military weapons of the day. O'Neill also stressed acquiring full stocks of weapons and equipment for the various circles.

The Brotherhood also directed a more formal military structure. The War Department of the Fenian Brotherhood in New York issued General Orders No. 4 on May 1, 1869. This ordered with "immediate effect" that the Brotherhood form a force of eight brigades, with each brigade containing three regiments of infantry, six companies of light cavalry, and one battery of light artillery. In each infantry regiment, there would be twelve companies of fusiliers or infantry of the line and six companies of voltigeurs or skirmishers. Each infantry company was to consist of a minimum of seventy-one officers and men. The cavalry companies would be a minimum of sixty-nine officers and men. Although the Fenian Brotherhood certainly earlier had developed its forces for conventional warfare, this order in practice meant that the armed structure of the Fenians took precedence over the "circles" structure, largely relegating the circles to a political role.

The same day in a separate circular, the War Department ordered all officers to report strength and equipment levels of their units, and that "officers disregarding the provisions of this Order shall be at once stricken from the rolls. . . ." Units were ordered to put their equipment in order. For units short of equipment, the headquarters offered the following: Breechloader rifles and complete accoutrements: $10; Jackets: $5; Pants: $3; Caps: $1; and Overcoats: $5 to $7. Military officers of General Staff "shall henceforth devote their time exclusively to the performance of that duty . . ."; public speeches and other distractions were prohibited.[28]

O'Neill faced two major obstacles to his plans. The first was the long-standing problem of all the Brotherhood's history: financial. The amount in the treasury as of September 11, 1868 was 23,447.58 dollars.[29] One estimate was that between October 1868 and April 1869 money on hand dropped from 20,000 dollars to about 3,800 dollars.[30] The total amount in treasury at the end of November 1869 reportedly was 1,129.58 dollars.[31]

Regular contributions had dropped significantly. The 1868 congress noted that only one-third of money pledged at the Cleveland congress about a year earlier had actually been paid.[32] There was some reflection of the financial difficulties—and the split between the wings of the Brotherhood—shown at the 1868 Fenian congress by the circles that were represented. Representatives were listed from the following circles: New York City: 16; Buffalo District (including surrounding towns): 10; other towns in New York State: 20; New Jersey: 9; Philadelphia: 17; elsewhere in Pennsylvania: 17; Ohio: 13; Massachusetts: 12; Rhode Island: 5; Connecticut: 6; Maine: 1; Vermont: 2; Illinois: 4; Colorado: 2; Iowa: 2; Maryland: 2; Delaware: 2; Nebraska: 2; Kentucky: 4; Tennessee: 4; Michigan: 2; Missouri: 1; and Washington D.C.: 2.[33] This can be compared with the figures cited earlier for the 1865 congress, which were both broader and larger. Although growth of circles occurred in some areas, the overall trajectory of circles appeared to be downward. The Senate resolved that it should call upon the "Irish race throughout the world" to contribute a one-dollar subscription; an assessment of five dollars for each member; and that all circles "be called on immediately to remit all moneys in their possession to Headquarters. . . ."[34] None of these measures, however, proved to have much impact on the overall financial situation.

In late 1869 and early 1870, dues from the circles seemed to be rather sporadic and very unpredictable month to month. There was a separate "war fund" from the circles that was collecting more money than regular dues for the Brotherhood. Even this, however, was highly variable in the money submitted. As of November 1869, 250 dollars had been collected for the formation of a cavalry regiment. All the contributions were from members in Vermont, where it was most likely such a force would be of use.[35] Likewise, "There are committees out in New York, Brooklyn, Phil'a, Troy, Buffalo, and other places, collecting exclusively for ammunition, and I think it safe in saying that there are fully three thousand dollars in the hands in Said Committees."[36] A letter to Frank Gallagher dated April 11, 1869, provided lists of circles and additional assessments that were imposed on them. The circles had until the end of August to raise the funds. It is not necessary to list all the circles and funds they were assessed, but a few can provide a feel for the amounts: Manhattan, $20,000; Western New York, $10,000; Utica, $2,000; Albany, $2,000; and Troy, $1,000.[37] From all indications, it is very doubtful that the Brotherhood ever received this amount of money from the circles.

Beyond income, actual costs for reequipping the Fenian army were greater than O'Neill initially thought. In many ways, his problems with weaponry appear akin to modern military procurement. As one example, in a letter to Frank Gallagher, a Centre in Buffalo and evidently a confidant, O'Neill noted that in at least one case, costs were more than 100 times what he had projected:

> [I believed] that the arms would be finished for about five hundred dollars ($500), but since that several thousand dollars have been paid for them. These arms have cost much more than I had any idea they were going to cost—about Sixty thousand dollars including freight and drayage to factory—and I believe there is still some money due Mr Meehan, but I do not know the amount, as has not yet furnished a full statement of his account. However they are now finished and paid for (except what may be due Mr Meehan) and are on the road to their destination. The freight, packing and unpacking at various points will cost considerable, I think however not more than two thousand five hundred dollars in all.[38]

Some of the expenses faced in rearming the force came unexpectedly and clearly flummoxed the leadership. As noted earlier, the US government had returned the weapons it had seized from the Fenians in 1866. This, however, came with a catch that was not fully recognized until 1868: "Under the head of 'Restored Arms' are included the charges for freight and storage of the arms seized by the United States Government in 1866—one of the stipulations of the Government, previous to giving back the arms, being that all back charges of the railroad and the express companies should be paid by the organization."[39] These costs certainly were much less than the cost of buying new weapons, but in the Brotherhood's financial straits, they certainly stung.

The second issue O'Neill faced was his relationship with the Fenian Senate. After John O'Neill was elected President of the Fenian Brotherhood in 1868, he became very focused on launching a fresh attack on Canada. He faced a problem, however, with the other Brotherhood leaders. In a reprise of the earlier O'Mahony-Roberts split, he became embroiled in a power struggle with a number of Fenian senators. He argued that "Without the honesty or manhood to leave the Organization and openly denounce its schemes as impracticable, they remained apparently faithful to the cause, but at the same time knew how to sow the seeds of dissension and distrust, and to vilify those who had embarked their whole fortune in the undertaking."[40] The rhetoric quickly became as heated as the earlier splits:

> In reply to your letter, I beg to state that some of the Senators are too much engaged in American politics to have the cause of Ireland much at heart. . . . Lately we have been trying, and with success, to get everything ready for an early movement. Seeing this, some of the Senators have resorted to throwing distrust in the rank and file, by saying that there is no money in the Treasury, and that we have no means of fighting. It was deemed right to warn the organization against these *hounds*. . . .[41]

This was O'Neill's narrative; from the senators' viewpoint, things undoubtedly appeared different. After the continuing military failures in Canada and the Ireland, even Fenian "true believers" had to think twice about what to do next. Simply trying similar operations as in 1866 had to be viewed with skepticism. Trying to square the circle of efforts being necessary to keep the Fenian Brotherhood relevant to the Irish nationalist cause versus simply wasting these efforts in further futile gestures was a difficult decision.

The O'Neill faction held the seventh Fenian congress in Philadelphia in November 1868, with about 180 circles represented. This congress called for fresh actions by the Brotherhood, but little else seemed to be resolved. The major practical result was purely procedural: "The Committee on Rules and Regulations beg respectfully to report: That the rules regulating the proceedings of the House of Representatives of the U.S. be adopted, as far as applicable, for the Government of the Congress of the Fenian Brotherhood."[42] One incident on January 8, 1870, further complicated O'Neill's position. His Secretary for Civil Affairs Patrick Keenan, argued with and then shot and wounded Senator Meehan, one of the main senate power brokers. Other senators began serious discussions about holding O'Neill indirectly responsible for this attack, and impeachment was considered. O'Neill avoided this proceeding, but the atmosphere became increasingly tense.

The senators called for holding an immediate convention in Chicago, which was held on April 11, 1866. At this convention, the Senate called for a delay in any further military preparations. In response, O'Neill unilaterally held his own convention in New York City on April 19, arguing it was more accessible to the delegates. At this convention, he received full authorization for his plans for a fresh Canadian operation. He justified his decision to hold a separate meeting in a circular:

> For a long time now I have been convinced that the Senate as a body did not mean to fight. I have felt that it was the purpose of its members to have the organization live on indefinitely, so that they might profit politically through their prominent connection with it, and to prolong its inactive life, the scheme of holding the Congress in Chicago or some other point far West was hit upon. Those interested knowing full well that the people could not be represented at said Congress, and that consequently they, holding the power, could make speedy fight impracticable.[43]

The New York convention seems to have been hand-picked by O'Neill for its members' loyalty. Even so, at least some of the delegates found O'Neill's overall approach less than impressive. One delegate argued that O'Neill's "speech was not what any intelligent congress would receive, it was not on the condition of the Brotherhood but all about the senate and himself."[44]

The competing New York and Chicago conventions bring up another point about the Fenian Brotherhood and its internecine power struggles. There seemed to be somewhat a geographical aspect to this. The eastern and western circles and their respective leaders appeared to have a pattern of disagreements and competition. During the period up through 1870, this was not a "clean" split, but certainly seemed to exist. New York City and Chicago—being the principal cities from which many of the leaders emerged—seemed to be the epicenters of the struggles for supreme power. Circles from smaller cities appeared to orbit in the gravity of these two cities, although again this was not completely geographically driven. After about 1870, this split between the two cities became even more pronounced.

However severe the split between O'Neill and his senators, he retained sufficient support to continue his invasion plans. The Fenian Brotherhood would have yet another attempt against Canada.

Chapter 11

1870: Invasion Redux

Soldiers, this is the advance-guard of the Irish-American army for the liberation of Ireland from the yoke of the oppressor. For your own country you enter that of the enemy. The eyes of your countrymen are upon you. Forward, March.

—Address of General O'Neill to Fenian troops
on the Canadian border[1]

O'Neill's initial plan centered on capturing St. Jean, Canada (called St. Johns by O'Neill).[2] This town was midway between the border (twenty-one miles) and Montreal (twenty-two miles further). His early scheme involved having a force of about 500 troops under command of General J.J. Donnelly make a dash for the town by rail, or if that was impossible, by foot, and either seize St. Jean or threaten it until reinforcements could arrive for an assault. Simultaneously, another force of 200 was to capture Richmond, Canada. The balance of the Fenian forces—intended by O'Neill to be at least 1,000—was to cross on the east side of the Richelieu River near Eccles Hill, Canada, and drive toward St. Jean, with another wing to the western side of the river advancing from Malone, New York to the same objective. From the point of capturing St. Jean, O'Neill's strategic intent seemed rather fuzzy: "In a further advance, we would, of course have to be guided by the number of reinforcements that might arrive, and by the number and disposition of the enemy."[3] St. Jean itself appeared to be of minimal strategic value; O'Neill's intention of capturing it seemed to be

143

more a matter of having an initial objective to aim for rather than based on its importance. In theory, Fenian troops holding St. Jean posed somewhat a threat to Montreal, being only twenty-two miles from that city, but trying to actually capture Montreal with at best only a few thousand troops was a chimera, particularly with little or no artillery. He also intended smaller raids to be conducted farther west all along the border, particularly in the Niagara region, to serve as distractions to the main operation.

According to O'Neill, he expected to have somewhere between 1,000 to 1,200 troops around St. Albans as his initial force on May 24, with a similar number of reinforcements within twenty-four hours. Some 1,000 to 1,500 troops were to be massed around Malone, New York. The first forces were to come from Massachusetts, Rhode Island, Vermont, and Northeastern New York; this appeared due more to their geographical location rather than their particular capabilities. O'Neill stated that he expected to have about 4,000 troops in total by the end of May 25. Planning on starting an offensive with only a portion of the troops actually assembled is normally not considered an optimal strategy, but O'Neill may have been realistic in his expectations. After the experience of 1866, the Fenians had to expect that large numbers of Fenians moving simultaneously would provoke a major response by the authorities. Trying to move them in smaller groups at least seemed to offer better chances of success in avoiding a quick American government reaction.

O'Neill made an unfortunate decision in his timing, choosing May 24 as the date to begin operations. This was Queen Victoria's Birthday. However much symbolic value an attack on that date might have, this also was the date when virtually every Canadian militia unit would be conducting ceremonies, hence would be activated. This meant it would be—and, in fact, was—easier to move them from parade to the field, rather than having to be assembled from their homes. The Canadian authorities chose a wise course and brought the troops together for the birthday ceremonies and only then notifying the militiamen that they were required for further services.

One issue that may have been salient in 1870 in contrast to 1866 was the quality and experience of the Fenian troops. Overall, the officers largely were the same, almost all Civil War veterans. Whether the same could be said for the soldiers may be questionable. With at least five years after discharge for most of the troops who had fought in the Civil War, many of the most reliable former soldiers probably had returned to civilian jobs and families. However dedicated to Irish independence, these Fenians were unlikely to be particularly eager for potentially long-term operations. The recruiting base was more likely to be younger militarily inexperienced youth looking for adventure or veterans who simply could not adjust to civilian life. Neither group represented a particularly strong base around which to organize a disciplined force.

In contrast to earlier operations, the Fenian forces had at least the potential for being better equipped in 1870. O'Neill had insisted that arms and other equipment be readily available. Le Caron (who had no particular reason to lie about it) claimed that he had prepositioned war material for at least 12,000 men on the ground near the Canadian border.[4] Persons living in the area and reporters noted considerable movement of cargo wagons moving crates of apparent weapons in late May around St. Albans and Malone. One additional asset the Fenians had in 1870 was artillery. This consisted of a "three-pounder" cannon. This was a light artillery piece and had the advantage of being easily moved. One cannon was unlikely to be massively significant in a battle, but it did provide an additional resource. At the least, its use against untrained troops could have an important psychological impact.

The Attack from St. Albans

O'Neill quickly had to come to terms with reality. He arrived in St. Albans in the early morning of May 24 and expected the trains to disgorge many hundreds of Fenians. Instead, he initially received some twenty-five to thirty from Massachusetts (commanded by a colonel), eighty to ninety from Northeast New York, and sixty-five from Vermont. Some reinforcements continued to arrive during the day of the May 24, but they remained in small numbers. O'Neill continued to rely on inaccurate newspaper reports on large numbers of Fenians approaching his area, however, and he decided to cross the border and hope for the best (and reinforcements). His new objective was Eccles Hill, in reality only a few hundred yards over the border, and in almost the same location as the Pigeon Hill objective in 1866.

Even in comparison to the earlier rather modest objectives, this offensive plan seemed particularly pointless. There was, however, a rather real concern for O'Neill. He feared the reaction of the US government to his plans more than he feared the Canadians: "I was very anxious to get the arms, etc., and a sufficient number of men to protect them on the other side to protect them on the other side beyond the reach of the United States authorities, whom I desired to evade."[5] At this point, O'Neill seemed to be

Title: Hope is not a plan

trying to achieve anything, no matter how modest, even a brief occupation of Canadian territory merely for propaganda purposes.

O'Neill insisted that operational security be tightened prior to this operation. Rather than the public pronouncements—and boasts—about Fenian plans, O'Neill was rather tight-lipped publicly about his specific intentions. He likewise tried to reduce the leaks from the lower-level members. In general orders of April 28, 1870, he specified that in moving to the operational area, "Officers and men must avoid the use of uniforms or any insignia that would distinguish them. Officers must not be recognized by military titles, and officers or men must not speak of Fenian matters [in transit]." In his later official report, O'Neill claimed that ". . . up to the last moment the enemy had no knowledge of our movements, so secretly had everything been managed."[6] The Fenian headquarters was by this point so thoroughly penetrated by British and Canadian intelligence operatives that these operational security measures were, in fact, moot, but they did indicate that the Fenian senior leaders at least had begun to learn lessons from earlier failures.

Based on the experience of the 1866 offensive, O'Neill based his planning on a delay in effective federal reaction, but did expect that such a response would, in fact, eventually occur. He wrote in his official report that he could "safely calculate" three days-worth of maneuvering before "the direct interference of the U.S. Government . . . and all of that time was allowed us."[7] This raises the question of what he actually expected to accomplish in three days.

A good indication of some of the morale issues surrounding the Fenian troops as the operations began was provided in a letter from a Fenian major who took part, Daniel Murphy of Connecticut. Somewhat oddly, this was included as an appendix to O'Neill's official report. Murphy noted that he initially opposed an operation in Canada, in part because he was unsure of support within the Fenians. "I went further, by informing that body [the Fenian Congress] that they could not depend on any men from Connecticut to inaugurate the movement, as I believed the Organization in that State to be demoralized, which assertion afterwards proved true." He argued that Fenian units that came to Malone were both slow in arriving and grossly understrength. He continued:

> On arriving at the front almost exhausted . . . [we saw] here
> and there were seated a few squads of men; some were lying
> around loose in a demoralized condition; and God knows, I
> could not blame them, for, perhaps some of them were told
> the same story that was told to me . . . but, whether they did

or not, in my humble opinion they were in no condition for an offensive movement. The first cheering news we received was that Gen. O'Neill had not men enough to cross the line, that the brave Gen. Lewis had deserted his post, and that the whole affair had gone up. We hoped against hope that we were not deceived by some one. . . . About 8 o'clock I received warning to prepare for marching orders at a moment's notice. For some time it was a question in my mind whether I should obey this order or not. . . . I finally concluded as the least of two evils to go to the front. . . .[8]

Major Murphy resigned from the Fenians after his experience in 1870. If his attitude at the start of the battle was typical of the Fenian officers, then it was futile for O'Neill and the more senior officers to expect much from their forces. Such attitudes certainly would have percolated downward among the troops, who could not be expected to be more motivated than their officers.

O'Neill established his headquarters at Franklin, Vermont, about ten miles from the border, with the troops camped at Hubbard's Farm, about one-half mile outside the village. Continuing to expect reinforcements, O'Neill postponed the attack from the night of May 24 to the morning of May 25. By this point, the expected upcoming battle had already drawn a horde of reporters and local tourists. It also brought US Marshal George P. Foster, who was in Vermont in response to President Grant's orders. Foster represented the initial practical Federal response to the Fenian attempt to cross the border.

In contrast to President Johnson's delays in 1866, Grant issued his proclamation condemning the Fenian plans on the intended day of operation itself. The proclamation was rather straightforward and direct:

May 24, 1870

Whereas it has come to my knowledge that sundry illegal military enterprises and expeditions are being set on foot within the territory and jurisdiction of the United States, with a view to carry on the same from such territory or jurisdiction against the people and district of the Dominion of Canada, within the dominions of her majesty the Queen of the United Kingdom of Great Britain and Ireland, with whom the United States are at peace:

Now, therefore, I, Ulysses S. Grant, President of the United States, do hereby admonish all good citizens of the United States, and all persons within the territory and jurisdiction of the United States, against aiding, countenancing, abetting, or taking part in such unlawful proceedings; and I do hereby warn all persons that by committing such illegal acts, they will forfeit all right to the protection of this Government, or to its interference in their behalf to rescue them from the consequences of their own acts; and I do hereby enjoin all officers in the service of the United States to employ all their lawful authority and power to prevent and defeat the aforesaid unlawful proceedings, and to arrest and bring to justice all persons who may be engaged therein.

In testimony whereof I have hereunto set my hand and caused the seal of the United States to be affixed.

Done at the city of Washington, this 24th day of May, in the year of our Lord 1870, and of the independence of the United States the ninety-fourth. [SEAL]

By the President: U.S. GRANT

HAMILTON FISH, Secretary of State.

US army units were ordered to the area, but there was a time lag. In the meantime, Marshal Foster wasted no time in carrying out his orders. He presented the proclamation to O'Neill, who reportedly not only rejected it, but also had some harsh—if unspecified in the historical record—words about the president. For want of any further practical actions immediately available, Foster also ordered O'Neill that he was required to keep the public roads clear.

The Canadians had excellent intelligence on Fenian intentions, but took some time to get their units in position. The initial force available immediately across the border from the projected Fenian route of advance was a private company of home guards led by Asa Westover. On May 23, two officers of this unit traveled to Franklin, Vermont, where they noted preparations for an offensive. After they returned north of the border, Westover activated his men and occupied Eccles Hill just north of the border. Selecting this hill as a defensive position was tactically wise because it dominated the road that was the logical route across the border.[9] After the initial home guard deployment, they soon were joined by other volunteer units.

About 10 A.M. on May 25, US Marshal Foster crossed the border to meet with the Canadians. He warned them of the expected attack and told them that US troops were on their way to enforce the neutrality laws. He also tried to pass along a message from O'Neill that the Fenians would obey the dictates of civilized warfare. Canadian Lieutenant Colonel Chamberlin, who had assumed command of the forces in the area, "said he could receive no messages from the Fenians, as they were mere pirates and marauders."[10] His messages delivered, Foster returned to the US side of the border.

As he was moving south, the Fenian column was moving north. There probably were about 176 Fenian troops in the initial advance.[11] O'Neill sent his advance guard in column formation on the road across the border, while keeping some troops around Richard's Farm, located (according to O'Neill's estimates) some twenty or thirty rods (110 to 165 yards) south of the border and about half a mile from the summit of Eccles Hill.[12] One miscalculation O'Neill made, however, was that the Canadian home guard had taken positions on the lower forward slope of Eccles Hill where they still had excellent fields of fire and were closer to the road leading across the border, even though still about 400 yards away from it. The home guard also was armed with very accurate sporting weapons rather than standard muskets.

As the Fenian column crossed the border, the Canadians opened fire and killed John Rowe, one of the Fenian soldiers, and wounded another. The members of the column took cover, and the advance stalled. Long-range firing by both sides continued with minimal results. O'Neill then ordered another group of soldiers to advance from a slightly different direction that provided more cover. This group also took fire, with one killed and two wounded. This advance also stalled, with the troops refusing to go further. Quoting O'Neill's account:

Finding that I could accomplish anything practical with these men, I had them to fall back a short distance out of range of the enemy's bullets, to await the arrival of the men from New York, under Col. Leddy, whom I looked for every moment. It was then that I made the following remarks to the men:

"Men of Ireland I am ashamed of you! You have acted disgracefully to-day; but you will have another chance of showing whether you are cravens or not. Comrades, we must not, we dare not go back with the stain of cowardice on us. Comrades, I will lead you again, and if you will not follow me, I will go with my officers and die in your front! I now leave you under charge of Boyle O'Reiley, and will go after reinforcements, and bring them up at once."

Given O'Neill's combat record, this speech likely was sincere. Having said that however, its impact on troops may not have been as intended. With his troops likely having at best shaky morale, expecting them to react well to their commander announcing that he is going to the rear for reinforcements may not have been the best approach.

O'Neill then returned to Richard's Farm where he tried to observe developments from inside the house.[13] Some gunfire, probably stray shots given the long range from the Canadians, hit the house, and the owner ordered O'Neill to leave. Once outside, O'Neill encountered Marshal Foster who drew his revolver and placed O'Neill under arrest. Foster and his deputy bundled him into a closed carriage and drove him through the Fenian camp. Despite a number of troops around Foster and the carriage, no one interfered with him, and he drove O'Neill to jail in St. Albans.

After O'Neill's arrest, some firing continued between the Canadians and Fenians, but neither side took any particular initiative. About 6 P.M., the Fenians began a disorganized retreat back along the border. Not long before this, the single Fenian cannon had fired a few ineffectual rounds toward the Canadians. For some inexplicable reason, the Fenians did not think to use their gun earlier in the fighting. The only real result of its final use was that it advertised its position to the Canadians. Seeing the Fenians falling back, the Canadians sent a detachment forward and captured the cannon, which they retained as a trophy. The other official Canadian trophy—and a rather gruesome one—of the battle was the bloody uniform of John Rowe, the first Fenian killed in the battle. The Canadian officers sent the uniform to the British Prince Arthur, who was serving with the Rifle Brigade in Canada. The casualty tally for the day's fighting was two Fenians killed, one later dying of wounds, and about ten wounded. The Canadians suffered no casualties.

The Malone Operation

The column launched from Malone, New York, had even less success. It did, however, initially provide a better operational environment for the Fenians.

A joke?

There were no local Canadian units immediately across the border, and some time would be required for them to reach the area. Likewise, there were no US troops in the immediate vicinity. Both these factors suggested that if the Fenian commanders moved fast and with initiative, they could face a good chance for launching a successful raid, even if short.

Fenian General J. H. Gleason, who previously had served in the Irish Brigade in the Civil War, was commander of the Fenian forces, but he resigned on May 26. He apparently had lost any confidence in the prospects for the operation. He was replaced by Colonel Owen Starr, who had been one of the regimental commanders in the 1866 operation and who had the reputation as one of the more aggressive Fenian commanders. On May 26, a small Fenian raiding party crossed the border and cut telegraph lines at Holbrook Corners, a village directly above the border. Another small group moved further to Hendersonville, about eight miles in road distance from Huntingdon, but this body of Fenians simply wandered through the area with no particular impact other than frightening the local population.

Starr's plan was very basic. He decided to move troops just over the border into Canada, establish defensive positions, and hope for reinforcements. With at most about 450 troops at hand, there was not much else he could do. Starr could hope that the Canadian (and US) response would take enough time so that enough additional Fenians would arrive to present a viable threat. Even with extensive reinforcements, it was extremely unlikely that the Fenians had the capability or capacity for practical operations, but his forces could at least win a propaganda victory by holding Canadian territory long enough to create embarrassment for the British government.

As a result, early morning on May 27, Starr marched his troops—or at least those willing to do so—a few hundred yards into Canadian territory. The Fenians (as in the Niagara campaign) then built breastworks from locally available fences. According to Senior, this was about 140 yards long and with the flanks well covered by the Trout River on one flank and heavy woods on the other.[14] It was on relatively high ground and had good fields of fire. The Fenian commanders again showed an excellent eye for terrain and how to take military advantage of it. All that was required was to have troops who were willing to stand their ground, at least for a while.

The Canadians quickly moved a column toward the area. The Canadians used a mix of Canadian militia and regular British units, and they outnumbered the Fenians by two or three to one. As the Canadian forces arrived in front of the Fenian lines, the militiamen opened fire at extremely long range, which was ineffectual. When the Canadians were about 400 yards from the breastworks, the Fenians loosed a volley. At that range, there was no possibility of accurate fire, especially given the weapons of the time. Unsurprisingly, no approaching Canadians were hit. The premature volley provided even further evidence of inexperienced and poorly trained troops. Evidently expecting some results from this volley and not surprisingly not seeing any, the Fenian troops panicked and fled from their position, abandoning much of their equipment. The Canadians pursued them to the border and then—after some militiamen reportedly tried to continue the pursuit across the borderline—halted. The entire engagement resulted in one Fenian killed, one wounded, and one captured; one Canadian was very lightly wounded. The main Fenian body had spent about an hour and a half in total inside Canada.

As the Fenians fled toward Malone, they encountered fresh Fenian forces arriving in the area. General Gleason had remained in Malone, and he exhorted the new troops to further efforts. This seemed to have no impact. General Meade, who had finally arrived in the area with a handful of troops, ended any further attempts on May 28 when he had General Gleason arrested. Adding to the Fenians' misery, President Grant refused to pay for Fenian travel home. Determining the financial problems of the Fenian troops and undoubtedly discerning the political advantages involved, William "Boss" Tweed of Tammany Hall offered to pay train fares for any Fenians requiring it. This ended the last serious Fenian Brotherhood effort at conventional military operations.

Chapter 12

The Withering of the Fenian Brotherhood: The Birth of "Fenianism"

If you are but true to this duty, if you are but true to nature, there are those among you, perhaps, will yet live to uplift Ireland's banner above the ruins of London.

—The Irish World, September 19, 1874

After the failure of 1870, the Fenian Brotherhood began a period of steady decline. The Senate faction met in Cincinnati on August 23, 1870, and abolished itself as the Fenian Brotherhood and renamed itself the United Irishmen. It pledged to support the IRB, and called for a directory to be cofounded with the Savage wing. The structure was for the directory to be comprised of seven members, three of whom would be from the Savage wing.

The Savage wing met in New York on August 30, 1870, with Savage reelected as president. It rejected a merger with the United Irishmen. It did, however, offer to consolidate groups if O'Neill agreed to accept the Savage wing's constitution. If so, then his wing would be offered two leadership positions. The problem with this proposal was that O'Neill was at that time a prisoner, serving a two-year sentence in Vermont for violating neutrality laws (a sentence for which he soon was pardoned). In practical terms, he was out of allies in the newly formed United Irishmen, and they had no particular reason to support such a merger.

President Grant pardoned O'Neill and the other Fenian officers in October 1870. These pardons seemed to be the result of cold-blooded

153

political calculations rather than any apparent sympathies. Particularly given the ever-increasing lack of support for the Brotherhood, releasing the leaders also was unlikely to result in its renaissance. O'Neill had lost most of his power in the Brotherhood after the Eccles Hill fiasco, but he continued to have influence. This residual sympathy led to O'Neill's last great adventure.

The Red River Operation

The political environment in which O'Neill launched his 1871 attempt requires some description. Western Canada—particularly what is now Manitoba—faced considerable unrest. Most of the population in the general area of the Red River by the beginning of the nineteenth century was what was called the Métis. These people emerged as early Europeans, particularly the French, moved into the area and intermixed with the native population. The mixed European–First Nation population developed its own culture and social structures. This particularly was the case in the Red River Valley area in the West that was called Rupert's Land. In the early nineteenth century, European settlers began encroaching on the Méti territory. Conflict was almost inevitable, especially because the Métis primarily were French–First Nation Catholics and the new settlers were in large part Scottish Presbyterians. After the confederation of Canada in 1867, the Anglophone colonial government in Ottawa moved to take control of the area and to incorporate it as the province of Manitoba.

This led to armed opposition by many of the Métis. Louis Riel became the leader of the opposition, and he led the so-called Red River Rebellion of 1869–1870, which was militarily inconsequential. The sole casualty was a settler whom Riel had executed. Riel's initial link to the Fenians was William Bernard O'Donoghue, who served as the treasurer of Riel's provisional government. It is probable that O'Donoghue had less interest in the Méti cause than he did in any anti-British movements that were available. O'Donoghue was born in Ireland, but emigrated to New York as a child. He later moved to the Red River, where he studied for the priesthood, but dropped out of his training. He became an early supporter of Riel. After the collapse of the uprising, he fled along with Riel to the US, and the two had a major falling-out. Even before his arrival in the US, O'Donoghue had made contact with John O'Neill.

O'Neill seemed to view the Red River area as a promising area for the Fenians to launch raids. As early as November 1869, O'Neill was pushing the plan for a Red River operation, with a follow-on request that the Buffalo Centre "send a *good man* out there at once."[1] In a subsequent letter marked "confidential," he provided further details of the efforts being made:

> I engaged a man at present in Missouri, Major Williams, and had sent him money and instructions the day before receiving your letter. I fully agree with you as to the importance of the country. There is now no objection on the part of the Ex. Com., M[r] Gibbons has always been for it, but the delay, first in getting the arms from the factory and then in locating them has been d____d annoying to me. Now, however, I have taken the matter into my own hands and will soon finish locating the arms. I hope that your Committees in Buffalo have been successful in collecting money for ammunition. You must see Justice Whalin and our friends generally and stir them up—Remember, Gallagher. that I build largely upon you for the desperate work before us, the eyes of the world is upon us and we must show what material we are made of—now amount of sophistry or subtle argument will serve us now—we have undertaken certain work—we must go through with it or stand aside and leave room for abler and better men; the world moves we cannot compel it to stand still.[2]

The Far West certainly was less important to O'Neill than was the impending raid into Quebec, but he clearly did not drop the idea of something being done in the West. After his release from prison, he resumed his focus in that direction. O'Neill pushed the plan of a Red River operation to the Fenian Brotherhood council, but they did not approve of any major efforts in that area. At the same time, however, they apparently had no objections to O'Neill conducting what essentially was a unilateral operation. They were unwilling to put a Brotherhood imprimatur on the plan, but seemed to be willing to see what O'Neill could accomplish.

O'Neill dutifully resigned from the Brotherhood and collected some weapons, probably from Fenian stocks. He and O'Donoghue, who began terming himself as president of the Republic of Red River, traveled West. At least in theory, their prospects looked good. The Métis were a disgruntled group who had shown the willingness to actively oppose the Canadian government. They were unlikely to provide active support in defense of the area. As the local governor wrote to Prime Minister John Macdonald:

I cannot count upon much, if any, aid from French half-breeds. They have not, I believe, any sympathy with the Fenian movement, but on the other hand, the bitter denunciation of the extreme English representation by the Liberal here and the Globe in Toronto, have aroused the worst feeling in them, and they would probably not be very sorry to see trouble.[3]

Likewise, there were only a handful of militiamen in the territory, and any reinforcements would take considerable time to arrive.

O'Neill and O'Donoghue assembled a small force of some thirty to forty-five soldiers of fortune for their effort. It is unclear how many were actually formal members of the Fenian Brotherhood; the leaders seemed to grab whoever was willing to go. They quickly ran into trouble even before trying to cross the border when the Méti leaders voted not to support any uprising. Nevertheless, on October 4, 1871, the group tried to cross the border and they seized a customs house near Pembina. The reason for the phrase "tried to cross" is that the border in that area was very poorly delineated, and it is most likely that the post actually was located on the American side of the border. The US army commander in the area, Captain (Brevet Colonel) Lloyd Wheaton, previously had heard reports of the presence of the quasi-Fenians and moved a party of thirty infantrymen to the area as fast as their wagons would carry them. As soon as O'Neill's group saw the soldiers, they fled in all directions. O'Neill and about a dozen others were soon captured by Wheaton's force. O'Donoghue fled north into Canada, but he was seized by some Métis who took him back across the border and turned him over to the Americans. There were some relatively half-hearted efforts by US authorities to try O'Neill and the others, but these were plagued by jurisdictional disputes and were abandoned. In many ways, the government seemed to feel that further trials were simply not worth the effort. This rather ludicrous expedition that probably never actually left the US was the last effort of O'Neill and the first generation of the Fenians.

The Slow Collapse of the Fenian Brotherhood

In late 1870, after repeated approaches from the American government, London decided to implement a widespread amnesty for Fenian prisoners in British prisons. The first batch of these Fenians—Jeremiah O'Donovan Rossa, John Devoy, Charles Underwood O'Connell, John McClure, and

Henry Mulleda, who were known as the "Cuba Five" for the name of the ship transporting them—arrived in New York on January 19, 1871. Their arrival generated a near frenzy by American politicians to fete them. In particular, competing political factions in New York City came close to blows over who would provide the best reception.[4] Perhaps wisely, the five Fenians tried to remain above the political blandishments, and they suggested that they would work with whoever supported Irish independence.

Many in the US and Ireland believed that the arrival of these formerly imprisoned Fenians, together with a number who arrived later, would reenergize the Fenian movement, particularly through helping to unify the various factions into a fresh movement. Some of the new arrivals clearly believed this themselves. As John Devoy stated: "Our aim will be to create an Irish party in this country, whose actions in American politics will have for its sole object the interests of Ireland. We will also hold aloof from all the different sections of Fenians. I may tell you that most of us are sick of the very issue of Fenianism, though as resolved as ever to work for the attainment of Irish independence."[5]

Several of the Cuba Five together with slightly later arrivals published their goals in a statement in the *Irish People* on March 18, 1871.[6] This manifesto stated that existing Irish nationalist organizations would be allowed to keep their "names and regulations," but would be required to send twenty-five percent of their revenue to a central treasury. This treasury was to be controlled by a central council with representatives from all the groups. The council in turn was to create a group called the Irish Confederation. One of the interesting aspects of the proposed Irish Confederation was its proposed leadership structure. The general council would come from the various American states, but the Directory of Five—clearly designed to have ultimate authority—was to be chosen from those who had been recently released from British prisons. Although unstated, this certainly implied an "Ireland first" approach by all the associated components of the Irish Confederation.

In response to this manifesto, the United Irishmen transferred its power to the new Confederation and John Savage resigned from his wing of the Brotherhood. A complication emerged as the Fenian Brotherhood held its tenth convention in New York on March 21, 1871. John O'Mahony had reemerged as a power broker within the group, and he resisted merging into a larger organization. As a result, the delegates at the convention rejected disestablishing the Fenian Brotherhood. The Irish Confederation itself found growth to be a slow prospect, relying primarily on clubs established in New

York City and Brooklyn. It finally collapsed in 1873, with its members either shifting to more peaceful groups such as the Home Rule Movement or rejoining the Brotherhood. Once again, unity in a single cause proved elusive.

Likewise, the Fenian Brotherhood remained in the doldrums, with its base of support mostly in New York and a small part of Massachusetts. O'Mahony returned to lead what was now frequently referred to as the Stephens wing of the Fenian Brotherhood in 1872. It continued as an organization, but seemed to have minimal impact. In what may have been gratifying to O'Mahony, given his struggles with the issue in the past, the twelfth Brotherhood convention held in New York in August 1873 declared that the group would never "join any organization or men in an attack on Canada, or on any other territory on this side of the Atlantic, except with the consent of the Government of the United States."[7] By 1874, the group's convention was reduced to only sixty delegates, and the only appreciable result of the convention was to call for the release of the remaining Fenian prisoners held by the British or transported to Australia. The 1876 convention called for the reinstatement of James Stephens as the leader of the IRB. Beyond this, and of considerably greater importance, decisions made at this meeting led to the creation of the "Skirmishing Fund" by O'Donovan Rossa, which is described in more detail later.

Reflecting the continuing loss of power (and perhaps patience) of the early leaders, John O'Mahony resigned as Head Centre in January 1877 and was succeeded in February by O'Donovan Rossa. He, in turn, resigned as Head Centre in August 1878, after raising 73,000 dollars for the Skirmishing Fund.[8] Although the Brotherhood continued to exist, a complication arose for the group. This was the emergence of another Irish nationalist group in the US that was partly an ally and partly a competitor.

The Clan na Gael

The Clan na Gael was also called the United Brotherhood in English. The formation of this organization actually came fairly early, in 1867, but its significance increased significantly after the Fenian fiasco of 1870. The reason that the Clan na Gael has to be discussed, even rather briefly, is that most of its leaders and a major portion of its followers had been members of the Fenian Brotherhood and continued to be viewed in the government's and public's eyes as Fenians. At times, in fact, some members seemed to drift between the two groups depending on the particular political or individual situation.

John Devoy detailed the early political initiatives in the formation of the Clan na Gael:

> The position of Chief Executive of the Irish Republican Brotherhood was filled by the unanimous election of Colonel Thomas J. Kelly. And, after a great deal of thought was given to the necessities of the Home Organization, a plan was prepared by me as Secretary, and presented to the Convention in the form of Resolutions, which were passed by an overwhelming vote. The chief provisions of this measure may be paraphrased as follows:
>
> 1. The Home Organization to be self-sustaining, each member paying into the local Circle a certain sum per week.
>
> 2. The American officers to be located in the various populous [sic] centres, according to the strength of the organization in each centre or city, and to be maintained by the funds of the local Circle or Circles.
>
> 3. One of the American officers thus assigned by Headquarters to any city was to serve as intermediary through whom the Executive could be reached without delay by the Centres of the local Circles.
>
> 4. The honest and deceived members of the "wings" in America, whose hatred of England was appealed to in order to lead them into channels of effort which in fact resulted in withdrawing their aid from the I. R. B., were now to be approached and organized into a new body—in America—the good men of the "wings" in America were to be selected and formed into a new American body, working directly with the Home Organization. The new organization in America to be known as the Clan-na-Gael.

These resolutions had other provisions, not necessary to cite here. The fourth provision went into active operation without delay, and soon after, the Napper Tandy Club was organized in New York, being the first Club of the Clan-na-Gael.[9]

According to Devoy, the Clan na Gael was formally founded by Jerome Collins in the home of James Sheedy in Hester Street New York on June

[handwritten note: Competition of Irish nationalist orgs. Hard to keep them straight.]

20, 1867, the anniversary of the birth date of Theobald Wolfe Tone, one of the earlier heroes of Irish rebellion in 1763. Collins proposed a plan to abduct Queen Victoria's grandson, Prince Arthur of Connaught, then holidaying in the US, and hold him as hostage in return for the release of Irish prisoners held by the British. In an evident attempt to reunite the main groups of the Irish nationalist movements, the plot was to use members of both wings of the Fenian Brotherhood and the IRB. This plan never got beyond the discussion stage, but suggested the future direction of Fenianism. As the Fenian Brotherhood became viewed as increasingly irrelevant to active measures supporting Irish nationalism, both former Fenians and new recruits who were looking for a militant approach to the independence struggle gravitated to the Clan. Its leader claimed by 1876 to have more than 11,000 members.[10]

The leaders of the Clan na Gael stressed secrecy both in its day-to-day activities and in its operational plans. In contrast to the American Fenian Brotherhood, it did not fight the label of "secret society," but in some ways seemed to revel in it. The group had secret identification signs, secret handshakes, and special secret initiation rites. Many contemporary observers suggested that many of the Clan's rituals were very similar to those of the Masons at the time, and this probably was a fair assessment. The effectiveness of the Clan na Gael's efforts to preserve secrecy might be illustrated by the fact that many of its secret rituals were described by Henri le Caron, who earlier had been a British agent operating against the Fenians. As the Clan became more significant, le Caron's British handlers reactivated him, and he rather quickly became a trusted member of the new group.

The Clan na Gael was led by an executive board, which in common with many of the secretive rituals was called the FC.[11] It was run by a chairman who was elected at an annual convention. Instead of using the Brotherhood's nomenclature of circles led by centers, the Clan used the terms "camps" and "guardians." Although in theory designed to coordinate all the other nationalist organizations, the Clan began to consume the American groups whole. The two wings of the Fenian movements in Ireland, the IRB and the Supreme Council, proved to be more difficult. The IRB was the toughest holdout, with Stephens demanding very tough conditions.[12] The Supreme Council after some negotiations did agree to form a union with the Clan, provided that the Americans provide financial assistance to the Irish nationalists. This alliance, however, remained on very shaky foundations.

The Catalpa Saga

The previous history of the Fenians and the IRB meant that even after the Clan na Gael became a separate organization, the Fenian links remained strong. One of the more dramatic episodes of the "neo-Fenianism" of the Clan had its antecedents in the 1867 rebellion. In the wake of the uprising, a number of Irish soldiers in the British army who had shown Fenian sympathies were court-martialed and sentenced to be transported to Australia. John Devoy in particular kept these soldiers in mind, particularly after he and an associate received letters from the Australian exiles asking not to be forgotten. Devoy had, in fact, personally recruited one of the soldiers. In 1874, he and the delegates at the Baltimore convention determined to do something to free the prisoners, who were held at Freemantle Prison in Australia.

The plan they devised is worthy of a Hollywood blockbuster. The whaling ship *Catalpa* was bought and fitted out for the rescue mission. The only person on board who initially knew the plot was the captain, George S. Anthony. The ship set out on April 27, 1875. Its first few months at sea were spent in the normal whaling areas in the Atlantic, and the crew actually spent the time hunting whales. The rationale was that this would provide good cover for the mission, plus it could provide profits from the sale of the whale oil to help defray the costs of the operation.

As the ship reached the Canary Islands, the new course for Australia would take the *Catalpa* out of any logical whaling routes, so Captain Anthony revealed the voyage's real purpose to his first mate, who agreed to follow the Captain's orders. The rest of the crew remained in the dark, however. The ship raced toward Australia, reaching Bunbury on March 27, 1876. In the meantime, Clan officials John J. Breslin and Thomas Desmond had been making arrangements inside Australia for the prison break. They made regular contact with the Fenian prisoners while they were on work details, and they coordinated a link-up between Captain Anthony and the six prisoners when he came ashore under very rough conditions. He and his shore crew were unable to make the initial rendezvous, but after avoiding British security officials, on April 17 the captain brought off the prisoners. On its way out of Australian waters, the *Catalpa* was intercepted by an armed British vessel that fired a shot across her bow. Captain Anthony pointed toward the US flag on the stern of the *Catalpa* and more or less dared the British captain to create a war. The British backed down, and the

Catalpa sailed on, reaching New York on August 19, 1876, to the expected hero's welcome.

The publicity given both to the return of the Cuba Five and the *Catalpa* rescue was very helpful to the Fenians. In a real sense, the Fenians may have gotten more advantage than the Clan na Gael due to the latter's insistence on secrecy. Even Clan operations were likely to be ascribed to the Fenians, especially given that many of the Clan members were former Fenians of one stripe or another and they continued to receive that label by the press and public. Within the Irish nationalist movement itself, the two movements tended to overlap for a few years, but the Clan appeared to be in a position to take charge of the movement in the US. It then, however, faced the same crisis as the Fenian Brotherhood did earlier: a major split in the leadership. John Devoy in New York began being challenged by Alexander Sullivan in Chicago. Virtually all historians have labeled Sullivan as being both crooked and a political opportunist. These views may very well be correct, but it also should be noted that Devoy was instrumental in writing the early narrative about the leadership struggle, which became intense. Devoy brought Sullivan up before a Clan tribunal for various financial crimes, but the trial was stacked with Sullivan's supporters, and he continued in his positions in Chicago and generally won the leadership struggle. The Clan continued to be an important player in the nationalist movement, but was weakened for a number of years. This helped lead to the reemergence of O'Donovan Rossa and the spread of "skirmishing."

The Fenian Terrorism Campaign

Although the IRB and Irish Americans operating in Ireland and England initially did not engage in widespread assassinations, there were a handful of early murders of informers and particularly "troublesome" police.[13] In general, however, most leaders focused on a "clean" struggle, even if this was ineffectual. O'Donovan Rossa sought to change all this through "skirmishing." In his mind—and in his statements—the use of "skirmishing" had a significantly different meaning than it does today; for him it meant terrorism directed against England. He made an effort to revive the Fenian Brotherhood in 1885 basically in an attempt to provide a regular funding stream for his bombing campaign. Rossa tied the Brotherhood closely to the *United Irishman* as its official organ. This newspaper was very militant, reflecting Rossa's statement that "This dynamite work will go on till Ireland if free, or till London is laid in ashes."[14]

O'Donovan Rossa was supported in the "skirmishing" aspirations by Patrick Ford, the editor of the Irish American newspaper, *The Irish World*. For example, an editorial in the December 4, 1875, proclaimed: "We must *take the offensive!* Action gives life, action gives health. At present the Irish cause is received with a hiss and a sneer. This is telling against us. A few bold and devoted heroes must spring up and show the world there is still power in Fenianism not only to scare, but to *hurt* England."[15] In addition to providing editorial support, the newspaper also provided the names of fund subscribers and how much they contributed in an effort to drum up more contributions. In a later edition, Ford was even more explicit about the ultimate goal:

> [Fenian operatives could enter] London unknown and unnoticed. When the night for action came . . . this little band would deploy, each man setting about his own allotted task, and no man save the captain of the band alone, knowing what any other man was to do, and *at the same instant strike with lightening* [sic] *the enemy of their land and race . . . in two hours from the word of command London would be in flames, shooting up to the heavens in fifty different places.*[16]

The strategy of conducting terrorist attacks certainly was not universally accepted by Irish nationalists, nor more specifically by Fenian leaders. Many argued against it on purely moral grounds, while others saw it as counterproductive to larger strategic goals. Some such as John Devoy seemed to be less concerned about either the morality or strategy than the fact that O'Donovan Rossa continued to be very public about his determination to continue the bombing. Certainly, an undercover campaign was not always aided by continual airing of the group's intentions.

Devoy and the Clan seemed to have mixed feelings about the terrorist campaign. Although generally condemning it in public, they seemed to have considerably more mixed feelings in private. In his later writing, Devoy suggested that no matter how unfortunate, terrorism worked:

> When William E. Gladstone in 1869 introduced the Bill to disestablish the Protestant Church in Ireland (in which the Irish people were not particularly interested) he admitted in his speech that his new outlook on Irish affairs was due to the intensity of Fenianism. His remarks on that occasion proved a stronger argument in favor of physical force—and even of Terrorism—

Too much detail. This is a mere postscript.

164   Rebels on the Niagara

on the part of Ireland to secure justice and freedom, than any Irishman ever made.[17]

O'Donovan Rossa's involvement in the bombing campaign was more than just rhetorical. He established the Brooklyn Dynamite School about 1881 or 1882 to teach bomb-making skills. Officially called the Mansonitor Manufacturing and Experimental Chemical Company as its cover identity, the school provided a month-long course for which it charged students 30 dollars. The chief instructor was "Professor Mezzeroff," a purported Russian bomb expert; in reality, he was Richard Rodgers, a Manhattan liquor salesman. Students who attended the school were expected to learn enough so that they could then go to England and train others in the finer arts of bomb making. Along with the students, bomb-making material flowed from the US to England. British security officials noted at the time that timers and detonating devices that they were able to intercept became increasingly sophisticated.

There was some coordination between the IRB Supreme Council and the American bombers, but this was far from perfect. Likewise, the Clan and O'Donovan Rossa established a modus vivendi; again, however, there were continual stresses in their relations. The actual bombing campaign in England and the convoluted politics surrounding it are too complex to cover in any detail. An excellent treatment of the bombings and British countermeasures—both of which became very brutal—is provided by Shane Kenna in *War in the Shadows: The Irish-American Fenians Who Bombed Victorian Britain.* The bombings lasted from 1881 to 1885, with a very mixed record of success. Perhaps the eeriest in terms of historical parallels to the 2005 London bombings was the simultaneous bombing of two London underground trains on October 30, 1883. Beyond this, targets included both government buildings and treasured landmarks. Throughout the bombings, Irish Americans were deeply involved in the campaign as leaders, smugglers, and coordinators.

Virtually every observer at the time termed the terrorist attacks as "Fenian bombings." In a real sense, any armed action by Irish or Irish Americans was ascribed to the Fenians. Given the backgrounds of many of the bombers and perhaps more importantly their leaders, this was virtually inevitable and, in fact, justified. At the same time, however, the Fenian Brotherhood itself had virtually collapsed as a coherent organization. In a real sense, the Fenian Brotherhood and the IRB had given birth to a philosophy and strategy that had moved beyond their control.

One further somewhat curious example of the continued relevance of the Fenian label was the so-called Fenian Ram, an early submarine built by John Holland, who became known in many circles as the father of the modern submarine. Holland, who was not shy about self-promotion, called this vessel Holland Boat Number II, but the press quickly labeled it as the *Fenian Ram*. It was launched in 1881 at the Delamater Iron Company in New York and was funded by the Skirmishing Fund. The submarine, operated by a three-person crew and armed with a 230mm pneumatic gun, was intended for use against British ships. It was launched and conducted a number of test dives. After a funding dispute between the Skirmishing Fund and Holland, members of the group stole the submarine and moved it to New Haven, Connecticut. They, however, found no one who actually could operate it, and they abandoned it. The *Fenian Ram* still exists and is on display at the Paterson Museum in New Jersey.

The Fates of the Fenian Leaders

Although the later years of some of the Fenian leaders already have been discussed, the fates of some of the others should be mentioned. James Stephens returned to the US in September 1871, where he got in the wine import business. This, however, was a failure, and he returned to France in 1874. He continued to be viewed as the "founding father" of the Fenian movement, an image that he certainly did not dissuade. As the Fenian Brotherhood began its descent into increasing irrelevancy, it turned to Stephens as somewhat a compromise candidate as leader. The January 27, 1876, convention not only reelected O'Mahony as Head Centre, but it also resolved that Stephens be restored to previous position as chief organizer. In January 1879, Stephens once again sailed to the US and assumed leadership of the Fenian Brotherhood. This was, however, a failure, and he returned to France at the end of 1880. Stephens was allowed to return to Ireland in 1891 (clearly indicating that the British government viewed him as a minimal threat), and he died there in 1901.

After Sweeny resigned from the Brotherhood in 1866, he was restored as an officer in the US army. There he rather quickly made brigadier general, and he retired in 1870. As noted earlier, Roberts had a very successful political career after his leadership of the Fenians. This also was the case with many lower-ranking members of the Brotherhood who became local political leaders in cities such as New York and Buffalo. John O'Neill may have had the longest-lasting memorial of any of the American Fenian leaders. After his failed foray into Western Canada, he established a town in Nebraska, which was named for him in 1874. The website of O'Neill, Nebraska, which bills itself as Nebraska's Irish Capital, prominently displays John O'Neill's history.

After resigning from the Fenian Brotherhood, John O'Mahony sank both into obscurity and poverty. Never wealthy, he ended his life in absolute penury. Even when offered financial assistance, O'Mahony generally refused to accept it. He died in New York City in a cold water flat in 1877 shortly after leaving office. Perhaps the only consolation he might have felt if he had known was that his body was returned to Dublin and interred with a major public ceremony. As John Devoy noted somewhat ruefully, "But the fine funeral was supposed to compensate for all this. No matter how the Irish treat a leader when living—and the treatment is often very bad—they never fail to give him decent burial."[18] Likewise, Jeremiah O'Donovan Rossa sank into severe alcoholism, but survived until 1915, dying in Staten Island. The return of his body to Ireland and his burial were attended with massive ceremony.

General Millen, the erstwhile senior Fenian military leader and British agent, became a correspondent for South American reporting for the *New York Herald*. He then returned to military adventures, joining the forces of Guatemala in their campaign against El Salvador. After the leader of the Guatemalans was killed in battle, Millen briefly returned to New York and then Mexico. He also resumed his work as a British spy, with his reporting continuing through the 1880s. Henri le Caron testified in open court during a trial in 1889 regarding Charles Stewart Parnell and his links with the Fenians. This meant that his career as an agent was at an end. He died in 1894.

Michael Scanlon, the "Fenian Poet," also faced financial difficulties with his candy business as a result of spending so much time publishing the *Irish Republic*. In 1873, he shut down the newspaper and joined the federal government in the State Department. In a few years, he became chief of the Bureau of Statistics. According to one (biased) source, he was temporarily demoted as a result of British pressure: "Information [he provided] was passed on to American businessmen and as a result the foreign trade of the United States was substantially increased to the detriment of British trade, a result entirely satisfying to Michael Scanlan. The British soon realised what was happening and used all their social and diplomatic influence to discredit Scanlan."[19] He retired in 1912 and died in 1917 in

Chicago. John Devoy was the longest lived of the Fenians. He lived to see the Irish Uprising of 1916 and the Irish War of Independence.

With the death of the founders, the Fenian Brotherhood passed into history. With a formal existence of less than thirty years, and effective for a much shorter period, the Brotherhood was relatively short-lived. Nevertheless, it was important not only for the overall Irish nationalist movement, but also for the US and more specifically New York State. The benign neglect shown by elements of the US government and the more active support by state and local officials toward the Brotherhood enabled the rise of a state within the state. However much the Fenians maintained their loyalty to the American and state governments—and this remained very solid—their military operations against both the Canadians and the British led to an immensely complicated situation for about two decades.

The Fenian Brotherhood also provided early examples of issues that later plagued both Irish nationalist movements and other groups: problems in coordinating transnational operations; in-fighting among the leadership; organizational splits; maintaining security; and bitter debates over the most promising strategies to achieve their goals. Although ultimately a failure, the Fenian Brotherhood remains an important element of American and New York nineteenth-century history and with significant impact on later Irish nationalism.

Appendix 1

The Fenian Constitutions of 1863 and 1865

Two constitutions are provided here. The first is the 1863 Fenian constitution under the O'Mahony regime and is reprinted here in full to enable a sense of the development of the organization under his control. Many of the provisions in the 1865 constitution are the same or only slightly changed, but there were some significant developments in respect to organization. The key changes included:

1. The removal of the need for the Head Centre to "be subject to the acknowledgment of the C. E. of the I. R. B."; that is, to be approved by James Stephens of the Irish Fenians.

2. The establishment of a Central Council.

3. The banning of religious discussions.

4. Strengthening the authority of the Head Centre and Central Council.

The second constitution is that of the Senate Wing of the Brotherhood under Roberts. This significantly changed the power dynamics of the organization.Beyond the predominance of power it gave to the Fenian Senate, it also provided a major increase in the controls over the financial processes of the group. After this constitution, O'Mahony continued to rule his wing under the earlier 1865 constitution.

One note should be provided on the sourcing. The first two constitutions are taken from proceedings of Fenian congresses, and they should be regarded as official. This version of the Roberts constitution was published in the *Chicago Tribune* of November 8, 1865. One section of the constitution was cut from the article, and it is an unofficial transcript of the document.

1863 Constitution and By-Laws

1. The Fenian Brotherhood.

The Fenian Brotherhood is a DISTINCT and INDEPEN-DENT organization. It is composed, in the first place, of Citizens of the United States of America of Irish birth and lineage; and, in the second place, of Irishmen and of Friends of Ireland living elsewhere on the American Continent and in the Provinces of the British Empire, wherever situated.

Its Headquarters are and shall be within the limits of the United States of America. Its members are bound together by the following general pledge:

2. General Pledge of Membership.

I . . . . .solemnly pledge my sacred word of honor as a truthful and honest man, that I will labor with earnest zeal for the liberation of Ireland from the yoke of England, and for the establishment of a Free and Independent Government on the Irish soil ; that I will implicitly obey the commands or my superior officers in the Fenian Brother hood; that I will faith-fully discharge my duties of membership as laid down in the Constitution and By-Laws thereof; that I will do my utmost to promote feelings of love, harmony, and kindly forbearance among all Irishmen; and that I will foster, defend and propagate the aforesaid Fenian Brotherhood to the utmost of my power.

3. Form of Organization.

The Fenian Brotherhood shall be sub-divided into State Organi-zations, Circles, and Sub-Circles. - it shall be directed and gov-erned by a Head Centre, to direct the whole organization; State

Centres to direct State Organizations; Centres, to direct Circles;
and Sub-Centres to direct Sub-Circles. The Head Centre shall be
assisted by a Central. Council of Five; by a Central Treasurer and
Assistant Treasurer; by a Central Corresponding Secretary and a
Central Recording Secretary; and by such intermediate officers
as the Head Centre may, from time to time, deem necessary for
the efficient working of the organization.

4. The Head Centre.

The Head Centre shall be elected annually by a General Congress
of Representatives of the Fenian Brotherhood, which Congress
shall be composed of the State Centres, and the Centres, together
with Elected Delegates from the several Circles of the organization—each Circle "in good standing " being entitled to elect
one Delegate. A Circle to be in good standing must have made
regular and satisfactory reports, through its Centre, to its State
Centre and Head Centre within a period of nine weeks previous
to a General Congress.

The election of the Head Centre shall be subject to the acknowledgment of the C. E. of the I. R. B.

5. The Central Council.

The Central Council shall consist of five Centres, who shall be
nominated by the Head Centre and elected at a General Congress.
– The Central Council shall, in whole or in part, be subject to
the call of the Head Centre when he may deem it expedient.

6. The Central Treasurer, Assistant Central Treasurer, Central
Corresponding Secretary, Central Recording Secretary.

The Central Treasurer and the Assistant Treasurer shall be nominated by the Head Centre and elected at a General Congress of
the Fenian Brotherhood. The Central Treasurer shall be required
to furnish bonds in such a manner as the Head Centre and
Central Council may direct, in order to secure to the pecuniary interests of the Fenian Brotherhood an absolute protection.

The Head Centre can, with the consent of the Central Council, remove or change the Central Treasurer.

The Central Treasurer shall pay to the order of the Head Centre such sums as he may have funded of the moneys of the Brotherhood, but he shall retain receipts as vouchers therefor, in order to exhibit a clear financial statement to the Central Council.

The Central Secretaries shall be appointed by the Head Centre.

7. State Centres.

State Centres shall, upon the recommendation of the majority of the Centres in the several States, be appointed and commissioned by the Head Centre, who shall also have the power of rejecting the appointment, and, with the assent of the Central Council, of changing or appointing State Centres. The State Centre shall control entirely the organization in his State. He shall establish Circles and communicate with all parties therein who desire instruction or advice. The State Centre shall make a consolidated report on the tenth of each month to the Head Centre, thoroughly explanatory of the condition of the organization of his State. He shall, if he deems proper, mark out a route in his State for an agent to traverse, with instructions to canvass and organize the same.

The consolidated report is appended in skeleton in the appendix to these By-Laws.

8. Centres.

Centres shall be elected by Circles, and after the approval of the Head Centre shall be commissioned by the State Centre; each commission being countersigned by the Head Centre. The Centre shall preside at all regular meetings of his Circle, and shall report upon the 2th of each month to the State Centre, setting forth the condition of his increase or decrease, with names, and the average attendance of members, the amount of moneys received, amount distributed for local expenditures, with the balance remitted, on the 25th, to the Head Centre.

The Centre shall be authorized to establish Sub-Circles, and to commission Sub-Centres, after their election by said Sub-Circles, with the approval of the State Centre.

9. Sub-Centres.

The Sub-Centre shall preside at all regular meetings of his Sub-Circle, and shall report once a month to his Centre upon whatever stated day the said Centre shall determine.

10. Sub-Circles.

Sub-Circles shall be established only in cities or towns where the number of members is so large as to interfere with efficient transaction of business. ' The Centre will make the partition of Sub-Circles, and hold a consolidated meeting of all his said Sub-Circles once in three months.

11. Presiding Officers.

In the absence of State Centres, Centres and Sub-Centres, the Chairman of the Committee of Safety shall preside at business meetings.

12. Treasurer of Circle or Sub-Circle.

A Treasurer shall be nominated and selected by each Circle and Sub-Circle. It shall be his duty to make up a financial report to be embodied in the monthly report of the Centre, on the 25th of each month. The balance on hand he shall forward to the Head Centre on the same stated day, every month, without fail.

13. Secretary of Circle or Sub-Circle.

A Secretary shall be nominated and elected by each Circle and Sub-Circle of the Fenian Brotherhood. It shall be his duty to make a faithful record of the proceedings of each meeting; he shall keep the financial accounts and shall sign all the official reports of his Circle or Sub-Circle, and shall in all things comport himself in accordance with the established duties of a Secretary.

14. The Committee of Safety

A Committee of Safety shall be established in each Circle and Sub-Circle. It shall consist of not less than Three nor more than Seven members, who shall be nominated by the Centre or Sub-Centre, and elected at a regular meeting of the Circle or Sub-Circle. This Committee shall have the power of receiving members, together with the power of expelling them; but in each case their action must be submitted for approval to a meeting of their Circle or Sub-circle. A vote of want of confidence in the Committee of Safety will necessitate. the immediate resignation of its members.

15. Admission of Members.

Every candidate for admission into the Fenian Brotherhood must be proposed two weeks before initiation.

16. Members in Good Standing.

Members in good standing are alone entitled to a voice in matters of business.

17. Meetings.

Each Circle and Sub-Circle of the Fenian Brotherhood shall meet once a week, for the transaction of business, at such time and place as may be deemed most in accordance with their interests and convenience. All discussions upon subjects connected with Religion or with American Politics, shall be peremptorily excluded from every meeting of the Fenian Brotherhood.

18. Dues and Initiation Fees.

The minimum established for the weekly dues is Five Cents for each member; the minimum for the initiation fee is One Dollar. Each Circle may, however, fix the amount of dues and initiation fees as may be deemed best for its interests.

19. Relations of Members and Officers of the Fenian Brotherhood.

Sub-Centres shall correspond with, and report to and be directed by Centres. Centres will correspond with, report to, and be directed by their State Centre. State Centres will correspond with, report to, and be directed by the Head Centre. No correspondence whatever can be held with Ireland or Europe on the business of the organization, except through the Head Centre. No communications on that business can be received in the United States from abroad except through the Head Centre. Any member, Sub-Centre, Centre, State Centre, or any officer whatever, derogating from this law shall be considered a traitor.

[20] Perfidy.

Perfidy on the part of a member or officer shall be punished by expulsion. Maligning the objects of the organization; Calumniating its officers or members; Conveying information to the enemy; Injuring seriously the organization by disgraceful conduct, shall constitute Perfidy. The names and descriptions of all persons guilty of Perfidy shall be sent by the Head Centre to all Circles throughout the United States, and to the C. E. in Ireland, to be there kept on record.

21. Members in Bad Standing.

Members who have not attended a meeting of their Circle or Sub-Circle for thirteen successive weeks, when their absence is not accounted for by a legitimate excuse, shall be considered in bad standing, and their names shall be stricken from the Roll of the Fenian Brotherhood. No member in bad standing shall enter into any Fenian Circle whatever until he has shown to the Committee of Safety of his previous Circle, sufficient cause to satisfy them of his firm resolve to act thenceforward the part of a truthful and steadfast Fenian.

Previous to his re-admission into the Brotherhood he shall pay a fine of not less than one dollar, and shall clear up all arrears of his weekly dues.

22. Men Coming from Abroad.

Men coming from abroad who represent themselves to be Fenian
Brothers, must be first recognized as such- by the Head Centre,
before admission to any Circle in the United States. Where it
is difficult to obtain this recognition, the Centre to whom the
party applies shall forward information and documents to the
State Centre, who will advise him in the case; otherwise the
applicant must be proposed in the regular manner, and be initiated as a new member.

23. Cards and Letters of Introduction.

When members change localities they shall carry a letter of
introduction and a certificate from the Centre of the Circle to
which they had been attached, to the Centre of the Circle to
which they are going. This will be taken up on presentation
and reported back to the Centre who issued it, and when found
correct, the member' shall be received forthwith. In places where
Circles are very large, cards may be issued to identify members.

24. Elections and Term of Office.

All the elected Officers of the several State organizations, Circles
and Sub-Circles of the Fenian Brotherhood shall hold office for
a period of not less than One Year from the date of their commissions, unless in case of resignation or dismissal.

25. Resignations and Dismissals.

Resignations, to be valid, must be, in the first instance, received
by a majority of the Circle or Sub-Circle of the resigning officer,
and next forwarded by his immediate superior to the Head
Centre for approval. Any officer of the Fenian Brotherhood may
be dismissed from his position for Perfidy, Neglect of Duty, or
Disobedience of Legitimate Orders, by a decree of his immediate
superior in command, or by a two-thirds vote of his constitu-
ents, subject, however, in each case, to the approval of the Head
Centre and a majority of the Central Council.

26. Jurisdiction of the Head Centre and Central Council.

The decision of the Head Centre, shall, with the written consent of the majority of the members of the Central Council be absolute and conclusive upon all points that are not specially provided for in these By-Laws, until the next annual session of the Congress of the Fenian Brother hood.

27. Annual Congress.

A Congress of the Fenian Brotherhood shall be held annually, during the month of November of each year, until the Independence of Ireland shall be thoroughly established. The Election of a Head Centre, Central Council, Central Treasurer and Assistant Central Treasurer, for the ensuing year, together with the confirmation of State Centres, for the same period, shall be made at the said annual Congress. It shall receive and confirm reports of the progress, strength, and pecuniary resources of the Fenian Organization during the current year, and shall make such alterations in its Constitution and By-Laws, as may be found necessary for its more efficient working. The said Annual Congress shall be held within the limits of the United States of America, at such place as shall seem fit to the Head Centre and Central Council.

28. Resolutions of the First Fenian Congress.

The Resolutions passed on the Fourth day of November, 1863, by the First Fenian Congress held in the City of Chicago, and State of Illinois, in the said month, and year, and, after mature deliberation, signed by the Centres, and Delegates there assembled, are, and shall be adopted as art of the Constitution and By-Laws of the Fenian Brotherhood.

29. Local By-Laws.

Each Circle shall have the power of enacting By-Laws for its special government. These shall be brief and comprehensive, and shall in no-wise conflict with the Constitution, and By-Laws of the Fenian Brotherhood. The Committee of Safety shall, in the first instance, prepare the said Local By-Laws, which shall be then sub mitted to the Circle for approval. The General Constitution and By-Laws together with the Resolutions of the First Fenian Congress, shall be read' once a month to the members of each Circle until they become thoroughly familiar with them.

1865 "Roberts Constitution"

We, the Fenians of the United States and other portions of America, in order to form a more perfect union, establish justice, insure domestic fraternity, and secure the blessings of liberty for the Irish race in Ireland, do ordain and establish this Constitution for the Fenian Brotherhood in the United States and other portions of America:

Article I.

SECTION 1. The Fenian Brotherhood is a distinct and independent organization.

It is composed, in the first place, of citizens of the United States of America, of Irish birth and lineage; and, in the second place, of Irishmen and friends of Ireland living on the American Continent and in the Provinces of the British Empire, wherever situated.

Its headquarters are, and shall be, within the limits of the United States of America.

SEC. 2. Its members are bound together by the following General Pledge.

I, _____ solemnly pledge by my sacred word of honor, as a truthful and honest man, that I will labor with earnest zeal for the liberation of Ireland from the yoke of England, and for the establishment of a free and independent government on the Irish soil; that I will implicitly obey the commands of my superior officers in the Fenian Brotherhood, in all things appertaining to my duty as a member thereof; that I will faithfully discharge my duties of membership as laid down in the Constitution and By-Laws thereof; that I will do my utmost to promote feelings of love, harmony, and kindly forbearance among all Irishmen; and that I will foster, defend and propagate the aforesaid Fenian Brotherhood to the utmost of my power.

SEC. 3. The Fenian Brotherhood shall be sub-divided into State, district and local Circles – States and districts to be district and controlled by State and district Centres, and local Circles by Centers who shall reside within the limits of their respective jurisdictions.

ARTICLE II.

SECTION 1. All legislative powers herein granted shall be vested in aa Congress of the Fenian Brotherhood of the United States and other portions of America, which shall consist of a Senate and a Representative body.

SEC. 2. The Representatives shall be delegates chosen every year by the Brotherhood in good standing, of the several States and districts. Delegates shall be apportioned among the several States and districts which may be included within the Union and other portions of America, according to their respective number of Circles, each Circle being entitled to one delegate for every one hundred members, more or less, but not less than ten, and one additional delegate for a fractional part of one hundred members exceeding fifty of such Circle.

SEC. 3. The Senate of the Fenian Brotherhood of the United States and other portions of America, shall be composed of fifteen (15) Senators; they shall be nominated by a committee of two from each State and district, elected by the delegates of each State and district in Congress assembled; and such nominees shall be elected by a two-thirds vote of said Congress.

SEC. 4. Each body shall elect its own presiding officers, and shall be the judge of the election returns and qualifications of its own members, and a majority of each body shall constitute a quorum for the transaction of business; but a smaller number may adjourn from day to day, and may be authorized to compel the attendance of absent members in such manner and under such penalties as such body may provide.

SEC. 5. Each body may determine the rules of its proceeding, punish its members for disorderly behavior, and, with the concurrence of two-thirds, expel a member.

SEC. 6. The Senate shall keep a journal, and furnish its members and the Secretary of the Brotherhood with a record of its proceedings; and said Secretary shall furnish such information as may be contained therein to the Representatives of the Brotherhood of the several States, excepting such parts as may, in their judgment, require secrecy.

SEC. 7. The Senate shall choose from their body a permanent President, who shall be Vice President of the Fenian Brotherhood, and in case of the death, impeachment, inability to act, or removal of the President of the Fenian Brotherhood of the United States, shall act as President of the Fenian Brotherhood.

SEC. 8. The Senate shall have the sole power to try all impeachments; when sitting they shall be on oath; and should it become necessary to try the President or Vice-President of the Fenian Brotherhood, the Senate shall elect its presiding officer pro tempore, and no person shall be convicted without the concurrence of two-thirds of the Senate.

No ex post facto laws shall be passed.

SEC. 9. Judgment inn [sic] cases of impeachment shall be final and at the discretion of the Senate.

The Senate shall meet in perpetual sessions while in officer, and organize within two days after their election, and shall have power to adjourn from time to time as they may determine.

SEC. 10. The General Congress shall assemble at least once in every year, and such meeting shall be on the first Tuesday of September, at such place as the President and Senate may deem fit.

SEC. 11. All propositions for raising revenue and fixing salaries of officers and employes [sic] of the Brotherhood shall originate in the Senate, and be referred to the President of the Fenian Brotherhood for ratification; if he approve[sic], he shall sign and return within twenty-four hours after the receipt thereof; if he do [sic] not approve he shall indorse his objection and return the same to that body, who shall enter his objections at large to that body, who shall enter his objections at large upon the journal, and proceed to reconsider. The President of the Senate then shall assemble the Senate, if not already assembled, and present the objections, and then, if the proposition receive a two-thirds vote, it shall become an ordinance; and, in failure to return within one day, the action of the Senate, by a two-thirds vote, shall become a law.

SEC. 12. The records of the voting, in all such cases, shall be taken and entered at large upon the journal of that body.

No salaried officer shall be a member of the Senate.

SEC. 12. [sic] No appropriation of money shall be made but by a vote of the Senate of the Fenian Brotherhood, subject to the conditions and qualifications laid down in Sec. 11, referring to raising revenue and fixing salaried officers.

ARTICLE III.

SECTION 1. The executive power of the Fenian Brotherhood shall be vested in the President, who shall hold his term of office for one year, and be elected for said term by a General Congress of the Senate and House of Delegates.

SEC. 2. Said Congress shall elect the President by ballot, and a quorum for this purpose shall consist of two-thirds of said

Senators and Delegates, but a majority of the whole shall be necessary to a choice.

SEC. 3. The President shall receive for his services a stated compensation, which shall be neither increased nor diminished during the period for which he shall have been elected.

SEC. 4. Before he enters upon the duties of his office, the President shall take the following oath or affirmation:

"I do solemnly swear (or affirm) that I will faithfully execute the duties of the office of President of the Fenian Brotherhood of the United States, and other portions of America, and will to the best of my ability preserve, protect and defend the Constitution of the Fenian Brotherhood."

SEC. 5. The President of the Fenian Brotherhood shall nominate a Secretary of Military Affairs, a Secretary of the Treasury, a Secretary of Naval Affairs, and a Secretary of Civil Affairs, whose nominations shall be approved by the Senate; and in case the President fail within a reasonable period to nominate such heads of bureaus, the Senate by a vote of two-thirds of their body shall fill such positions, having previously given the President twenty-four hours notice of their intention to do so; and such heads of such departments, are hereby constituted a board of advisers to the Executive, and in case of a disagreement between them and the Executive upon any point involving the welfare of the Brotherhood, the same shall be referred to the Senate, whose decision on the point shall be final until the assembling of the next Congress.

SEC. 6. The President shall have power, by and with the advice and consent of the Senate, to make arrangements and treaties with persons or powers friendly to the objectives of the Fenian Brotherhood, and shall by and with the advice and consent of the Senate, appoint all envoys and ambassadors, and all other officers of the Fenian Brotherhood, whose appointments are not herein otherwise provided for, and which may be established under the provisions of this Constitution.

SEC. 7. In case any vacancy should occur in any of the departments, or State Centres, by death, resignation or dismissal, such vacancy shall be filled by the President with the approval and consent of the Senate, such appointee to hold the office during the unexpired term.

SEC. 8. The President may on extraordinary occasions convene both houses, or either of them, and in case of disagreement between them, with respect to the time of adjournment, each body may adjourn to such time and place as they shall deem proper.

SEC. 9. The President shall receive envoys and other public ministers. He shall take care that the laws be faithfully executed, and shall commission the Central officers and State Centres.

SEC. 10. The President, Vice President and all civil officers of the Fenian Brotherhood shall be removed from office and expelled, on impeachment for and conviction of treason, bribery, or other high crimes and misdemeanors.

[Newspaper: *Article IV. relates to State and District organizations, the details of which possess no general interest. Section 18, however, is a curiosity:*]

SEC. 18. Communications on official matters passing between the Fenian Brotherhood and the I. H. [Stephens], and any *State or Power* [italics in original] whatever, shall, previous to despatch [sic], or immediately on receipt, be submitted to the President of the Fenian Brotherhood, the President of the Senate, and, if necessary, the Cabinet and Senate. Communications from the I. R. shall be received in the first instance by the President, and, as before provided, laid immediately before the Senate. Communications from the I. R. shall be received in the first instance by the President, and, as before provided, laid immediately before the Senate. No communication shall be had by the President of the Senate, Secretaries of Bureaux, or any official, with the I. R., or any Power, save by and with the knowledge or consent of the President, or the order of a two-third vote of the Senate.

Secretary Of The Treasury

He shall be appointed by the President, by and with the consent and approval of the Senate, and shall have full supervision and control of the Financial Department, shall daily audit the accounts of all officers thereof, and make weekly reports of the receipts and expenditures in the same to the President and Senators. He shall employ such additional assistance as he may find necessary by and with the consent and approval of the Senate.

Agent Of The Irish Republic

He shall be appointed by the President, by and with the consent and approval of the Senate, and be subordinate to and under the control of the Secretary of the Treasury, shall sign all Bonds as Agent of the Irish Republic on receipt of voucher from the Treasurer that thee moneys therefor have been received by him, which voucher he shall file in his department. He shall also assist as Secretary for the Secretary of the Treasury, and make out a daily statement of the business of his office for the examination and auditing of the Secretary of the Treasury.

Subscription Agent

He shall be appointed by the President, by and with the consent and approval of the Senate, and shall be subordinate to and under control of the Secretary of the Treasury. He shall receive all orders for Bonds, and on receipt thereof take the letters unopened to the Treasurer and Corresponding Secretary, in whose presence they shall be opened. He shall receive blank Bonds, and a voucher for the amount of moneys contained therein -- these letters or orders shall be retained by him, and filed in his department. He shall take said blank Bonds to the agent of the Irish Republic, presenting said agent with the Treasurer's receipt or voucher; and, on the said agent signing said bonds, he shall receive, stamp and issue the same to parties ordering them, keeping a receipt book or other voucher, which shall state the date, number, amount and description of bonds, by whom ordered, on whose account, how dispatched and when.

Treasurer

He shall be appointed by the President, by and with the consent and approval of the Senate, and give bonds to amount of five hundred thousand dollars, to be approved of by the President and Senate, which shall consist of bonds, mortgages on real estate, and other collaterals. He shall be under the supervision and control of the President, and Secretary of the Treasury, and may be removed on the recommendation of the President by a vote of two-thirds of the Senate. He shall receive all moneys of the organization from all sources, and pay out no moneys without an order from the Secretary of the Treasury. Said order must fully explain the object the money is required for; and, if a bill, it must be attached and the items explained therein. He shall in case of doubt refuse to pay until a majority of the Secretaries of the Bureaux shall so order by their indorsement. He shall be guided in payments by, and pay nothing foreign to the following heads, viz:

First – Remittances to I. R., on order of the President and President of the Senate.

Second – Secret service, by indorsement of the Head of Military Department.

Third – Organizing expenses, by indorsement of the Secretary of the Treasury.

Fourth – Salaries of officers, by indorsement of Secretaries of their respective Departments.

Fifth – Military envoys, by indorsement of the Head of that Department, or his deputy during his absence.

Sixth – Naval affairs, by indorsement of Secretary of that Department.

He shall render a daily statement of the receipts and expenditures, under their respective heads, for the examination and auditing of the Secretary of the Treasury.

He shall allow the Agent of the Irish Republic to examine his books, for the purpose of perfecting weekly statements to be furnished by the Secretary of the Treasury to the President and Senators.

He shall be entitled to employ an Assistant Treasurer, to be appointed by the President, by and with the consent and approval of the Senate, who shall give bonds in an amount sufficient to satisfy the Secretary of the Treasury, and whose business it shall be to keep the books of this department and superintend the same.

The Treasurer shall give to the Secretary of the Treasury a power of attorney for and in the name of the Assistant Treasurer, to be used only in case of accident to the Treasurer (or his blank check, as he may elect), for which the Secretary of the Treasury shall give him a bond of indemnity that it shall not be used improperly.

The Treasurer shall give a receipt for all moneys received from the several Circles and other sources (exclusive of bonds) to the Corresponding Secretary, who shall remit said receipts to the proper parties, keeping a record of his correspondence. All letters shall be opened in the presence of the Treasurer or Assistant Treasurer, Subscription Agent and Corresponding Secretary.

Corresponding Secretary

There shall be a Corresponding Secretary, who shall be under the supervision and control of the Secretary of the Treasury. He shall be appointed by the President, by and with the consent and approval of the Senate. He shall receive all correspondence connected with his department, in the presence of the Subscription Agent and Treasurer. He shall file all letters in his department from the several Circles and other sources, not connected with or in reference to the issue of bonds of the Irish Republic. He shall take receipts from the Treasurer for all money received (exclusive of subscriptions for bonds), and remit them to the proper parties.

Appendix 2

A Fenian Soldier's Account of 1866

The Buffalo Courier on May 29, 1893, published an account by one aged Fenian veteran of the raid. This later was reprinted Frank H. Severance, editor, Publications of The Buffalo Historical Society, Volume XXV, Buffalo: The Buffalo Historical Society, 1921, pp. 271–274. The newspaper did not identify the Fenian beyond the fact that he was a prominent citizen of Buffalo. According to the veteran, beyond the organized forces that crossed the border, other Fenians crossed somewhat independently (and at various dates) and generally created mischief. As with any veteran's account told long after the event, at least some of it almost certainly amounts to "war stories." As one of the few existing accounts by the Fenian rank and file, however, it is worth quoting at length:

> The Second New York Mounted Rifles [says our veteran raider] were organized in Buffalo late in the summer of 1862. Most of the boys who joined were from Erie and Niagara counties, though some hailed from farther east in the State. . . . There were forty of the company more hare-brained than the rest, and I was one of them. Five or six were of French descent, and the rest were Irish by birth or parentage. We were "the Fenian Forty." The French boys, myself included, were just as Irish as the rest; and when the regiment was mustered out in '66, we were in fine condition to fill up with enthusiasm for Fenianism, which was just beginning to be greatly agitated. The love of fresh excitement was as great as for the cause, and perhaps,

as someone remarked at the time, we were Fenians because we still had our old army jackets of blue with the most beautiful green binding and slashings on them. At any rate, we made our plans. We heard that a crossing was to be made by the main body of Fenians soon, and we determined to be the first of the aggressive forces. On the night of the 20th of May [this date may be subject to error], 1866, the Fenian Forty, in the full uniform of the Second Mounted Rifles, armed to the teeth with guns and sabres, and all our old accoutrements, congregated at the foot of Genesee street. All had come alone by roundabout ways, and our gathering was secret.

A dozen rowboats lay moored to the wharf. To whom they belonged we never knew. We silently manned them, muffled the oarlocks with our handkerchiefs, and without a sound pulled out into the river. We landed at Fort Erie, the first Fenian invaders. We pushed the boats out into the current to conceal the evidence of our landing, and started our raid.

Our object was plain. We were to capture and hold, money, horses and stores for the army that was yet to come. For fear that our whereabouts might be discovered if we remained so nearly opposite Buffalo, we immediately marched up the lake shore about ten miles, and began operations. We scoured the Canadians' farms from the lake back into the country half a dozen miles, and the length of the territory covered reached from Fort Erie a dozen miles westward.

In the first place, we captured enough horses for our own accommodation, and the farmers were obliged to furnish us all the food that we wanted for ourselves and our horses. We had had experience enough in the South to show us what should be captured in a raid like this. We harmed no one; there was no occasion for it. The 'Canucks' imagined, seeing our uniforms, that the United States had gone to war with Canada, and they made no resistance. We took money from the people only when they had a superfluity of it; such cases however were quite frequent. We made one old miser give up $200, and that was a lot of money then. We got along finely with our enterprise. A good quantity of horses and fodder was hidden in some isolated barns, and we had several stands of muskets in readiness for the coming forces. Finally we exhausted the horse and provender supply and started down toward the river. This was about ten days after our landing at Fort Erie. As we were marching we were met by Mike Mahany, whom we had sent the day previous down toward the river on a scout. He told us of the disastrous battle of Limestone Ridge, where several of O'Neill's boys were killed and wounded, and that the forces on the other side of the river had been ordered by the Government to disperse to their homes. The United States gunboat Michigan was lying in the middle of the river protecting the comparatively small force of Fenians from the British troops and preserving peace.

There was no use in going any further, and we decided that neither the Canadian authorities nor anybody else should ever have the satisfaction of knowing all the preparations we had made for an invasion that had proved a fiasco. We rode back to the western end of the territory which we had looted, gave back to the farmers what money we had taken, and further delighted them by telling them where they could find the 'borrowed' supplies, including the horses other than those we were riding. We restored all our remaining booty to its first owners. The fun was over, and we did not wish to profit by the misfortunes of these petty farmers. We rode down to Windmill Point, and I, being captain of the troop, ordered the horses set free. They scattered quickly, and no doubt galloped speedily home. We found fifteen rowboats at the beach.

We had considerable quantities of bedding, including many gay-colored spreads and comfortables [sic]. With these and some saplings we rigged the boats, and putting our Irish flag above my "flagship," we bade farewell to the land that we had wished to make the great "Irish Republic."

Appendix 3

General Sweeney's Proclamation to the Canadians in 1866

June 5

General Sweeney to the people of Canada:

We come among you as the foes of British rule in Ireland. Exiled from that native land of ours by the oppression of British aristocracy and legislation, our people hunted down to the emigrant ships, or worse, to that charnel of Government institutions, the poor-house; our countrymen torn from their families and friends and hurried in droves into the prison pens of England and Ireland; our country subjected to a foreign tyranny, which disenfranchises the mass of the Irish people and makes poverty and misery the sad rule of their condition, covering our fair land with paupers' graves and wretched hovels, eliciting from the liberal minds of England herself expressions of shame for the Government and indignation for the people.

We have taken up the sword to strike down the oppressors red, to deliver Ireland from the tyrant, the despoiler, the robber. We have registered our oaths upon the altar of our country in the full view of Heaven, and sent up our vows to the throne of Him who inspired them. Then, looking about us for the enemy, we find him here [italics in original] – here in your midst where he is most vulnerable and convenient to our strength; and have sworn to stretch forth the armed hand of Ireland and grapple with him. The battle has commenced, and we pledge ourselves to all the sacred memories of struggling liberty, to follow it up at any cost to either of two alternatives – the absolute political independence and liberty of Ireland or the demolition of our armies.

We have no issue with the people of these provinces, and wish to have none but the most friendly relations. Our weapons are for the oppressors of Ireland. Our blows shall be directed only against the power of England; her privileges alone shall we invade, not yours. We do not propose to divest you of a solitary right you now enjoy. We will assail and asperse only the rights that are claimed and enjoyed by the Government of Great Britain – the right to make her American possessions the field, and base of operations in a war against an enemy. We come to install ourselves in her possessions, and turn them against her in a war for Irish freedom. We are here, neither as murderers nor robbers, for plunder or spoliation. We are here as the Irish army of liberation; the friends of liberty against despotism, of democracy against aristocracy, of the people against their oppressors, of the ballot against the privileges of class, of progress and development against right or wrong; to conduct this contest according to the laws known to honorable warfare, in a manner worthy of the high object we aim for; and the sublime sentiments that actuated us. In a word, our war is with the armed power of England, and not with the people, not with these provinces. Against England upon land and sea, until Ireland is free! And all who raise an arm to defend her, to frustrate or defeat us, belong to the common enemy, and as such will be dealt with. As we know how to recognize the services of our friends, so also do we know how to punish the depredations of our foes. Our work for Ireland accomplished, we leave to your own free ballots to determine your natural and political standing and character, and shall rejoice to see, and assist to make, these limitless colonies spring from the foot of a foreign throne as free and independent, as proud as New York, Massachusetts, or Illinois. To that yearning for liberty and aspiration after natural independence which swells the breast of every true son of every land, to your own manliness we leave those questions for settlement, confident that the dwarfed development of your vast resources and natural wealth, made the chilling influences of English supremacy in wretched contrast with the national dignity and stupendous material prosperity of your neighboring people of the United States, under the stimulus of self-government and democratic institution, constitutes a stronger argument in favor of cooperation with us, and of the revolution in your political condition which this comparison suggests, that any discussion of the questions involved which we could offer here.

To Irishmen throughout these Provinces we appeal, in the name of seven centuries of British iniquity and Irish misery and suffering – in the name of our murdered sires, our desolate homes, our desecrated altars, our millions of famine graves, our insulted name and race – to stretch forth the hand of brotherhood in the holy cause of fatherland, and smite the tyrant where we can in his work of murdering our nation and exterminating our people. We conjure you, our countrymen who, from misfortunes inflicted by the very tyranny you are serving, or from any other cause, have been forced to enter the ranks of the enemy, not to be the willing instrument of your country's death or degradation. If Ireland still speaks to you in the truest impulses of your hearts, Irishmen, obey her voice! If you would not be miscreants, recreant to the first principles of your nature, engraven upon the very corner-stone of your being, raise not the hand of the matricide to strike down the banner of Erin! No uniform, and surely not the blood-dyed coat of England, can emancipate you from the natural law that binds your allegiance to Ireland, to liberty, to right, to justice. To the friends of Ireland, of freedom, of humanity, of the people, we offer the olive branch of peace and honest grasp of friendship. Take it, Irishmen, Frenchmen, Americans – take it all and trust it.

To all who marched to the call of the enemy, and rally under his standard to aid or abet his cause, we the sword in as firm and earnest a gripe [sic] as ever did its work upon a foeman. We wish to meet with friends, we are prepared to meet with enemies. We shall endeavor to merit the confidence of the former, and the latter can expect from us but the leniency of a determined though generous foe, and the restraints and relations imposed by civilized warfare.

T. W. Sweeney

Major General commanding the Armies of Ireland.

Notes

Foreword

1. John O'Leary, *Recollections of Fenians and Fenianism*, vol. 1 (London: Downey & Co, 1896), 80–81.

2. David A. Wilson, "The Fenians in Canada" (Ottawa: Library and Archives Canada, n.d.), 1.

3. Anthony Tyler D'Angelo, "The 1866 Fenian Raid on Canada West: A Study of Colonial Perceptions and Reactions towards the Fenians in the Confederation Era." Master's thesis, Queen's University, Kingston, Ontario, Canada, 2009, 43. Italics in original.

4. Susannah J. Ural, *The Harp and the Eagle: Irish-American Volunteers and the Union Army, 1861–1865* (New York: NYU Press, 2006), 13.

Chapter 1

1. John O'Leary, *Recollections of Fenians and Fenianism*, vol. 2 (London: Downey & Co, 1896), 39.

2. Joseph Denieffe, *A Personal Narrative of the Irish Revolutionary Brotherhood* (New York: Gael Publishing Company, 1906), viii. The various Irish nationalist movements frequently emphasized efforts to ally with enemies of Britain. In the case of the Russians, little momentum was achieved before the end of the Crimean War. Russia was a favored candidate as an ally for the Fenians, who approached Russian representatives several times during the period of the group's existence, seemingly every time Russo-British relations hit a rough patch.

3. Denieffe, 2–3.

4. In contemporary accounts, this group also was known as the Irish Revolutionary Brotherhood both by outsiders and at times by some of its members. It is unclear if this was simply confusion or if the group used slightly different titles at different periods.

5. John Savage, *Fenian Heroes and Martyrs* (Boston: Patrick Donohoe, 1868), 55.

6. O'Leary, 102. Other sources indicate that he was in an asylum for a brief time.

7. "The Fenian Explosion; Brief Sketch of the Origin and Progress of the Movement. The Fenian Senate Busy Yesterday," *New York Times* (December 13, 1865).

8. *New York Times* (April 11, 1866), 4.

9. For the lower estimate, *The Cleveland Leader* (September 29, 1865). It also claimed, however, that the circles were increasing by 100 circles per month. For the higher estimate, "The Fenian Explosion; Brief Sketch of the Origin and Progress of the Movement. The Fenian Senate Busy Yesterday," *New York Times* (December 13, 1865).

10. *Proceedings of the Second National Congress of the Fenian Brotherhood Held in Cincinnati, Ohio, January 1865* (Philadelphia: James Gibbons, 1865), 16–22. "Bad standing" represented those circles that had not kept up with their required dues.

11. *Proceedings of the First National Convention of the Fenian Brotherhood Held in Chicago, Illinois November 1863* (Philadelphia: James Gibbons, 1863), 8–9. Cited as *Chicago Proceedings* hereafter.

12. *Chicago Proceedings*, 50; *Cincinnati Proceedings*, 39.

13. Stanley Lebergott, "Wage Trends, 1800–1900," *Trends in the American Economy in the Nineteenth Century* (Princeton, NJ: Princeton University Press, 1960), 462.

14. Anonymous, *The Fenian Raid at Fort Erie, June the First and Second 1866* (Toronto: W.C. Chewett and Co., 1866), 14–15.

15. *New York Daily Tribune* (August 4, 1865), 8.

16. William D'Arcy, *The Fenian Movement in the United States: 1858–1886* (Washington: Catholic University of America Press, 1947), 16.

17. Letter from Michael Doheny. Cited in Marta Ramón-García, "Square-Toed Boots and Felt Hats: Irish Revolutionaries and the Invasion of Canada (1848–1871)," *Estudios Irlandeses* 5 (2010), 84.

18. Kenneth A. Scherzer, *The Unbounded Community: Neighborhood Life and Social Structure in New York City, 1830–1875* (Durham, NC: Duke University Press, 1992), 199.

19. Anonymous, *The Fenian Raid at Fort Erie*, 12.

20. John O'Leary, vol. 1, 100.

21. Fred C. Wexler, *The Tammany Regiment: A History of the Forty-Second New York Volunteer Infantry, 1861–1864* (Bloomington, IN: iUniverse, 2016), 463–464 (Kindle edition). He provides the example of Michael Doheny, the first Lieutenant Colonel of this regiment, who served for only about two months at the beginning of the war as the unit was being recruited. Doheny was both a very prominent Fenian and a veteran of the 1848 Irish uprising. A number of other prominent

Fenians were early recruits, and in fact Doheny's son continued to serve as an officer in the regiment. Although somewhat predating the events in this book, some militia units in fact first were organized as Irish nationalist militias before becoming "regularized" militia units. A particular example of this was the Irish Fusileers, subsequently becoming the Mitchell Guards, Company C, 9th Regiment, New York State Militia. For details, see Joseph Denieffe, v.

22. *Proceedings of the Second National Congress of the Fenian Brotherhood Held in Cincinnati, Ohio, January 1865* (Philadelphia: James Gibbons, 1865), 22. Cited as *Cincinnati Proceedings* hereafter.

23. Wexler, 4794 (Kindle edition).

24. *Cincinnati Proceedings*, 6.

25. Wexler, 5481 (Kindle edition). This was somewhat of a "hard luck" unit. It took over 50 percent casualties at Antietam, and continued to bleed casualties throughout the campaigns in Northern Virginia. Its remaining strength of about 102 officers and troops were humiliatingly captured by the Confederates on June 22, 1864, near Petersburg, Virginia, and spent the remainder of the war as prisoners. As a reflection of the officer casualties suffered by the unit, the senior officer in the regiment that day was a first lieutenant.

26. Wexler, 4145 (Kindle edition). Wexler also notes (location 5236) that one of the members of the 42nd captured in 1864 was Corporal Thomas Sylvanus, also known as Ching Lee or Ye Way Lee, a Chinese from Hong Kong. This might be one of the few occasions during the Civil War in which a Chinese served as a regular member of the military, much less a noncommissioned officer; there reportedly were about three Chinese who rose to the rank of corporal in all the Federal forces.

27. "The Fenians.; A Card from Archbishop Purcell," *New York Times* (March 5, 1865).

28. Letter by D. Dunne, D.D., V.G., *The Chicago Republican* (December 4, 1865).

29. *Buffalo Commercial Advertiser* (July 29, 1867).

30. *Chicago Proceedings*, 33–34; *Cincinnati Proceedings*, 53.

31. Letter from John O'Mahony, April 4, 1859. Quoted in O'Donovan Rossa, *Rossa's Recollections* (Mariner's Harbor, NY: O'Donovan Rossa, 1898), 301–302.

32. Oliver Rafferty, "Fenianism in North America in the 1860s: The Problems for Church and State," *History* (1999), 263, offers a useful table of the bishops of North America and their relative relationships with the Brotherhood.

33. For example, see the biographical sketch of Thomas Murray, the Fenian Treasurer in Buffalo, who also was "one of the founders and a life-long member of the Immaculate Conception Church, Buffalo." Rev. Thomas Donohue, *History of the Catholic Church in Western New York* (Diocese of Buffalo, Buffalo: Catholic Historical Publishing Co., 1904), 404.

34. *Cincinnati Proceedings*, 52.

35. Peter Vronsky, *Ridgeway: The American Fenian Invasion and the 1866 Battle that Made Canada* (Toronto: Allen Lane, 2011), 266.

36. *Brooklyn Daily Eagle* (March 10, 1865), 2, at the Brooklyn Public Library. Accessed at Bklyn.newspapers.com. It might also be noted that in Ireland, the IRB also had a number of Protestant members, although probably less in percentage terms than in the US. See John Devoy, *Recollections of an Irish Rebel* (New York: Chase D. Young Company, 1929), 28, 33.

37. For an excellent examination of this sectarian issue, see Anthony Tyler D'Angelo, "The 1866 Fenian Raid on Canada West: A Study of Colonial Perceptions and Reactions towards the Fenians in the Confederation Era." Master's thesis, Queen's University, Kingston, Ontario, Canada, September, 2009.

38. *Chicago Proceedings*, 47.

39. *Cincinnati Proceedings*, 39.

40. *Chicago Proceedings*, 10.

41. For an academic approach to this issue, see Mitchell Snay, "The Imagined Republic: The Fenians, Irish American Nationalism, and the Political Culture of Reconstruction," *Proceedings of the American Antiquarian Society* (2004), 291–313.

42. *The Buffalo Courier*, "That Mysterious Fenian Congress in Buffalo" (July 25, 1865).

Chapter 2

1. James Stephens, *The Birth of the Fenian Movement: American Diary 1859*, edited by MartaRamón (Dublin: University College Press Dublin, 2009), 52.

2. Desmond Ryan, *The Fenian Chief: A Biography of James Stephens* (Coral Gables, FL: University of Miami Press, 1967), 49–51.

3. John Devoy, *Recollections of an Irish Rebel* (New York: Chase D. Young Company, 1929), 26.

4. Devoy, 27.

5. O'Donovan Rossa, *Rossa's Recollections* (Mariner's Harbor, NY: O'Donovan Rossa), 1898, 304.

6. John O'Leary, *Recollections of Fenians and Fenianism*, vol. 1 (London: Downey & Co, 1896), 113.

7. Ryan, 62. This letter probably was written in autumn 1856.

8. Stephens, *American Diary*.

9. Letter to Michael Doheny, January 1, 1858, in W.S. Neidhardt, *Fenianism in North America* (University Park, PA: Pennsylvania State University Press, 1975), 4.

10. Devoy, 19.

11. Joseph Denieffe, *A Personal Narrative of the Irish Revolutionary Brotherhood* (New York: Gael Publishing Company, 1906), 28.

12. O'Leary, 135.

13. Stephens, *American Diary*, 18.

14. Ibid., 70.

15. Both eventually did play a role with the Brotherhood, albeit briefly. Meagher joined the Fenians officially in 1863, but never played much of a role: "[H]is Fenian commitment seems to have been based on the Brotherhood's usefulness to himself rather than the reverse." (Stephens, *American Diary*, 72). Mitchel also briefly acted as the Fenian financial agent in Paris in 1866, but remained only a few months before leaving, apparently in despair and/or disgust with the financial arrangements.

16. Ryan, 84.

17. Anonymous, *James Stephens, Chief Organizer of the Irish Republic: Embracing an Account of the Origin and Progress of the Fenian Brotherhood* (New York: George W. Carleton, 1856), 44.

18. Stephens, *American Diary*, 8.

19. Ibid., 56.

20. The full letter is quoted in Rossa, 269–281.

21. William D'Arcy, *The Fenian Movement in the United States: 1858–1886* (Washington: Catholic University of America Press, 1947), 33.

22. O'Leary, 135.

23. Denieffe, 60.

24. Neidhardt, 15.

25. O'Leary, 213.

26. Anonymous, *James Stephens*, 55–56.

27. Brian Jenkins, *Fenians and Anglo-American Relations During Reconstruction* (Ithaca: Cornell University Press, 1969), 85–87.

28. O'Leary, 130.

29. Devoy, 26.

30. Devoy, 55.

31. Letter of instructions by John O'Mahony to Captain Thomas J. Kelly, March 17, 1865. Denieffe, 186–187.

32. For excerpts from these reports, see D'Arcy, 70–78.

33. Neidhardt, 41.

34. It should be noted that not everyone would agree as to the relative unimportance of the Canadian Fenians. For example, Richard Brown, *Famine, Fenians and Freedom: 1840–1882* (Southampton, UK: 2012) (Kindle edition) argues as to the widespread presence of Fenians in the various Canadian provinces. The counterargument is that except for the small group of Canadian Fenians who were arrested trying to reach the Campobello operations, there is no evidence of attempts for operations by the Canadian Fenians. Their main focus seemed to be supporting Irish-Canadian interests against the Canadian Orangemen; this typically involved either infiltrating or supporting—with the verbiage depending upon one's political viewpoint—the much larger Hibernian Order. One incident that led many

to overstress the significance of the Canadian wing was the assassination in 1868 of popular Canadian Parliamentarian Thomas D'Arcy McGee, a major opponent of the Fenians. His purported assassin, Patrick J. Wheelan who was tried and hanged for the crime, was a Catholic and a Fenian sympathizer, but there were no indications that the Fenians actually had anything to do with the assassination.

Chapter 3

1. "AFFAIRS IN THE WEST.; Political Movements. The Fenian Fair Miscellaneous" (*New York Times*, April 2, 1864).

2. Ibid.

3. Jenkins, 23.

4. For example, see "Secretary Seward and the Fenians" (*New York Times*, October 20, 1865). For a detailed examination of US-British relations over Ireland, see David Sim, *A Union Forever: The Irish Question and U.S. Foreign Relations in the Victorian Age* (Ithaca, NY: Cornell University Press, 2013). Brian Jenkins, *Fenians and Anglo-American Relations During Reconstruction* (Ithaca: Cornell University Press, 1969), 44–46, also examines Seward's stance. There still is some question as to whether Seward, who seemed to be genuinely sympathetic to at least some form of Irish nationalism, was actually supportive of the Fenians or whether he simply was trying to maximize practical political support.

5. Le Caron, *Twenty-Five Years in the Secret Service: The Recollections of a Spy* (London: William Heinemann, 1892), 665–674 (Kindle edition).

6. Peter Vronsky, "Conspiracy Theory: The 'Chinese Colleagues' and the Seward-Bruce Anglo-American Secret Détente to Contain the Fenian Invasion of Canada, 1865–1866" (May, 2016). www.investigativehistory.org/articles.

7. Jenkins, 129.

8. Ibid., 273.

9. Thirty-ninth Congress, first Session, House of Representatives EX DOC No. 154, "Release of Fenian Prisoners. Message from the President of the United States" (July 26, 1866). The House of Representatives had passed a resolution calling for the release of the Fenian prisoners in Canada.

10. John Barlet Brebner, *North Atlantic Triangle: The Interplay of Canada, the United States, and Great Britain* (New Haven: Yale University Press, 1945), 165.

11. Brebner, 170–171. In fairness, this was not completely one-sided. In 1849, severe rioting broke out in Montreal following the passage of a bill that included reimbursement for former members of the 1837 and 1838 rebellions in Canada. After widespread destruction, leading merchants of the city signed a petition to have the province annexed to the US. Although the petition certainly did not succeed and was rather quickly withdrawn, it helped drive a push toward

separate "side deals" on opening up trade between the separate provinces and the US. Brebner, 150–154.

12. Jenkins, 191.

13. For examples, see *Correspondence Related to the Fenian Invasion and the Rebellion of the Southern States*, printed by Order of Parliament (Ottawa: Hunter, Rose, and Company, 1869), 1–15. Hereafter referred to as *Correspondence*.

14. *Correspondence*, 1–7.

15. Letter from Mr. Consul Denis Donohoe to Lord Lyons, Buffalo, July 5, 1864. *Correspondence*, 11.

16. Brebner, 161.

17. *Correspondence*, 35.

18. Ibid., 35.

19. Ibid., 36.

20. Ibid., 40.

21. Brebner, 160, notes, "A curious sidelight on this crisis is that, when some of the British officers were prevented by the winter closure of the St. Lawrence from reaching Canada quickly, the American Government allowed them to proceed from Portland across Maine by rail."

22. For the diplomatic responses to the legal drama, see *Correspondence*, 119–132. For a particularly strong US note, see the communique from Secretary of State Seward, 139.

23. Jenkins, 49–69.

24. Peter Vronsky, "Conspiracy Theory: The 'Chinese Colleagues' and the Seward-Bruce Anglo-American Secret Détente to Contain the Fenian Invasion of Canada, 1865–1866" (May 2016). www.investigativehistory.org/articles.

Chapter 4

1. *Blackwood's Magazine*, vol. 190 (September 1911), 392.

2. It might be ironic that O'Mahony wrote to Stephens on March 17, 1865 that "You will be glad, perhaps, to learn that I have at last got a C.C. [Central Council] that is perfectly free from any special favoritism toward me. . . . This is what I like, as I find them to be nearly all earnest, practical men in the cause." In *The Gael* 23, no. 11 (November 1904), 367.

3. *Brooklyn Daily Eagle*, December 11, 1865, 2, at Brooklyn Public Library. Accessed at Bklyn.newspapers.com.

4. *New York Times*, "The Fenian Brotherhood: Unexpected Explosion in the Cabinet and Senate," (December 11, 1865).

5. Other sources date the year of his immigration as 1832.

6. D'Arcy, 81.

7. *Cincinnati Proceedings*, 13.

8. Ibid., 5.

9. Ibid., 8.

10. Draft of letter from John O'Mahony to John Mitchel when the latter was being sent to France as a financial agent for the Fenian Brotherhood, November 10, 1865. Cited in Joseph Denieffe, *A Personal Narrative of the Irish Revolutionary Brotherhood* (New York: Gael Publishing Company, 1906), 200–203.

11. *The Brooklyn Daily Eagle* (May 24, 1865), 3.

12. Headquarters, Fenian Brotherhood, "Military Organization of the Fenian Brotherhood" (New York, October 21, 1865), section 8.

13. "Military Organization," section 9.

14. Adjutant General's Office, War Department, Fenian Brotherhood, "General Orders No. 2" (New York, November 20, 1865), 1.

15. *Proceedings of the Fifth National Convention of the Fenian Brotherhood at Troy, New York* (September 1866, Philadelphia: n.p., 1866), 21.

16. John Devoy, *Recollections of an Irish Rebel* (New York: Chase D. Young Company, 1929), 90.

17. John Savage, *Fenian Heroes and Martyrs* (Boston: Patrick Donohoe, 1868), 67.

Chapter 5

1. *Saint John Morning News*.

2. Ryan, 188.

3. Ibid.

4. John Devoy, *Recollections of an Irish Rebel* (New York: Chase D. Young Company, 1929), 42–43.

5. Although too convoluted to go into in any depth in this book, the legal status of Irish Americans in both the United Kingdom and Canada was an ongoing diplomatic war between the US and Britain. The US government viewed naturalized citizens as being US, with the full rights of citizenship in place. The British government on the other hand did not recognize such naturalization and treated "hyphenated" Americans as British subjects for purposes of the law. It took a number of years to resolve this legal battle. Jenkins covers this issue in great detail throughout his book, *Fenians and Anglo-American Relations During Reconstruction*. The naturalization issue also created an impact on domestic politics. In a sarcastic, but likely somewhat accurate observation, the *New York Tribune* wrote that mass naturalization of the Irish took place before elections, involving ceremonies "with no more solemnity than, and quite as much celerity as, is displayed in converting swine into pork in a Cincinnati Packing house." Jenkins, 95.

6. *Brooklyn Daily Eagle* (August 16, 1885), 11, at the Brooklyn Public Library. Accessed at Bklyn.newspapers.com.

7. Devoy, 59. Years later, Meehan was shot and wounded by a disgruntled fellow Fenian, apparently for personal reasons.

8. Leon O'Broin, *Fenian Fever: An Anglo-American Dilemma* (New York: New York University Press, 1971), 13.

9. Devoy, 73–77.

10. For details of the prison break, see Denieffe, 208–211. Devoy, one of the main planners of the break, also provides details on 78–87.

11. Denieffe, 127.

12. D'Arcy, 74. The Fenians never actually commissioned privateers.

13. Cited in Robert L. Dallison, *Turning Back the Fenians: New Brunswick's Last Colonial Campaign* (Fredericton, New Brunswick: Goose Lane [New Brunswick Military Heritage Project], 2006), 220 (Kindle edition).

14. Ibid., 246.

15. Ibid., 380.

16. Ibid., 807.

17. Letter, to: "My dear Gallagher" From: John O'Neill, October 7, 1868. Accessed at http://digital.library.villanova.edu.

18. For a copy of an undated list of code words, see the Catholic University of America at http://cuislandora.wrlc.org/.

19. Letter from Kelly to O'Mahony, Cork, May 1, 1865. *The Gael* 23, no. 11 (November 1904), 367.

20. Quoted in Leon O'Broin, *Fenian Fever: An Anglo-American Dilemma* (New York: New York University Press, 1971), 48.

21. Ibid., 50. For other details of Millen's recruitment and years as a British agent, see Kenna, 6881–6930.

22. "Revelations by a Fenian General," *Wellington Independent* 21, no. 2492 (March 14, 1867), 5.

23. Le Caron, *Twenty-Five Years in the Secret Service: The Recollections of a Spy* (London: William Heinemann, 1892), 866 (Kindle edition). Le Caron provides a copy of the IOU in his book.

24. D'Arcy, 145, provides an interesting if perhaps somewhat sarcastic note on this: "In 1867 at the Cleveland convention of the Roberts wing a proposal was made that [the Fenian Sisterhood] be admitted to the Fenian Brotherhood. This the tight-lipped Fenians rejected on the ground that women were unable to keep a secret."

25. Rossa, 264.

26. "Fenians—O'Mahoney Fenians activities in Eastport," *The Morning Free-man* (April 12, 1866).

27. There is some question as to the name of this vessel. In his telegraph to General Grant, General Meade identified the name as *E. H. Pray*. Both vessels were on the registry during this period.

28. Doyle later was appointed lieutenant governor of New Brunswick, then promoted to lieutenant general and appointed as commander of British forces in Canada.

29. Dallison, 986 (Kindle edition).

30. *The Papers of Ulysses S. Grant* 16, no. 1866, 111.

31. Debates in the Cabinet were in the best traditions of passing the buck. Each cabinet secretary argued that another agency bore responsibility for resolving the problem. Secretary of the Navy Gideon Welles, for example, in his diary noted that "I observe that these men are very chary about disturbing the Fenians and I do not care to travel out of the line of duty to relieve them." Gideon Wells, *Diary of Gideon Welles*, 3 vols. (Boston: Houghton Mifflin, 1911), 486.

32. David C. Newton and Kenneth J. Pluskat, eds., *The Lost Civil War Diaries: The Diaries of Corporal Timothy J. Regan* (Victoria, British Columbia: Trafford Publishing, 2003), 283. Entry date of April 16, 1866.

33. For a vivid description of this incident, see Dallison, 1213–1234 (Kindle edition).

34. "Fenians—Failure of O'Mahoney's plan for Campobello," *The Morning Freeman* (May 10, 1866).

35. Anonymous, *James Stephens, Chief Organizer of the Irish Republic: Embracing an Account of the Origin and Progress of the Fenian Brotherhood* (New York: George W. Carleton, 1866), 98.

Chapter 6

1. Speech by Thomas Sweeny in January 1866 in Buffalo. Cited in W.S. Neidhardt, *Fenianism in North America* (University Park, PA: Pennsylvania State University Press, 1975), 34.

2. Both in Neidhardt, 53–54.

3. Joseph Denieffe, *A Personal Narrative of the Irish Revolutionary Brotherhood* (New York: Gael Publishing Company, 1906), 218–219

4. The text of this general order is in appendix 2.

5. Unless otherwise noted, all these details are from Thomas Sweeny, *Official Report of General T. W. Sweeny, Secretary of War* (New York, September 1866).

6. For example, a letter dated March 23, 1866, noted that 3,000 muskets were in preparation for shipment; the same letter included attempts to buy light artillery. Denieffe, 222. Elsewhere, correspondence was exchanged about the purchase and storage of two million rounds of .58 caliber (the standard musket round at the time) ammunition. Denieffe, 234. Another letter dated May 3, 1866, broke down the distribution of weapons to the circles and the availability of remaining stocks: to J.F. Scanlon, Chicago: 620; to J.W. Fitzgerald, Cincinnati, Ohio 100; to Philip Breen, St. Clair, Schuylkill Co., Pa 40; to Samuel Mulvill, Bergen Point, NJ 20; to Cornelius Finn 20; to Peter Higgins, Cleveland, Ohio 20; to John Egan, Elizabethport, NJ 20; to Ed. Fitzwilliam. Watertown, Mass 20; to P.J. Kelly, Newburg, NY 40; total issued from New York 900. On hand in New York subject to orders 1,100.

The following were issued from Bridesburg:

To John Nealon, Carbondale, Pa 80; to M.J. Philben, Wilkesbarre, Pa 80; to J.E. Clark, Pittstown, Pa 80; to Bryan Fallon, Archibald, Pa 20; to P. Regan, Oswego, NY 480; to Thomas McLean, Cincinnati, Ohio 480; to W. Fleming, Troy, NY 480; to C.I. King. Corrv. Pa 20; to D. McGowan, East St. Louis, 111 40; to Owen Gavigan, Auburn, NY 40; to P. O'Day, Buffalo, NY 1,000; to John Barret, Dunkirk, NY 480; to M.J. Cronin, Erie, Pa 840; to J. O'Farrell, Baltimore, Md 100. Denieffe, 233.

7. A letter from a US sailor then in Buffalo sent a letter dated April 9, 1866, to Sweeny concerning the strength of the armed guards on the Welland Canal in Canada; this was a logical objective for the Fenians if they invaded Canada. On May 9, 1866, similar reporting on defenses around Windsor was submitted. Interestingly, the report also included details about US forces around Detroit. Denieffe, 237.

8. Peter Vronsky, *Ridgeway: The American Fenian Invasion and the 1866 Battle that Made Canada* (Toronto: Allen Lane, 2011), 29, 84.

9. John O'Neill, *Official Report of the Battle of Ridgeway, Canada West, Fought June 2d. 1866* (New York: John J. Foster, 1870), 37.

10. Published in full in Denieffe, 238–239.

11. Reprinted in Frank H. Severance, ed., *Publications of The Buffalo Historical Society* vol. 25 (Buffalo: The Buffalo Historical Society, 1921), 267.

12. May 30 cable from British Consul in Buffalo to the Canadian government. Cited in Alexander Somerville, *Narrative of the Fenian Invasion of Canada* (Hamilton, Canada West: Joseph Lyte, 1866), 12.

13. *New York Times* (May 31, 1866).

14. *Buffalo Express* (May 31, 1866), 1.

15. Neidhardt, 37.

16. Vronsky, 44–45, does a detailed order of battle for the Fenian units and derives a total strength of 1,059. There might be some question as to how many of these troops actually stayed with their unit after they crossed the border. Vronsky does agree with the usual estimate of 800 at Ridgeway.

17. O'Neill, *Official Report*, 38.

18. Lieutenant Colonel George T. Denison, *Soldiering in Canada: Recollections and Experiences* (London: MacMillan and Company, 1900), 85.

Chapter 7

1. Canadian troops claimed after the battle that the Fenians were armed with repeating rifles. Although the Fenians earlier had tried to obtain some of these weapons, there is absolutely no evidence that any Fenians were armed with these at Ridgeway or Fort Erie. The misconception likely arose because the Fenian troops simply were proficient enough with the loading procedures for the muskets

that they could get through the process much more quickly than the Canadians were accustomed to.

2. *New York Tribune* (Monday June 4, 1866), 1.

3. John O'Neill, *Official Report of the Battle of Ridgeway, Canada West, Fought June 2d. 1866* (New York: John J. Foster, 1870), 38.

4. Peter Vronsky, *Ridgeway: The American Fenian Invasion and the 1866 Battle that Made Canada* (Toronto: Allen Lane, 2011), 54.

5. David C. Newton and Kenneth J. Pluskat, eds., *The Lost Civil War Diaries: The Diaries of Corporal Timothy J. Regan* (Victoria, British Columbia: Trafford Publishing, 2003), 286. Also, Somerville, 21.

6. Vronsky, 54.

7. The other artillery battery had guns but not the "traces" required to haul the guns to the field. Despite this issue being known, Colonel Peacocke inspected that battery on March 8, 1866, and publicly announced, "The Hamilton battery was in a state of highest efficiency, ready for any emergency." Alexander Somerville, *Narrative of the Fenian Invasion of Canada* (Hamilton, Canada West: Joseph Lyte, 1866), 45.

8. Colonel George T. Denison, *Soldiering in Canada: Recollections and Experiences* (London: MacMillan and Company, 1900), 88.

9. Somerville, 78.

10. Ibid., 53.

11. Denison, 98.

12. Vronsky, 66.

13. Andrew McIntosh, an ensign in No. 5 Company, cited in Hereward Senior, *The Last Invasion of Canada: The Fenian Raids, 1866–1870* (Toronto: Dundurn Press, 1991), 1030 (Kindle edition).

14. Field Marshal Viscount Wolseley, *The Story of a Soldier's Life*, vol. 2 (1903), 2117–2124 (Kindle edition). As a regular soldier, Wolseley might be expected to denigrate the Canadian militia officers, but in various locations he both praises their "common sense" (which he compared very positively in contrast to most British regular officers) and criticizes their lack of experience.

15. Vronsky, 67.

16. Ibid., 76.

17. Denison, 89.

18. There are some rather large discrepancies in the strength numbers provided by various authors of the two units. MacDonald states that the naval contingent consisted of three officers and forty-three men and the artillery battery three officers and fifty-nine men. John A. MacDonald, *Troublous Times in Canada: A History of the Fenian Raids of 1866 and 1870* (Toronto: W.S. Johnston, 1910), 43. The lower numbers for the naval contingent seem to be more logical.

19. It was already noted that the Fenians had learned from their Civil War experiences both the importance of and the ability to build quick field expedient

protection. Somerville provided a good detailed description of the sorts of field fortifications the Fenians used in Canada: "A [fence] rail was cut in three pieces; the ends sharpened, and driven into the ground in form like an x. Two of these x's supported a rail horizontally set at a height of about three feet. From that two or more rails slanted downward to the ground, from the position in which sharp-shooters were to be screened. Then a lower roof of rails was laid longitudinally and horizontally on these, beginning on the ground, rising to the higher level. Then an upper roof was laid by pieces placed transversely to the former, and as closely together as they would lie. This roof sloped from three feet high to the ground at an angle of about thirty degrees, or less. It was intended that rifle bullets, hitting it from the direction in which the opposing force might come, would glance off over the heads of sharpshooters ensconced behind. Some of these screens were four feet high in rear, others only two, generally they were elevated three feet. The different sections of screens were regulated by the length of rails, and were not placed con-tinuously end to end, but were advanced, like detached columns twelve or twenty yards before others, and much scattered." Somerville, 31–32.

20. The specific wording was "Be cautious in feeling your way, for fear obstacles should prevent a junction. . . ." Booker inquiry in MacDonald, 205.

21. Vronsky, 98–100.

22. Much of the evidence cited for this was in letters exchanged between some Canadian officers and O'Neill sometime after the event. Read at face value, O'Neill's response to the Canadians (who initiated the exchange) suggests that the Fenians were hard-pressed and on the verge of losing. Read more carefully, however, his account seems to be much more a matter of trying to pay compliments to a former foe.

23. The full proceedings of the court of inquiry are in MacDonald as an appendix, 197–246.

24. MS of Mr. William J. McElroy "only surviving Veteran" living in Buffalo, NY. Undated and no page numbers. McElroy was a Canadian militiaman who later emigrated to Buffalo. Manuscript held at the Library, Buffalo History Museum.

25. MacDonald, 245.

26. Hereward Senior, *The Last Invasion of Canada: The Fenian Raids, 1866–1870* (Toronto: Dundurn Press, 1991), 1202 (Kindle edition).

27. John A. MacDonald, *Troublous Times in Canada: A History of the Fenian Raids of 1866 and 1870* (Toronto: W. S. Johnston, 1910), 211.

28. The 13th Battalion later was renamed the Royal Hamilton Light Infantry (Wentworth Regiment).

29. Vronsky, 205.

30. Ibid., 188.

31. Denison was one of the first to see Dennis after his arrival at Peacocke's camp. For a full description, see Denison, 100–102. According to Denison, Dennis also quickly disappeared in a similar situation during Riel's Rebellion in 1870, 103.

32. *New York Tribune* (Monday June 4, 1866), 1.

33. For a photo of what may be the only surviving Fenian uniform jacket, see Lar Joye, "The Wearing of the Green: Fenian Uniform from Canada, 1870," *History Ireland* 16, no. 6 (Nov.–Dec., 2008), 51. The buttons on the uniform have the design of "IRA" surrounded by shamrocks. This may be the first use of the title "Irish Republican Army."

34. MS of Mr. William J. McElroy "only surviving Veteran" living in Buffalo, NY. Undated and no page numbers. McElroy was a Canadian militiaman who later emigrated to Buffalo. Manuscript held at the Library, Buffalo History Museum.

35. The *Buffalo Examiner*, which had reporters covering the Fenians, had very conflicting stories on Fenian behavior in Canada. Some reports indicated widespread looting, while others suggested overall good behavior. One issue might be common in most wars of the period: camp followers and others who followed the actual forces. The *Buffalo Examiner* reported on June 3, 1866, that "about a dozen of the Buffalo roughs visited Fort Erie and held high carnival here, insulting men and women, and taking what they could lay their hands upon. During the night they entered the clothing store of Messrs. Kirby & Co., and after maltreating three young men . . . carried off the greater portion of the contents of the store, conveyed them across to the American side of the river, and deposited them in a shed. This morning Collector Thomson discovered the goods, and seized them, and the Custom House authorities in Buffalo have now charge of the them."

36. Somerville, 25–26.

37. Ibid., 21.

38. Ibid., 28–29.

39. Vronsky, 161.

40. Denison, 106–107.

Chapter 8

1. One note might be made about Ogdensburg and its spelling. It initially was spelled "Ogdensburgh," but the "h" was dropped after it was incorporated in 1817. Many contemporary sources, however, continued to use the final "h" for a number of years.

2. "An English View of the Fenians," *Brooklyn Daily Eagle* (March 10, 1865), 4. Accessed at Bklyn.newspapers.com.

3. Ibid.

4. Ibid.

5. Spear's name commonly has been spelled several ways, with variants including "Spears" and "Spier."

6. Neidhardt, 79.

7. Senior, 1723.

8. Thomas R. Roberts to Brown Chamberlain, editor of Montreal *Gazette*, quoted in Senior, 1685.

9. Neidhardt, 80. Some newspapers at the time claimed that Canadian troops had crossed the border while pursuing the Fenians. These claims caused considerable public protest, but they apparently were bogus.

10. *Buffalo Express* (June 6, 1866). This might be contrasted with the governor of Maine during the Campobello Raid, who sent state forces to the area for violations of the neutrality act.

Chapter 9

1. *New York Tribune* (Monday June 4, 1866), 1.

2. *New York Times* (June 1, 1866), 5, 1.

3. This is based on a report in the *New York Tribune*, June 4, 1866. There is some debate as to its accuracy, with some arguing that the report actually meant General Meade, who certainly was there. In any event, General Grant certainly was actively engaged in issuing orders for an active response.

4. Cited in *New York Tribune* (June 4, 1866), 1.

5. Peter Vronsky, *Ridgeway: The American Fenian Invasion and the 1866 Battle that Made Canada* (Toronto: Allen Lane, 2011), 28.

6. *New York Tribune* (June 4, 1866), 1.

7. Ibid.

8. *Herkimer Democrat* (June 20, 1866), 4.

9. *Buffalo Express* (June 4, 1866), 1.

10. Vronsky, *Ridgeway*, 37–38.

11. O'Neill's number is very exact, but not necessarily accurate. Many of his strength figures for the Fenians are considerably below those cited elsewhere.

12. O'Neill, *Official Report of the Battle of Ridgeway, Canada West, Fought June 2d. 1866* (New York: John J. Foster, 1870), 40–41.

13. Gideon Wells. *Diary of Gideon Welles*, 3 vols. (Boston: Houghton Mifflin, 1911), 520.

14. *New York Tribune* (June 4, 1866), 1.

15. William D'Arcy, *The Fenian Movement in the United States: 1858–1886* (Washington: Catholic University of America Press, 1947), 166.

16. *Buffalo Express*, June 5, 1866.

17. For details of these trials, see George R. Gregg and E.P. Roden, *Trials of the Fenian Prisoners at Toronto Who Were Captured at Fort Erie, C.W., in June 1866* (Toronto: Leader Steam-Press, 1867).

18. For example, see letters Lord Monck to Sir Bruce, no. 52, Ottawa, June 11, 1866, 143; Lord Monck to Mr. Cardwell, no. 53, Ottawa, June 14, 1866. *Correspondence Related to the Fenian Invasion and the Rebellion of the South-*

ern States (Order of Parliament: Ottawa, Hunter, Rose & Company, 1869), 143–144.

Chapter 10

1. *Proceedings of the Fifth National Convention of the Fenian Brotherhood at Troy, New York, September 1866* (Philadelphia: n.p., 1866), 11 Brevet promotions were common in nineteenth-century military. They were honorary promotions without the seniority or actual permanent rank of regular promotions, and were awarded to officers for bravery or other distinguished service during wartime. In some cases, officers with a permanent rank of captain could rise as high as brevet brigadier general.

2. *Troy Proceedings*, 8.

3. *The Public Ledger* (Saint John's, Newfoundland) (September 21, 1866), 3.

4. *Troy Proceedings*, 16.

5. Ibid., 27.

6. Ibid., 22. There literally were pages of similar diatribe against O'Mahony and Stephens.

7. *New York Herald* (October 9, 1866), 6.

8. The level of disdain and apparent disgust by the American military leaders toward these deserters was shown by their hanging rather than being executed by firing squad. Hanging was considered to be a much more dishonorable death.

9. Desmond Ryan, *The Fenian Chief: A Biography of James Stephens* (Coral Gables, FL: University of Miami Press, 1967), 238.

10. Ryan, 239.

11. It is virtually certain that the American Ambassador had no clue about Cluseret's role with the Fenians. It is much less clear that this was the case with the New York governor.

12. John Devoy, *Recollections of an Irish Rebel* (New York: Chase D. Young Company, 1929), 96.

13. Brian Jenkins, *Fenians and Anglo-American Relations During Reconstruction* (Ithaca: Cornell University Press, 1969), 222–223.

14. Denieffe, 138–139.

15. John Devoy, *Recollections of an Irish Rebel* (New York: Chase D. Young Company, 1929), 66. Devoy also noted one other problem for McCafferty: "McCafferty was born in Sandusky, Ohio, had lived many years in the South, and his manner of speech puzzled them," 67.

16. Devoy, 63–67, provides details of the soldiers in British regiments whom he claimed to be loyal to the Fenians.

17. There was a wave of trials for potentially disloyal soldiers in 1866, in which 180 "Fenian soldiers" were arrested. For details, see Richard Brown, *Famine, Fenians and Freedom: 1840–1882* (Southampton, UK, 2012), 7242–7262 (Kindle edition).

18. F. Hugh O'Donnell, *A History of the Irish Parliamentary Party* (New York: Longmans, Green, & Co., 1910), 5–6.

19. D. O'Sullivan Official Report, *Proceedings of the Senate and House of Representatives of the Fenian Brotherhood in Joint Convention at Philadelphia, PA, November 24, 25, 26, 27, 28 and 29, 1868* (New York: D.W. Lee, 1868), 20.

20. As with many issues, there are debates about what actually happened during this incident, with some claiming it to be an accidental shooting; in either event, there was blood shed.

21. Devoy, 240.

22. *Marx and Engels on Ireland* (Moscow: Progress Publishers, 1971).

23. For a more detailed biography of Burke, see Quinlivan and Rose, 8–9.

24. Marx and Engels, 150.

25. Letter from John Mitchel to "M. Moynhan": February 19, 1867. *The Gael*, vol. 23, no. 11 (November 1904), 371.

26. D'Arcy, 231.

27. *Brooklyn Eagle* (February 27, 1867), 2.

28. War Department, Head-Quarters Fenian Brotherhood, New York (May 1, 1869).

29. Proceedings of the Senate and House of Representatives of the Fenian Brotherhood in Joint Convention at Philadelphia, PA, November 24, 25, 26, 27, 28 and 29 (New York: D.W. Lee, 1868), 20.

30. Jenkins, 293.

31. Neidhardt, 113.

32. 1868 Proceedings, 16.

33. Ibid., 50–54.

34. Ibid., 8.

35. Financial Report of the Treasurer of the Fenian Brotherhood November, 1869.

36. Letter, to: F.B. Gallagher Esq. From: F. Renehan, April 11, 1869. http://digital.library.villanova.edu.

37. Ibid.

38. Letter, to: F.B. Gallagher Esq. From: John O'Neill, December 16, 1869. http://digital.library.villanova.edu.

39. Circular: "Head-Quarters Fenian Brotherhood, Treasury Department." From: Patrick Keenan, March 18, 1868.

40. Gen. John O'Neill, *Official Report of Gen. John O'Neill on the Attempt to Invade Canada* (New York: John J. Foster, 1870), 5.

41. What seems to be a form letter, to: P. Meehan Esq From: James Keenan (Secretary of Civil Affairs), February 21, 1870. http://digital.library.villanova.edu. Italics in original.

42. *Proceedings of the Senate and House of Representatives of the Fenian Brotherhood in Joint Convention at Philadelphia, PA, November 24, 25, 26, 27, 28 and 29, 1868* (New York: D.W. Lee, 1868), 4.

43. Neidhardt, 114.

44. Letter, to: [Frank] Gallagher, From: Col. William Clingen, April 21, 1870. http://digital.library.villanova.edu.

Chapter 11

1. Le Caron, *Twenty-Five Years in the Secret Service: The Recollections of a Spy* (London: William Heinemann, 1892), 951–961 (Kindle edition).

2. O'Neill, *Official Report*, 15–16.

3. Ibid., 16.

4. Le Caron, 932.

5. O'Neill, 17.

6. Ibid., 16.

7. O'Neill, *Official Report*, 34.

8. Ibid., 45–46.

9. The home guard also reportedly offered to the mayor of Franklin that they cross the border and seize the weapons being moved there for the Fenians. They argued that being a private security force, they could act independently. This offer was refused. Hereward Senior, *The Last Invasion of Canada: The Fenian Raids, 1866–1870* (Toronto: Dundurn Press, 1991), 2196 (Kindle edition).

10. Senior, 2221.

11. This figure is from O'Neill, *Official Report*, 19. He tended to underestimate his strength in his reports, but this likely is a rather close approximation. Some further Fenian troops arrived in the area during the day, but they did not see any particular action.

12. A note on spelling. Senior, whose coverage of the 1870 raid is very detailed, titles this as "Rykert's" farm. The spelling used here is that of O'Neill and earlier analysts of 1870.

13. The following account differs somewhat from that of O'Neill in his official report and is based more on other accounts that appear more accurate. One interesting aspect of O'Neill's report is that he insisted that Foster's "conduct throughout has been that of a gentleman."

14. Senior, 2362.

Chapter 12

1. Letter, to: "My dear Mr. Gallagher." From: John O'Neill, November 27, 1869. Letter, to: "My dear Mr. Gallagher." From: John O'Neill, December 2, 1869.

2. Letter, to: "My dear Gallagher." From: John O'Neill, December 24, 1869.

3. Senior, 2489.

4. D'Arcy, 370–372.

5. Ibid., 372.

6. Ibid., 373.

7. Ibid., 388.

8. Ibid., 398.

9. Devoy, 249–250.

10. Shane Kenna, *War in the Shadows: The Irish-American Fenians Who Bombed Victorian Britain* (Kildare, Ireland: Merrion, 2014), 440 (Kindle edition).11. The Clan na Gael did the same thing with any titles for which it used abbreviations. They simply used the next letters of the alphabet to refer to the abbreviated title. For example, the [E]xecutive [B]oard became "FC"; the [U]nited [B]rotherhood became "VC," and so on. Exactly what the point of this was remains questionable.

12. According to the Clan negotiator, Stephens demanded (among other things) that he be in charge of all movements; be supported financially "in a manner befitting his position"; the executive board of the Clan to resign; and "No strollers from America to be permitted on the other side under pains of execution. . . ." Stephens later denied making these rather exorbitant demands, but they seemed to fit his earlier behavior. Kenna, 476–492.

13. Leon O'Broin. *Fenian Fever: An Anglo-American Dilemma* (New York: New York University Press, 1971), 222–223.

14. D'Arcy, 406.

15. Quoted in Kenna, 736. Italics in original.

16. Ibid., 772. Italics in original.

17. Devoy, 250.

18. Ibid., 271.

19. Micheál De Burca, editor, "Life and Poems of Michael Scanlan: The Fenian Poet" (Kilmallock, Ireland: The Abbey Printing Works 1969), 4.

Bibliography and Suggested Readings

Primary Sources

Adjutant General's Office, War Department, Fenian Brotherhood, "General Orders No. 2," New York, November 20, 1865.

Anonymous. *The Fenian Raid at Fort Erie, June the First and Second 1866*. Toronto: W.C. Chewett and Co., 1866. Basically an expanded newspaper report, useful for the immediate media response to the attack.

Correspondence Related to the Fenian Invasion and the Rebellion of the Southern States. Printed by Order of Parliament, Printed by Hunter, Rose, and Company, Ottawa, 1869. The bulk of the papers are on issues surrounding the Canadian response to the Civil War, but also includes exchanges about the Fenians.

Denieffe, Joseph. *A Personal Narrative of the Irish Revolutionary Brotherhood*. New York: The Gael Publishing Company, 1906. This provides insights from a fairly senior Fenian, together with copies of a number of letters, orders, and the like produced by the Fenians.

Denison, Lieutenant Colonel George T. *Soldiering in Canada: Recollections and Experiences*. London: MacMillan and Company, 1900. A cavalry commander who served in the 1866 operation. He also was the president of the courts of inquiry examining Ridgeway and Fort Erie battles.

Devoy, John. *Recollections of an Irish rebel*. New York: Chase D. Young Company. Memoir by a key member of the IRB, later to be very involved in the American Irish nationalist movements. 1929.

Gregg, George R., and E.P. Roden. *Trials of the Fenian Prisoners at Toronto Who Were Captured at Fort Erie, C.W., in June 1866*. Toronto: Leader Steam-Press, 1867. Very detailed coverage of these trials.

Headquarters, Fenian Brotherhood, *Military Organization of the Fenian Brotherhood*. New York, October 21, 1865.

Index to the Executive Documents. Printed by Order of the Senate, for the Second Session of the Fortieth Congress, 1867–1868. Washington: Government Printing Office, 1868. Contains many primary source documents on the US response to the Fenians.

215

Le Caron, Henri. *Twenty-Five Years in the Secret Service: The Recollections of a Spy.*
London: William Heinemann, 1892. Although many of the details he provides of his activities cannot be verified, and some of his assertions are either
questionable or wrong, this memoir offers a thoroughly entertaining account
of nineteenth-century intelligence operations, in this case against the Fenians
and successor Irish groups. The basics of his story are confirmed elsewhere.

MacDonald, John A. *Troublous Times in Canada: A History of the Fenian Raids of
1866 and 1870.* Toronto: W. S. Johnston, 1910. Long a standard history of
the battles from the Canadian side, he was a veteran of both campaigns. Also
includes the courts of inquiry for both Booker and Dennis. Although very
jingoistic in tone, remains useful.

McElroy, William J. Account of the "only surviving Veteran" living in Buffalo, NY.
Undated two-page manuscript of a Canadian militiaman who moved to Buffalo later in life. Available at Buffalo History Museum.

Newton, David C., and Kenneth J. Pluskat, eds. *The Lost Civil War Diaries: The
Diaries of Corporal Timothy J. Regan.* Victoria, British Columbia: Trafford
Publishing, 2003. Some interesting contemporary observations of the Fenians
by an Irish American soldier.

O'Donovan Rossa [Jeremiah]. *Rossa's Recollections.* Mariner's Harbor, NY: O'Donovan
Rossa, 1898. Memoir by one of the leading Irish Fenians. Much of the book,
which can be rather frustrating in its lack of structure, deals with his ancestors
and family life, but it also is of use for internal Fenian dynamics.

O'Leary, John. *Recollections of Fenians and Fenianism.* London: Downey & Co,
1896. An important memoir by a senior Fenian.

O'Neill, General John. *Official Report of Gen. John O'Neill on the Attempt to Invade
Canada.* New York: John J. Foster, 1870. His apologia for the 1870 campaign;
very useful both for the military and internal political issues surrounding the
fiasco. Also includes his official report on the 1866 invasion, which focuses
rather more on military issues.

The Papers of Ulysses S. Grant, vol. 16: 1866. Contains cables and other correspondence to and from General Meade and others regarding means of control
of the Fenians.

*Proceedings of the First National Convention of the Fenian Brotherhood Held in Chi-
cago, Illinois, November 1863.* Philadelphia: James Gibbons, 1863. Both this
and the following reports provide not only the Fenian Constitution, but also
all the public resolutions of the conventions. Essential sources for the public
face of the Fenians at the time.

*Proceedings of the Second National Congress of the Fenian Brotherhood Held in Cincin-
nati, Ohio, January 1865.* Philadelphia: James Gibbons, 1865.

Proceedings of the Fifth National Convention of the Fenian Brotherhood at Troy, New
York, September 1866, Philadelphia: no publisher provided, 1866.

Proceedings of the Senate and House of Representatives of the Fenian Brotherhood in Joint Convention at Philadelphia, PA, November 24, 25, 26, 27, 28 and 29, 1868. New York: D.W. Lee, 1868.

Savage, John. *Fenian Heroes and Martyrs.* Boston: Patrick Donohoe, 1868. The writer became president of the Fenian Brotherhood. This book essentially is a propaganda document, but offers some interesting profiles of well-known Fenians.

Stephens, James. *The Birth of the Fenian Movement: American Diary 1859*, edited by Marta Ramón. Dublin: University College Press Dublin, 2009. A key primary source for the establishment of the Fenians.

Wells, Gideon. *Diary of Gideon Welles*, 3 vols. Boston: Houghton Mifflin, 1911. Very limited coverage of the administration's response to the Fenians, but those entries are very helpful in understanding the internal Cabinet response.

Wolseley, Field Marshal Viscount. *The Story of a Soldier's Life*, vol. II. Originally published in 1903, Kindle edition. Chapters 34, and 36–38 cover his time in Canada during the 1860s through 1870. Chapter 35, although not on Canada, describes his visit to Confederate forces during the Civil War and is also of interest.

Secondary Sources

Anonymous. *James Stephens, Chief Organizer of the Irish Republic: Embracing an Account of the Origin and Progress of the Fenian Brotherhood.* New York: George W. Carleton, 1866. More of a hagiography than biography, this book offers a useful contemporary account of Stephens and the Fenian Brotherhood as of 1866. With a short foreword by Stephens, it seems to represent the "party line."

Brebner, John Barlet. *North Atlantic Triangle: The Interplay of Canada, the United States, and Great Britain.* New Haven: Yale University Press, 1945. Although not focused on the Fenians, provides a good survey of major diplomatic issues among the two countries and colony.

Brown, Richard. *Famine, Fenians and Freedom: 1840–1882.* Southampton, UK: 2012 (Kindle edition). Provides details on the precursors to the Fenian movement, particularly the 1848 uprising. Also useful in its account of the various conflicts among the Irish nationalist groups and Fenian structures in Canada and Australia.

Dallison, Robert L. *Turning Back the Fenians: New Brunswick's Last Colonial Campaign.* Fredericton, New Brunswick: Goose Lane (New Brunswick Military Heritage Project), 2006. Although not particularly helpful at the larger political level, this book provides the most detailed examination of the Campobello Island operation. It is particularly detailed on the use of the Canadian militia forces in defending against the Fenians.

D'Angelo, Anthony Tyler. "The 1866 Fenian Raid on Canada West: A Study of Colonial Perceptions and Reactions Towards the Fenians in the Confederation Era." Master's thesis, Queen's University, Kingston, Ontario, Canada, 2009. A very useful paper on the sectarian issues surrounding the Canadian Fenians.

D'Arcy, William. *The Fenian Movement in the United States: 1858–1886.* Washington, DC: Catholic University of America Press, 1947. Although now somewhat dated, this remains one of the best political studies of the Fenian Brotherhood. Essential reading.

De Burca, Micheál, ed. *Life and Poems of Michael Scanlan: The Fenian Poet.* Kilmallock, Ireland: The Abbey Printing Works, 1969.

Dixon, R., ed. *Marx and Engels on Ireland.* Moscow: Progress Publishers, 1971. Translated by Angela Clifford, K. Cook, and B. Bean. Although somewhat peripheral to the main themes in this book, their take on Ireland and the Fenians is interesting.

Donhue, Father Thomas. *History of the Catholic Church in Western New York.* Diocese of Buffalo, Buffalo: Catholic Historical Publishing Co., 1904.

Gantt, Jonathan. *Irish Terrorism in the Atlantic Community, 1865–1922.* New York: Palgrave Macmillan, 2010. Attempts to show that the Fenians were a terrorist organization from the early days of the group.

Jenkins, Brian. *Fenians and Anglo-American Relations During Reconstruction.* Ithaca: Cornell University Press, 1969. The best secondary source for an examination of diplomatic and internal political issues within the US administration over the Fenians.

Kenna, Shane. *War in the Shadows: The Irish-American Fenians Who Bombed Victorian Britain.* Kildare, Ireland: Merrion, 2014, Kindle edition. Useful examination of the later stages of Fenianism.

Lebergott, Stanley. "Wage Trends, 1800–1900," *Trends in the American Economy in the Nineteenth Century.* Princeton, NJ: Princeton University Press, 1960.

Neidhardt, W. S. *Fenianism in North America.* University Park, PA: Pennsylvania State University Press, 1975. A Canada-centric examination of the Fenians.

O'Broin, Leon. *Fenian Fever: An Anglo-American Dilemma.* New York: New York University Press, 1971. Focuses on the British government's reactions.

O'Concubhair, Pádraig, *The Fenians Were Dreadful Men: The 1867 Rising.* Cork: Mercier Press, 2011. A good study of the rebellion.

F. Hugh O'Donnell. *A History of the Irish Parliamentary Party.* New York: Longmans, Green, & Co., 1910.

Pease, Zephaniah. *The Catalpa Expedition.* New Bedford, MA: George S. Anthony, 1897. Much of the book is based on interviews with Captain Anthony, who led the expedition. A thoroughly enjoyable read, although certainly slanted toward the Irish involved.

Quinlivan, Patrick, and Paul Rose. *The Fenians in England, 1865–1872: A Sense of Insecurity.* London: John Calder, 1982. A modern pro-Fenian treatment of the Manchester and Clerkenwell incidents and the subsequent trials.

Rafferty, Oliver. "Fenianism in North America in the 1860s: The Problems for Church and State." *History*, 1999, 257–277. Further examination of Fenian-Church relations.

Ramón-García, Marta. "Square-Toed Boots and Felt Hats: Irish Revolutionaries and the Invasion of Canada (1848–1871)." *Estudios Irlandeses* No. 5, 2010, 81–91.

Ryan, Desmond. *The Fenian Chief: A Biography of James Stephens.* Coral Gables, FL: University of Miami Press, 1967. Written by a veteran of the 1916 uprising, this volume offers a nationalistic but reasonably balanced examination of Stephens's life.

Scherzer, Kenneth A. *The Unbounded Community: Neighborhood Life and Social Structure in New York City, 1830–1875.* Durham, NC: Duke University Press, 1992. General background.

Senior, Hereward. *The Last Invasion of Canada: The Fenian Raids, 1866–1870.* Toronto: Dundurn Press, 1991, Kindle edition. A good military examination of these campaigns.

Severance, Frank H., ed. *Publications of The Buffalo Historical Society*, vol. XXV. Buffalo: The Buffalo Historical Society, 1921. Provides some anecdotal material on the Fenians in Buffalo in 1866.

Sim, David. "Filibusters, Fenians, and a Contested Neutrality: The Irish Question and U.S. Diplomacy, 1848–1871. *American Nineteenth Century History*, vol. 12, no. 3, September 2011, 265–287. A briefer diplomatic study.

Sim, David. *A Union Forever: The Irish Question and U.S. Foreign Relations in the Victorian Age.* Ithaca, NY: Cornell University Press, 2013. Useful for diplomatic issues.

Snay, Mitchell. "The Imagined Republic: The Fenians, Irish American Nationalism, and the Political Culture of Reconstruction." *Proceedings of the American Antiquarian Society*, 2004, 291–313.

Somerville, Alexander. *Narrative of the Fenian Invasion of Canada.* Hamilton, Canada West: Joseph Lyte, 1866. One of the first published accounts of the Ridgeway battle, and very influential on the historical narrative. In later years, Somerville renounced his own treatment of Booker and acknowledged that it was somewhat a hatchet job against him. Nevertheless, many elements of the book remain very useful.

Ural, Susannah J. *The Harp and the Eagle: Irish-American Volunteers and the Union Army, 1861–1865.* New York: NYU Press, 2006. Excellent examination of the period leading up to the rise of the Fenians.

Vronsky, Peter. *Ridgeway: The American Fenian Invasion and the 1866 Battle that Made Canada.* Toronto: Allen Lane, 2011. A somewhat revisionist and very detailed treatment of the battle.

Vronsky, Peter. "Conspiracy Theory: The 'Chinese Colleagues' and the Seward-Bruce Anglo-American Secret Détente to Contain the Fenian Invasion of Canada, 1865–1866." May, 2016, www.investigativehistory.org/articles. Important recent scholarship on the issue.

Walker, Mabel Gregory. *The Fenian Movement*. Colorado Springs: Ralph Myles Publisher, 1969. The sections on US politics surrounding the Fenians are of some use, but the remainder should be read with caution.

Wexler, Fred C. *The Tammany Regiment: A History of the Forty-Second New York Volunteer Infantry, 1861–1864*. Bloomington, IN: iUniverse, 2016. Kindle edition. This book provides a good micro-level study of one of the Irish units in the American Civil War and some of its connections with the Fenian movement.

Wilson, David A. "The Fenians in Canada." Ottawa: Library and Archives Canada, undated. A good short introduction.

Useful Websites

http://digital.library.villanova.edu/. Villanova University. Contains papers of Frank Gallagher, a Fenian Senator in Buffalo, New York, with many letters, receipts, and official documents. Very useful, particularly for day-to-day operations of the Fenians in the 1868–1869 period.

http://cuislandora.wrlc.org/islandora/object/achc-fenian%3A1. Catholic University of America. Many important digital Fenian documents.

http://www.fenians.org/index.htm. Provides links to many public domain documents, particularly on the 1866 Ridgeway battle.

Newspapers and Periodicals

The following are the primary newspapers used for this book:

The Gael. Particularly in the late nineteenth and earlier twentieth centuries, this journal published a number of letters from the papers of earlier senior Fenian leaders.

Brooklyn Daily Eagle

Buffalo Express

New York Times

New York Tribune

Herkimer Democrat

As noted in the text, any newspaper from the period must be used with considerable caution. Many of the stories are filled with rumors, exaggerations, and general inaccuracies. They are most useful for their coverage of speeches, ceremonies, and the like, and for general color of the period.

Index